Theodor Adorno

Verso

Minima Moralia

Reflections from Damaged Life

Translated from the German by E. F. N. Jephcott

Minima Moralia was first published
by Suhrkamp Verlag, Frankfurt am Main 1951
© Suhrkamp Verlag 1951

This translation first published 1974
©NLB 1974
Verso Editions 1978
Thirteenth impression 2002

Verso
UK: 6 Meard Street, London W1F 0EG
USA: 180 Varick Street, New York, NY 10014-4606

ISBN 0 86091 704 5
Printed in Great Britain by
The Bath Press, Bath

For Max

In gratitude
and promise

PART TWO

1945

Publisher's Note

The German text of *Minima Moralia* has no footnotes. Adorno's extensive use of literary, musical, philosophical and idiomatic allusions is, however, an integral device of the whole formal structure and style of the book. Explanations of these has seemed essential, where prior knowledge could not reasonably be assumed in English-speaking readers. This edition therefore includes brief decipherments of those implicit or explicit references or citations where a clarification appeared to be necessary. All such footnotes have been added by NLB. The decision when to insert them has often proved difficult. But in general, familiarity with works or figures in German literary history has been assumed to be less widespread among Anglo-Saxon audiences than French references: hence, at risk of superfluity for readers conversant with the former, more information has been provided where echoes of it are concerned. A special problem has arisen with the titles to the aphorisms. These comprise six languages in the original – German, English, French, Italian, Latin and Greek. The latter four have been rendered exactly in the form in which Adorno composed them, with accompanying notes. The titles in English, no longer directly visible in translation, are the following: *They, the people, Tough Baby, English spoken, Golden Gate, I.Q., Wishful thinking,* and *Who is who* (Nos. 7, 24, 26, 104, 126, 127, 138). Whether in titles or text, the great majority of the allusions in *Minima Moralia,* as will be seen, involve irony or inversion.

All actual quotations – for example, from Hegel or Nietzsche, Goethe or Proust – have been newly translated from the original, and footnoted to standard native editions; to help English-speaking readers locate the passages concerned, however, translated editions have been added in brackets in the notes. The only exceptions, where existing English-language translations have been used, are the quotations from Marx and Lukàcs towards the end of the book.

The melancholy science from which I make this offering to my friend relates to a region that from time immemorial was regarded as the true field of philosophy, but which, since the latter's conversion into method, has lapsed into intellectual neglect, sententious whimsy and finally oblivion: the teaching of the good life. What the philosophers once knew as life has become the sphere of private existence and now of mere consumption, dragged along as an appendage of the process of material production, without autonomy or substance of its own. He who wishes to know the truth about life in its immediacy must scrutinize its estranged form, the objective powers that determine individual existence even in its most hidden recesses. To speak immediately of the immediate is to behave much as those novelists who drape their marionettes in imitated bygone passions like cheap jewellery, and make people who are no more than component parts of machinery act as if they still had the capacity to act as subjects, and as if something depended on their actions. Our perspective of life has passed into an ideology which conceals the fact that there is life no longer.

But the relation between life and production, which in reality debases the former to an ephemeral appearance of the latter, is totally absurd. Means and end are inverted. A dim awareness of this perverse *quid pro quo* has still not been quite eradicated from life. Reduced and degraded essence tenaciously resists the magic that transforms it into a façade. The change in the relations of production themselves depends largely on what takes place in the 'sphere of consumption', the mere reflection of production and the caricature of true life: in the consciousness and unconsciousness of individuals. Only by virtue of opposition to production, as still not wholly encompassed by this order, can men bring about another more worthy of human beings. Should the appearance of life, which the sphere of consumption itself defends for such bad reasons, be once entirely effaced, then the monstrosity of absolute production will triumph.

Nevertheless, considerations which start from the subject remain false to the same extent that life has become appearance. For since the overwhelming objectivity of historical movement in its present phase consists so far only in the dissolution of the subject, without yet giving rise to a new one, individual experience necessarily bases itself on the old subject, now historically condemned, which is still for-itself, but no longer in-itself. The subject still feels sure of its autonomy, but the nullity demonstrated to subjects by the concentration camp is already overtaking the form of subjectivity itself. Subjective reflection, even if critically alerted to itself, has something sentimental and anachronistic about it: something of a lament over the course of the world, a lament to be rejected not for its good faith, but because the lamenting subject threatens to become arrested in its condition and so to fulfil in its turn the law of the world's course. Fidelity to one's own state of consciousness and experience is forever in temptation of lapsing into infidelity, by denying the insight that transcends the individual and calls his substance by its name.

Thus Hegel, whose method schooled that of *Minima Moralia*, argued against the mere being-for-itself of subjectivity on all its levels. Dialectical theory, abhorring anything isolated, cannot admit aphorisms as such. In the most lenient instance they might, to use a term from the *Preface* to the *Phenomenology of Mind*, be tolerated as 'conversation'. But the time for that is past. Nevertheless, this book forgets neither the system's claim to totality, which would suffer nothing to remain outside it, nor that it remonstrates against this claim. In his relation to the subject Hegel does not respect the demand that he otherwise passionately upholds: to be in the matter and not 'always beyond it', to 'penetrate into the immanent content of the matter'.[1] If today the subject is vanishing, aphorisms take upon themselves the duty 'to consider the evanescent itself as essential'. They insist, in opposition to Hegel's practice and yet in accordance with his thought, on negativity: 'The life of the mind only attains its truth when discovering itself in absolute desolation. The mind is not this power as a positive which turns away from the negative, as when we say of something that it is null, or false, so much for that and now for something else; it is this power only when looking the negative in the face, dwelling upon it.'[2]

The dismissive gesture which Hegel, in contradiction to his own insight, constantly accords the individual, derives paradoxically

1. *Phänomenologie des Geistes, Werke* 3, Frankfurt 1970, p. 52 (*The Phenomenology of Mind*, London 1966, p. 112).
2. *Phänomenologie des Geistes*, p. 36 (*The Phenomenology of Mind*, p. 93).

enough from his necessary entanglement in liberalistic thinking. The conception of a totality harmonious through all its antagonisms compels him to assign to individuation, however much he may designate it a driving moment in the process, an inferior status in the construction of the whole. The knowledge that in pre-history the objective tendency asserts itself over the heads of human beings, indeed by virtue of annihilating individual qualities, without the reconciliation of general and particular – constructed in thought – ever yet being accomplished in history, is distorted in Hegel: with serene indifference he opts once again for liquidation of the particular. Nowhere in his work is the primacy of the whole doubted. The more questionable the transition from reflective isolation to glorified totality becomes in history as in Hegelian logic, the more eagerly philosophy, as the justification of what exists, attaches itself to the triumphal car of objective tendencies. The culmination of the social principle of individuation in the triumph of fatality gives philosophy occasion enough to do so. Hegel, in hypostasizing both bourgeois society and its fundamental category, the individual, did not truly carry through the dialectic between the two. Certainly he perceives, with classical economics, that the totality produces and reproduces itself precisely from the interconnection of the antagonistic interests of its members. But the individual as such he for the most part considers, naively, as an irreducible datum – just what in his theory of knowledge he decomposes. Nevertheless, in an individualistic society, the general not only realizes itself through the interplay of particulars, but society is essentially the substance of the individual.

For this reason, social analysis can learn incomparably more from individual experience than Hegel conceded, while conversely the large historical categories, after all that has meanwhile been perpetrated with their help, are no longer above suspicion of fraud. In the hundred and fifty years since Hegel's conception was formed, some of the force of protest has reverted to the individual. Compared to the patriarchal meagreness that characterizes his treatment in Hegel, the individual has gained as much in richness, differentiation and vigour as, on the other hand, the socialization of society has enfeebled and undermined him. In the period of his decay, the individual's experience of himself and what he encounters contributes once more to knowledge, which he had merely obscured as long as he continued unshaken to construe himself positively as the dominant category. In face of the totalitarian unison with which the eradication of difference is proclaimed as a purpose in itself, even part of the social force of liberation may have temporarily withdrawn to the individual sphere. If critical theory lingers there, it is not only with a bad conscience.

All this is not meant to deny what is disputable in such an attempt. The major part of this book was written during the war, under conditions enforcing contemplation. The violence that expelled me thereby denied me full knowledge of it. I did not yet admit to myself the complicity that enfolds all those who, in face of unspeakable collective events, speak of individual matters at all.

In each of the three parts the starting-point is the narrowest private sphere, that of the intellectual in emigration. From this follow considerations of broader social and anthropological scope; they concern psychology, aesthetics, science in its relation to the subject. The concluding aphorisms of each part lead on thematically also to philosophy, without ever pretending to be complete or definitive: they are all intended to mark out points of attack or to furnish models for a future exertion of thought.

The immediate occasion for writing this book was Max Horkheimer's fiftieth birthday, February 14th, 1945. The composition took place in a phase when, bowing to outward circumstances, we had to interrupt our work together. This book wishes to demonstrate gratitude and loyalty by refusing to acknowledge the interruption. It bears witness to a *dialogue intérieur*: there is not a motif in it that does not belong as much to Horkheimer as to him who found the time to formulate it.

The specific approach of *Minima Moralia*, the attempt to present aspects of our shared philosophy from the standpoint of subjective experience, necessitates that the parts do not altogether satisfy the demands of the philosophy of which they are nevertheless a part. The disconnected and non-binding character of the form, the renunciation of explicit theoretical cohesion, are meant as one expression of this. At the same time this ascesis should atone in some part for the injustice whereby one alone continued to perform the task that can only be accomplished by both, and that we do not forsake.

Minima Moralia

Life does not live

Ferdinand Kürnberger

For Marcel Proust. – The son of well-to-do parents who, whether from talent or weakness, engages in a so-called intellectual profession, as an artist or a scholar, will have a particularly difficult time with those bearing the distasteful title of colleagues. It is not merely that his independence is envied, the seriousness of his intentions mistrusted, and that he is suspected of being a secret envoy of the established powers. Such suspicions, though betraying a deep-seated resentment, would usually prove well-founded. But the real resistances lie elsewhere. The occupation with things of the mind has by now itself become 'practical', a business with strict division of labour, departments and restricted entry. The man of independent means who chooses it out of repugnance for the ignominy of earning money will not be disposed to acknowledge the fact. For this he is punished. He is not a 'professional', is ranked in the competitive hierarchy as a dilettante no matter how well he knows his subject, and must, if he wants to make a career, show himself even more resolutely blinkered than the most inveterate specialist. The urge to suspend the division of labour which, within certain limits, his economic situation enables him to satisfy, is thought particularly disreputable: it betrays a disinclination to sanction the operations imposed by society, and domineering competence permits no such idiosyncrasies. The departmentalization of mind is a means of abolishing mind where it is not exercised *ex officio,* under contract. It performs this task all the more reliably since anyone who repudiates the division of labour – if only by taking pleasure in his work – makes himself vulnerable by its standards in ways inseparable from elements of his superiority. Thus is order ensured: some have to play the game because they cannot otherwise live, and those who could live otherwise are kept out because they do not want to play the game. It is as if the class from which independent intellectuals have defected takes its revenge, by pressing its demands home in the very domain where the deserter seeks refuge.

Grassy seat.[1] – Our relationship to parents is beginning to undergo a sad, shadowy transformation. Through their economic impotence they have lost their awesomeness. Once we rebelled against their insistence on the reality principle, the sobriety forever prone to become wrath against those less ready to renounce. But today we are faced with a generation purporting to be young yet in all its reactions insufferably more grown-up than its parents ever were; which, having renounced before any conflict, draws from this its grimly authoritarian, unshakeable power. Perhaps people have at all times felt the parental generation to become harmless, powerless, with the waning of its physical strength, while their own generation already seemed threatened by the young: in an antagonistic society the relation between generations too is one of competition, behind which stands naked power. But today it is beginning to regress to a state versed, not in the Oedipus complex, but in parricide. One of the Nazis' symbolic outrages is the killing of the very old. Such a climate fosters a late, lucid understanding with our parents, as between the condemned, marred only by the fear that we, powerless ourselves, might now be unable to care for them as well as they cared for us when they possessed something. The violence done to them makes us forget the violence they did. Even their rationalizations, the once-hated lies with which they sought to justify their particular interest as a general one, reveal in them an inkling of the truth, an urge to resolve a conflict whose existence their children, proof against all uncertainty, cheerfully deny. Even the outdated, inconsistent, self-doubting ideas of the older generation are more open to dialogue than the slick stupidity of Junior. Even the neurotic oddities and deformities of our elders stand for character, for something humanly achieved, in comparison to pathic health, infantilism raised to the norm. One realizes with horror that earlier, opposing one's parents because they represented the world, one was often secretly the mouthpiece, against a bad world, of one even worse. Unpolitical attempts to break out of the bourgeois family usually lead only to deeper entanglement in it, and it sometimes seems as if the fatal germ-cell of society, the family, were at the

1. Allusion to the lines of a well-known German song: *Der liebste Platz den ich auf Erden hab',/das ist die Rasenbank am Elterngrab* (The dearest spot I have on earth/is the grassy seat by my parents' grave).

same time the nurturing germ-cell of uncompromising pursuit of another. With the family there passes away, while the system lasts, not only the most effective agency of the bourgeoisie, but also the resistance which, though repressing the individual, also strengthened, perhaps even produced him. The end of the family paralyses the forces of opposition. The rising collectivist order is a mockery of a classless one: together with the bourgeois it liquidates the Utopia that once drew sustenance from motherly love.

3

Fish in water. – Since the all-embracing distributive machinery of highly-concentrated industry has superseded the sphere of circulation, the latter has begun a strange post-existence. As the professions of the middle-man lose their economic basis, the private lives of countless people are becoming those of agents and go-betweens; indeed the entire private domain is being engulfed by a mysterious activity that bears all the features of commercial life without there being actually any business to transact. All these nervous people, from the unemployed to the public figure liable at any moment to incur the wrath of those whose investment he represents, believe that only by empathy, assiduity, serviceability, arts and dodges, by tradesmen's qualities, can they ingratiate themselves with the executive they imagine omnipresent, and soon there is no relationship that is not seen as a 'connection', no impulse not first censored as to whether it deviates from the acceptable. The concept of connections, a category of mediation and circulation, never flourished best in the sphere of circulation proper, the market, but in closed and monopolistic hierarchies. Now that the whole of society is becoming hierarchical, these murky connections are proliferating wherever there used still to be an appearance of freedom. The irrationality of the system is expressed scarcely less clearly in the parasitic psychology of the individual than in his economic fate. Earlier, when something like the maligned bourgeois division between professional and private life still existed – a division whose passing one almost now regrets – anyone who pursued practical aims in the private sphere was eyed mistrustfully as an uncouth interloper. Today it is seen as arrogant, alien and improper to engage in private activity without any evident ulterior motive. Not to be 'after' something is almost suspect: no help to others in the rat-race is acknowledged unless legitimized by counter-claims. Countless people are making, from the aftermath of the liquidation of professions, their profession. They are the nice folk, the good mixers liked by all, the just, humanely excusing all mean-ness and scrupulously proscribing any non-standardized impulses as sentimental. Indispensable for their knowledge of all the channels and plug-holes of power, they divine its most secret judgements and live by adroitly propagating them. They are found in all political camps, even where the rejection of the system is taken for granted, and has thereby produced a slack and subtle conformism of its own. Often they win sympathy by a certain good-naturedness, a kindly involvement in other people's lives: selflessness as specu-lation. They are clever, witty, full of sensitive reactions: they have refurbished the old tradesman's mentality with the day before yesterday's psychological discoveries. They are capable of every-thing, even love, yet always faithlessly. They deceive, not by instinct, but on principle, valuing even themselves as a profit begrudged to anyone else. To intellect they are bound both by affinity and hatred: they are a temptation for the thoughtful, but also their worst enemies. For it is they who insidiously attack and despoil the last retreats of resistance, the hours still exempt from the demands of machinery. Their belated individualism poisons what little is left of the individual.

4

Final serenity. – A newspaper obituary for a businessman once contained the words: 'The breadth of his conscience vied with the kindness of his heart.' The blunder committed by the bereaved in the elevated language reserved for such purposes, the inadvertent admission that the kind-hearted deceased had lacked a conscience, expedites the funeral procession by the shortest route to the land of truth. If a man of advanced years is praised for his exceptional serenity, his life can be assumed to comprise a succession of in-famies. He has rid himself of the habit of getting excited. Breadth of conscience is passed off as magnanimity, all-forgiving because all-too-understanding. The *quid pro quo* between one's own guilt and that of others, is resolved in favour of whoever has come off best. After so long a life one quite loses the capacity to distinguish who has done what harm to whom. In the abstract conception of universal wrong, all concrete responsibility vanishes. The black-guard presents himself as victim of injustice: if only you knew, young man, what life is like. But those conspicuous midway through life by an exceptional kindness are usually drawing advances on such serenity. He who is not malign does not live serenely but with a peculiarly chaste hardness and intolerance. Lacking appropriate objects, his love can scarcely express itself except by hatred for the inappropriate, in which admittedly he comes to resemble what he hates. The bourgeois, however, is tolerant. His love of people as they are stems from his hatred of what they might be.

5

How nice of you, Doctor.[1] – There is nothing innocuous left. The little pleasures, expressions of life that seemed exempt from the responsibility of thought, not only have an element of defiant silliness, of callous refusal to see, but directly serve their diametrical opposite. Even the blossoming tree lies the moment its bloom is seen without the shadow of terror; even the innocent 'How lovely!' becomes an excuse for an existence outrageously unlovely, and there is no longer beauty or consolation except in the gaze falling on horror, withstanding it, and in unalleviated consciousness of negativity holding fast to the possibility of what is better. Mistrust is called for in face of all spontaneity, impetuosity, all letting oneself go, for it implies pliancy towards the superior might of the existent. The malignant deeper meaning of ease, once confined to the toasts of conviviality, has long since spread to more appealing impulses. The chance conversation in the train, when, to avoid dispute, one consents to a few statements that one knows ultimately to implicate murder, is already a betrayal; no thought is immune against com-munication, and to utter it in the wrong place and in wrong agree-ment is enough to undermine its truth. Every visit to the cinema leaves me, against all my vigilance, stupider and worse. Sociability itself connives at injustice by pretending that in this chill world

1. *Herr Doktor, das ist schön von Euch*: humble thanks of an old peasant to Faust for consorting with a popular crowd at Easter (Goethe's *Faust*, Part One).

we can still talk to each other, and the casual, amiable remark contributes to perpetuating silence, in that the concessions made to the interlocutor debase him once more in the person of speaker. The evil principle that was always latent in affability unfurls its full bestiality in the egalitarian spirit. Condescension, and thinking oneself no better, are the same. To adapt to the weakness of the oppressed is to affirm in it the pre-condition of power, and to develop in oneself the coarseness, insensibility and violence needed to exert domination. If, in the latest phase, the condescending gesture has been dropped and only the adaptation remains visible, this perfect screening of power only allows the class-relationship it denies to triumph more implacably. For the intellectual, inviolable isolation is now the only way of showing some measure of solidarity. All collaboration, all the human worth of social mixing and participation, merely masks a tacit acceptance of inhumanity. It is the sufferings of men that should be shared: the smallest step towards their pleasures is one towards the hardening of their pains.

6

Antithesis. – He who stands aloof runs the risk of believing himself better than others and misusing his critique of society as an ideology for his private interest. While he gropingly forms his own life in the frail image of a true existence, he should never forget its frailty, nor how little the image is a substitute for true life. Against such awareness, however, pulls the momentum of the bourgeois within him. The detached observer is as much entangled as the active participant; the only advantage of the former is insight into his entanglement, and the infinitesimal freedom that lies in knowledge as such. His own distance from business at large is a luxury which only that business confers. This is why the very movement of withdrawal bears features of what it negates. It is forced to develop a coldness indistinguishable from that of the bourgeois. Even where it protests, the monadological principle conceals the dominant universal. Proust's observation that in photographs, the grandfather of a duke or of a middle-class Jew are so alike that we forget their difference of social rank, has a much wider application: the unity of an epoch objectively abolishes all the distinctions that constitute the happiness, even the moral substance, of individual existence. We record the decline of education, and yet our prose, measured against that of Jacob Grimm or Bachofen,[1] has in common with the culture industry cadences unsuspected by us. Nor do we any longer have the same command of Latin and Greek as Wolf or Kirchhoff.[2] We point at the decline of civilization into illiteracy, and ourselves forget the art of letter-writing, or of reading a text from Jean Paul as it must have been read in his time. We shudder at the brutalization of life, but lacking any objectively binding morality we are forced at every step into actions and words, into calculations that are by humane standards barbaric, and even by the dubious values of good society, tactless. With the dissolution of liberalism, the truly bourgeois principle, that of competition, far from being overcome, has passed from the objectivity of the social process into the composition of its colliding and jostling atoms, and therewith as if into anthropology. The subjugation of life to the process of production imposes as a humiliation on everyone something of the isolation and solitude that we are tempted to regard as resulting from our own superior choice. It is as old a component of bourgeois ideology that each individual, in his particular interest, considers himself better than all others, as that he values the others, as the community of all customers, more highly than himself. Since the demise of the old bourgeois class, both ideas have led an after-life in the minds of intellectuals, who are at once the last enemies of the bourgeois and the last bourgeois. In still permitting themselves to think at all in face of the naked reproduction of existence, they act as a privileged group; in letting matters rest there, they declare the nullity of their privilege. Private existence, in striving to re-semble one worthy of man, betrays the latter, since any resemblance is withdrawn from general realization, which yet more than ever before has need of independent thought. There is no way out of entanglement. The only responsible course is to deny oneself the ideological misuse of one's own existence, and for the rest to conduct oneself in private as modestly, unobtrusively and

1. Jacob Grimm (1785–1863): founder of German philology as a systematic discipline, as well as collector of German folk-tales. Johann Jakob Bachofen (1815–87): romantic historian of ancient law and myth, author of the famous work *Das Mutterrecht* (1861).

2. Friedrich-August Wolf (1759–1824): classical philologist who first investigated the origins of Homeric poetry – a friend of Goethe and Humboldt. Adolf Kirchhoff (1826–1905): German classical scholar of the later nineteenth century.

unpretentiously as is required, no longer by good upbringing, but by the shame of still having air to breathe, in hell.

7

They, the people. – The circumstance that intellectuals mostly have to do with intellectuals, should not deceive them into believing their own kind still more base than the rest of mankind. For they get to know each other in the most shameful and degrading of all situations, that of competing supplicants, and are thus virtually compelled to show each other their most repulsive sides. Other people, particularly the simple folk whose qualities the intellectual is so fond of stressing, generally encounter him in the role of those with something to sell, yet who have no fear of the customer ever poaching on their preserves. The car mechanic, the barmaid, have little difficulty in abstaining from effrontery: courtesy is in any case imposed on them from above. If, conversely, illiterates come to intellectuals wanting letters written for them, they too may receive a tolerably good impression. But the moment simple folk are forced to brawl among themselves for their portion of the social product, their envy and spite surpass anything seen among *literati* or musical directors. In the end, glorification of splendid underdogs is nothing other than glorification of the splendid system that makes them so. The justified guilt-feelings of those exempt from physical work ought not become an excuse for the 'idiocy of rural life'. Intellectuals, who alone write about intellectuals and give them their bad name in that of honesty, reinforce the lie. A great part of the prevalent anti-intellectualism and irrationalism, right up to Huxley, is set in motion when writers complain about the mechanisms of competition without understanding them, and so fall victim to them. In the activity most their own they have shut out the consciousness of *tat twam asi*.[1] Which is why they then scuttle into Indian temples.

8

If knaves should tempt you. – There is an *amor intellectualis* for kitchen personnel, a temptation for those engaged in theoretical

1. 'Thou art this': mystic pantheist formula of the Upanishads.

28

or artistic work to relax their spiritual demands on themselves, to drop their standards, to indulge, in their subject-matter and its expression, all kinds of habits that lucid appraisal has rejected. Since there are no longer, for the intellectual, any given categories, even cultural, and bustle endangers concentration with a thousand claims, the effort of producing something in some measure worthwhile is now so great as to be beyond almost everybody. The pressure of conformity weighing on all producers further diminishes their demands on themselves. The centre of intellectual self-discipline as such is in the process of decomposition. The taboos that constitute a man's intellectual stature, often sedimented experiences and unarticulated insights, always operate against inner impulses that he has learned to condemn, but which are so strong that only an unquestioning and unquestioned authority can hold them in check. What is true of the instinctual life is no less of the intellectual: the painter or composer forbidding himself as trite this or that combination of colours or chords, the writer wincing at banal or pedantic verbal configurations, reacts so violently because layers of himself are drawn to them. Repudiation of the present cultural morass presupposes sufficient involvement in it to feel it itching in one's finger-tips, so to speak, but at the same time the strength, drawn from this involvement, to dismiss it. This strength, though manifesting itself as individual resistance, is by no means of a merely individual nature. In the intellectual conscience possessed of it, the social moment is no less present than the moral super-ego. Such conscience grows out of a conception of the good society and its citizens. If this conception dims – and who could still trust blindly in it – the downward urge of the intellect loses its inhibitions and all the detritus dumped in the individual by barbarous culture – half-learning, slackness, heavy familiarity, coarseness – comes to light. Usually it is rationalized as humanity, desire to be understood by others, worldly-wise responsibility. But the sacrifice of intellectual self-discipline comes much too easily to its maker for us to believe his assurance that it is one. The most striking example is that of intellectuals whose material situation has changed: no sooner have they only perfunctorily persuaded themselves of the need to earn money by writing and that alone, than they turn out trash identical in all its nuances to what, with ample means, they had most passionately abjured. Just as once-rich emigrés are often as self-indulgently miserly on foreign soil as they always wanted to be at home, so the impoverished in spirit march joyously into the inferno that is their paradise.

9

Promise me this, my child.[1] – The immorality of lying does not consist in the offence against sacrosanct truth. An appeal to truth is scarcely a prerogative of a society which dragoons its members to own up the better to hunt them down. It ill befits universal untruth to insist on particular truth, while immediately converting it into its opposite. Nevertheless, there is something repellent about a lie, and awareness of this, though inculcated by the traditional whip, yet throws light on the gaolers. Error lies in excessive honesty. A man who lies is ashamed, for each lie teaches him the degradation of a world which, forcing him to lie in order to live, promptly sings the praises of loyalty and truthfulness.[2] This shame undermines the lying of more subtly organized natures. They do it badly, which alone really makes the lie a moral offence against the other. It implies his stupidity, and so serves to express contempt. Among today's adept practitioners, the lie has long since lost its honest function of misrepresenting reality. Nobody believes anybody, everyone is in the know. Lies are told only to convey to someone that one has no need either of him or his good opinion. The lie, once a liberal means of communication, has today become one of the techniques of insolence enabling each individual to spread around him the glacial atmosphere in whose shelter he can thrive.

10

Divided-united. – Marriage, living on as an abject parody in a time that has removed the basis of its human justification, usually serves today as a trick of self-preservation: the two conspirators

1. *Vor allem eins, mein Kind*: allusion to the lines of the late romantic poet Robert Reinick (1805–52), *Vor allem eins, mein Kind, sei treu und wahr,/ lass nie die Lüge deinen Mund entweihen* (Above all else, my child, be loyal and true / and never let a lie profane your mouth).
2. *Üb' immer Treu' und Redlichkeit*: phrase from a *Lied* set by Mozart.

deflect outward responsibility for their respective ill-doing to the other while in reality existing together in a murky swamp. The only decent marriage would be one allowing each partner to lead an independent life, in which, instead of a fusion derived from an enforced community of economic interests, both freely accepted mutual responsibility. Marriage as a community of interests unfailingly means the degradation of the interested parties, and it is the perfidy of the world's arrangements that no-one, even if aware of it, can escape such degradation. The idea might therefore be entertained that marriage without ignominy is a possibility reserved for those spared the pursuit of interests, for the rich. But the possibility is purely formal, for the privileged are precisely those in whom the pursuit of interests has become second nature – they would not otherwise uphold privilege.

22

With all my worldly goods. – Divorce, even between good-natured, amiable, educated people, is apt to stir up a dust-cloud that covers and discolours all it touches. It is as if the sphere of intimacy, the unwatchful trust of shared life, is transformed into a malignant poison as soon as the relationship in which it flourished is broken off. Intimacy between people is forbearance, tolerance, refuge for idiosyncrasies. If dragged into the open, it reveals the moment of weakness in it, and in a divorce such outward exposure is inevitable. It seizes the inventory of trust. Things which were once signs of loving care, images of reconciliation, breaking loose as independent values, show their evil, cold, pernicious side. Professors, after separation, break into their wives' flats to pilfer objects from writing desks, and well-endowed ladies denounce their husbands for tax-evasion. If marriage offers one of the last possibilities of forming human cells within universal inhumanity, the universal takes revenge in the breakdown of marriage, laying hands on what had seemed excepted from the rule, subjugating it to the alienated orders of rights and property and deriding those who had lived in delusive security. Just what was most protected is cruelly requisitioned and exposed. The more 'generous' the couple had originally been, the less they thought of possessions and obligations, the more abominable becomes their humiliation. For it is precisely in the realm of the legally undefined that strife, defamation and endless conflict of interests flourish. The whole sombre base on which the institution of marriage rises, the husband's barbarous power over the property and work of his wife, the no less barbarous sexual oppression that can compel a man to take life-long responsibility for a woman with whom it once gave him pleasure to sleep – all this crawls into the light from cellars and foundations when the house is demolished. Those who once experienced the good universal in restrictively belonging to each other, are now forced by society to consider themselves scoundrels, no different from the universal order of unrestricted meanness outside. The universal is revealed in divorce as the particular's mark of shame, because the particular, marriage, is in this society unable to realize the true universal.

12

Inter pares. – In the realm of erotic qualities a reversal of values seems near completion. Under liberalism, up to our own times, married men from good society, unsatisfied by their correct spouses of sheltered upbringing, were wont to indemnify themselves with chorus girls, *bohémiennes*, Viennese *süsse Mädel* ['sweet wenches'] and *cocottes*. With the rationalization of society this possibility of irregular bliss has disappeared. The *cocottes* have died out, the equivalent of '*süsse Mädel*' probably never existed in Anglo-Saxon and other countries with a technical civilization; but the chorus girls and the bohemians now parasitically grafted to mass culture, are so thoroughly imbued with its reasoning that he who voluptuously flees to their anarchy, the free control of their own exchange value, risks waking up under the obligation, if not of engaging them as assistants, at least of recommending them to a film magnate or script-writer of his acquaintance. The only women still able to indulge in anything resembling uncalculating love are now these very ladies whose husbands once forsook them for the tiles. While they remain as tedious to their husbands, through the latters' fault, as their mothers were, they can at least bestow on others what they are otherwise denied by all. The long-since frigid libertine represents business, while the correct, well-brought-up wife stands yearningly and unromantically for sexuality. So at last society ladies achieve the honour of their dishonour, at the moment when there are no longer either society or ladies.

13

Protection, help and counsel. – Every intellectual in emigration is, without exception, mutilated, and does well to acknowledge it to himself, if he wishes to avoid being cruelly apprised of it behind the tightly-closed doors of his self-esteem. He lives in an environment that must remain incomprehensible to him, however flawless his knowledge of trade-union organizations or the automobile industry may be; he is always astray. Between the reproduction of his own existence under the monopoly of mass culture, and impartial, responsible work, yawns an irreconcilable breach. His language has been expropriated, and the historical dimension that nourished his knowledge, sapped. The isolation is made worse by the formation of closed and politically-controlled groups, mistrustful of their members, hostile to those branded different. The share of the social product that falls to aliens is insufficient, and forces them into a hopeless second struggle within the general competition. All this leaves no individual unmarked. Even the man spared the ignominy of direct co-ordination bears, as his special mark, this very exemption, an illusory, unreal existence in the life-process of society. Relations between outcasts are even more poisoned than between long-standing residents. All emphases are wrong, perspectives disrupted. Private life asserts itself unduly, hectically, vampire-like, trying convulsively, because it really no longer exists, to prove it is alive. Public life is reduced to an unspoken oath of allegiance to the platform. The eyes take on a manic yet cold look of grasping, devouring, commandeering. There is no remedy but steadfast diagnosis of oneself and others, the attempt, through awareness, if not to escape doom, at least to rob it of its dreadful violence, that of blindness. Utmost caution is called for, particularly in the choice of private acquaintances, as far as choice still remains. Above all, one should beware of seeking out the mighty, and 'expecting something' of them. The eye for possible advantages is the mortal enemy of all human relationships; from these solidarity and loyalty can ensue, but never from thoughts of practical ends. Hardly less dangerous are the mirror-images of

33

the mighty, lackeys, flatterers and cadgers, who ingratiate themselves with those better off than they in an archaistic manner that
can flourish only in the economically extraterritorial circumstances
of emigration. While they may bring their protector trivial advantages, they drag him down the moment he accepts them, as he is
ceaselessly seduced to do by his own helplessness in a strange
country. If in Europe the esoteric gesture was often only a pretext
for the blindest self-interest, the concept of austerity, though
hardly ship-shape or watertight, still seems, in emigration, the
most acceptable lifeboat. Only a few, admittedly, have a seaworthy
example at their disposal. To most boarders, it threatens starvation
or madness.

14

Le bourgeois revenant. – Absurdly, the Fascist regimes of the first
half of the twentieth century have stabilized an obsolete economic
form, multiplying the terror needed to maintain it now that its
senselessness is blatant. Thereby has private life also been marked.
With the strengthening of external authority the stuffy private
order, particularism of interests, the long-outdated form of the
family, the right of property and its reflection in character, have
also re-consolidated themselves. But with a bad conscience, a
scarcely concealed awareness of untruth. Whatever was once good
and decent in bourgeois values, independence, perseverance, forethought, circumspection, has been corrupted utterly. For while
bourgeois forms of existence are truculently conserved, their
economic pre-condition has fallen away. Privacy has given way
entirely to the privation it always secretly was, and with the stubborn adherence to particular interests is now mingled fury at being
no longer able to perceive that things might be different and better.
In losing their innocence, the bourgeois have become impenitently
malign. The caring hand that even now tends the little garden as if
it had not long since become a 'lot', but fearfully wards off the
unknown intruder, is already that which denies the political refugee
asylum. Now objectively threatened, the subjectivity of the rulers
and their hangers-on becomes totally inhuman. So the class realizes
itself, taking upon itself the destructive will of the course of the
world. The bourgeois live on like spectres threatening doom.

Le nouvel avare. – There are two kinds of avarice. One, the archaic type, is the passion that spares oneself and others nothing; its physiognomic traits have been immortalized by Molière, and explained as the anal character by Freud. It is consummated in the miser, the beggar with secret millions, who is like the puritanical mask of the unrecognized caliph in the fairy-tale. He is related to the collector, the manic, finally to the great lover, as Gobseck is to Esther.[1] He is still occasionally to be found as a curiosity in local columns of newspapers. The miser of our time is the man who considers nothing too expensive for himself, and everything for others. He thinks in equivalents, subjecting his whole private life to the law that one gives less than one receives in return, yet enough to ensure that one receives something. Every good deed is accompanied by an evident 'is it necessary?', 'do I have to?' This type are most surely revealed by the haste with which they 'avenge' kindness received, unwilling to tolerate, in the chain of exchange acts whereby expenses are recovered, a single missing link. Because with them everything is done in a rational above-board manner, they are, unlike Harpagon and Scrooge, neither to be convicted nor converted. They are as affable as they are implacable. If need be, they will place themselves irrefutably in the right and transform right into wrong, whereas the sordid mania of stinginess had the redeeming feature that the gold in the cash-box necessarily attracted thieves, indeed, that its passion was stilled only in sacrifice and loss, as is the erotic desire for possession in self-abandonment. The new misers, however, indulge their asceticism no longer as a vice but with prudence. They are insured.

On the dialectic of tact. – Goethe, actuely aware of the threatening impossibility of all human relationships in emergent industrial society, tried in the *Novellen* of *Wilhelm Meister's Years of Travel* to present tact as the saving accommodation between alienated human beings. This accommodation seemed to him inseparable

1. The miser and the courtesan in Balzac's *Splendeurs et Misères des Courtisanes*: Gobseck was Esther's great-uncle.

from renunciation, the relinquishment of total contact, passion and unalloyed happiness. The human consisted for him in a self-limitation which affirmatively espoused as its own cause the ineluctable course of history, the inhumanity of progress, the withering of the subject. But what has happened since makes Goethean renunciation look like fulfilment. Tact and humanity – for him the same thing – have in the meantime gone exactly the way from which, as he believed, they were to save us. For tact, we now know, has its precise historical hour. It was the hour when the bourgeois individual rid himself of absolutist compulsion. Free and solitary, he answers for himself, while the forms of hierarchical respect and consideration developed by absolutism, divested of their economic basis and their menacing power, are still just sufficiently present to make living together within privileged groups bearable. This seemingly paradoxical interchange between absolutism and liberality is perceptible, not only in *Wilhelm Meister*, but in Beethoven's attitude towards traditional patterns of composition, and even in logic, in Kant's subjective reconstruction of objectively binding ideas. There is a sense in which Beethoven's regular recapitulations following dynamic expositions, Kant's deduction of scholastic categories from the unity of consciousness, are eminently 'tactful'. The precondition of tact is convention no longer intact yet still present. Now fallen into irreparable ruin, it lives on only in the parody of forms, an arbitrarily devised or recollected etiquette for the ignorant, of the kind preached by unsolicited advisers in newspapers, while the basis of agreement that carried those conventions in their human hour has given way to the blind conformity of car-owners and radio-listeners. The demise of the ceremonial moment seems at first sight to benefit tact. Emancipated from all that was heteronomous and harmfully external, tactful behaviour would seem one guided solely by the specific nature of each human situation. Such emancipated tact, however, meets with the difficulties that confront nominalism in all contexts. Tact meant not simply subordination to ceremonial convention: it was precisely the latter all later humanists unceasingly ironized. Rather, the exercise of tact was as paradoxical as its historical location. It demanded the reconciliation – actually impossible – between the unauthorized claims of convention and the unruly ones of the individual. Other than convention there was nothing by which tact could be measured. Convention represented, in however etiolated a form, the universal which made up the very substance of the individual claim. Tact is the discrimination of differences. It consists in conscious deviations. Yet when, emancipated, it confronts the individual as an absolute, without anything universal from which to be differentiated, it fails to engage the individual and finally wrongs him. The question as to someone's health, no longer required and expected by upbringing, becomes inquisitive or injurious, silence on sensitive subjects empty indifference, as soon as there is no rule to indicate what is and what is not to be discussed. Thus individuals begin, not without reason, to react antagonistically to tact: a certain kind of politeness, for example, gives them less the feeling of being addressed as human beings, than an inkling of their inhuman conditions, and the polite run the risk of seeming impolite by continuing to exercise politeness, as a superseded privilege. In the end emancipated, purely individual tact becomes mere lying. Its true principle in the individual today is what it earnestly keeps silent, the actual and still more the potential power embodied by each person. Beneath the demand that the individual be confronted as such, without preamble, absolutely as befits him, lies a covetous eagerness to 'place' him and his chances, through the tacit admissions contained in each of his words, in the ever more rigid hierarchy that encompasses everyone. The nominalism of tact helps what is most universal, naked external power, to triumph even in the most intimate constellations. To write off convention as an outdated, useless and extraneous ornament is only to confirm the most extraneous of all things, a life of direct domination. That the abolition of even this caricature of tact in the rib-digging *camaraderie* of our time, a mockery of freedom, nevertheless makes existence still more unbearable, is merely a further indication of how impossible it has become for people to co-exist under present conditions.

17

Proprietary rights. – It is the signature of our age that no-one, without exception, can now determine his own life within even a moderately comprehensible framework, as was possible earlier in the assessment of market relationships. In principle everyone, however powerful, is an object. Even the profession of general no longer offers adequate protection. No agreements, in the Fascist era, are binding enough to secure headquarters against air attacks, and commandants observing traditional caution are hanged by Hitler and beheaded by Chiang Kai-shek. It follows directly from this that anyone who attempts to come out alive – and survival itself has something nonsensical about it, like dreams in which, having experienced the end of the world, one afterwards crawls from a basement – ought also to be prepared at each moment to end his life. This is the mournful truth that has emerged from Zarathustra's exuberant doctrine of freely-chosen death. Freedom has contracted to pure negativity, and what in the days of *art nouveau* was known as a beautiful death has shrunk to the wish to curtail the infinite abasement of living and the infinite torment of dying, in a world where there are far worse things to fear than death. – The objective end of humanism is only another expression for the same thing. It signifies that the individual as individual, in representing the species of man, has lost the autonomy through which he might realize the species.

18

Refuge for the homeless. – The predicament of private life today is shown by its arena. Dwelling, in the proper sense, is now impossible. The traditional residences we grew up in have grown intolerable: each trait of comfort in them is paid for with a betrayal of knowledge, each vestige of shelter with the musty pact of family interests. The functional modern habitations designed from a *tabula rasa,* are living-cases manufactured by experts for philistines, or factory sites that have strayed into the consumption sphere, devoid of all relation to the occupant: in them even the nostalgia for independent existence, defunct in any case, is sent packing. Modern man wishes to sleep close to the ground like an animal, a German magazine decreed with prophetic masochism before Hitler, abolishing with the bed the threshold between waking and dreaming. The sleepless are on call at any hour, unresistingly ready for anything, alert and unconscious at once. Anyone seeking refuge in a genuine, but purchased, period-style house, embalms himself alive. The attempt to evade responsibility for one's residence by moving into a hotel or furnished rooms, makes the enforced conditions of emigration a wisely-chosen norm. The hardest hit, as everywhere, are those who have no choice. They live, if not in slums, in bungalows that by tomorrow may be leaf-huts, trailers, cars, camps, or the open air. The house is past. The bombings of European cities, as well as the labour and concentration camps, merely proceed as executors, with what the immanent development of technology had long decided was to be the fate of houses. These are now good only to be thrown away like old food cans. The possibility of residence is annihilated by that of socialist society, which, once missed, saps the foundations of bourgeois life. No individual can resist this process. He need only take an interest in furniture design or interior decoration to find himself developing the arty-crafty sensibilities of the bibliophile, however firmly he may oppose arts-and-crafts in the narrower sense. From a distance the difference between the Vienna Workshops and the Bauhaus is no longer so considerable. Purely functional curves, having broken free of their purpose, are now becoming just as ornamental as the basic structures of Cubism. The best mode of conduct, in face of all this, still seems an uncommitted, suspended one: to lead a private life, as far as the social order and one's own needs will tolerate nothing else, but not to attach weight to it as to something still socially substantial and individually appropriate. 'It is even part of my good fortune not to be a house-owner', Nietzsche already wrote in the *Gay Science*.[1] Today we should have to add: it is part of morality not to be at home in one's home. This gives some indication of the difficult relationship in which the individual now stands to his property, as long as he still possesses anything at all. The trick is to keep in view, and to express, the fact that private property no longer belongs to one, in the sense that consumer goods have become potentially so abundant that no individual has the right to cling to the principle of their limitation; but that one must nevertheless have possessions, if one is not to sink into that dependence and need which serves the blind perpetuation of property relations. But the thesis of this paradox leads to destruction, a loveless disregard for things which necessarily turns against people too; and the antithesis, no sooner uttered, is an ideology for those wishing with a bad conscience to keep what they have. Wrong life cannot be lived rightly.

1. Friedrich Nietzsche, *Werke* (ed. Schlechta), Munich 1955, Vol II, p. 154 (*The Joyful Wisdom*, Edinburgh–London 1910, p. 203).

Do not knock. – Technology is making gestures precise and brutal, and with them men. It expels from movements all hesitation, deliberation, civility. It subjects them to the implacable, as it were ahistorical demands of objects. Thus the ability is lost, for example, to close a door quietly and discreetly, yet firmly. Those of cars and refrigerators have to be slammed, others have the tendency to snap shut by themselves, imposing on those entering the bad manners of not looking behind them, not shielding the interior of the house which receives them. The new human type cannot be properly understood without awareness of what he is continuously exposed to from the world of things about him, even in his most secret innervations. What does it mean for the subject that there are no more casement windows to open, but only sliding frames to shove, no gentle latches but turnable handles, no forecourt, no doorstep before the street, no wall around the garden? And which driver is not tempted, merely by the power of his engine, to wipe out the vermin of the street, pedestrians, children and cyclists? The movements machines demand of their users already have the violent, hard-hitting, unresting jerkiness of Fascist maltreatment. Not least to blame for the withering of experience is the fact that things, under the law of pure functionality, assume a form that limits contact with them to mere operation, and tolerates no surplus, either in freedom of conduct or in autonomy of things, which would survive as the core of experience, because it is not consumed by the moment of action.

20

Struwwelpeter. – When Hume, confronting his worldly compatriots, sought to defend epistemological contemplation, the 'pure philosophy' forever in disrepute among gentlemen, he used the argument: 'Accuracy is, in every case, advantageous to beauty, and just reasoning to delicate sentiment.'[1] That was itself pragmatic, and yet it contains implicitly and negatively the whole truth about the spirit of practicality. The practical orders of life, while pur-

1. David Hume, *An Enquiry Concerning Human Understanding*, Chicago 1963, pp. 6–7.

porting to benefit man, serve in a profit economy to stunt human qualities, and the further they spread the more they sever everything tender. For tenderness between people is nothing other than awareness of the possibility of relations without purpose, a solace still glimpsed by those embroiled in purposes; a legacy of old privileges promising a privilege-free condition. The abolition of privilege by bourgeois reason finally abolishes this promise too. If time is money, it seems moral to save time, above all one's own, and such parsimony is excused by consideration for others. One is straightforward. Every sheath interposed between men in their transactions is felt as a disturbance to the functioning of the apparatus, in which they are not only objectively incorporated but with which they proudly identify themselves. That, instead of raising their hats, they greet each other with the hallos of familiar indifference, that, instead of letters, they send each other inter-office communications without address or signature, are random symptoms of a sickness of contact. Estrangement shows itself precisely in the elimination of distance between people. For only as long as they abstain from importuning one another with giving and taking, discussion and implementation, control and function, is there space enough between them for the delicate connecting filigree of external forms in which alone the internal can crystallize. Reactionaries like the followers of Jung have noticed something of this. 'It is,' we read in one of G. R. Heyer's *Eranos* essays 'a distinguishing habit of people not yet fully formed by civilization, that a topic may not be directly approached, indeed, for some time not even mentioned; rather the conversation must move towards its real object as if by itself, in spirals.'[1] Instead of this, the straight line is now regarded as the shortest distance between two people, as if they were points. Just as nowadays house-walls are cast in one piece, so the mortar between people is replaced by the pressure holding them together. Anything different is simply no longer understood, but appears, if not as a Viennese speciality with a head-waiterly tinge, then as childish trustfulness or an illicit advance. In the form of the few sentences about the health of one's wife that prelude the business discussion over lunch, the utilitarian order has taken over and assimilated even its opposite. The taboo on talking shop and the inability to talk to each other are in reality the same thing. Because everything is business, the latter is unmentionable like rope in a

1. Gustav-Richard Heyer (1890–1967): psychologist disciple of Jung.

hanged man's home. Behind the pseudo-democratic dismantling of ceremony, of old-fashioned courtesy, of the useless conversation suspected, not even unjustly, of being idle gossip, behind the seeming clarification and transparency of human relations that no longer admit anything undefined, naked brutality is ushered in. The direct statement without divagations, hesitations or reflections, that gives the other the facts full in the face, already has the form and timbre of the command issued under Fascism by the dumb to the silent. Matter-of-factness between people, doing away with all ideological ornamentation between them, has already itself become an ideology for treating people as things.

21

Articles may not be exchanged. – We are forgetting how to give presents. Violation of the exchange principle has something non-sensical and implausible about it; here and there even children eye the giver suspiciously, as if the gift were merely a trick to sell them brushes or soap. Instead we have charity, administered beneficence, the planned plastering-over of society's visible sores. In its organized operations there is no longer room for human impulses, indeed, the gift is necessarily accompanied by humiliation through its distribution, its just allocation, in short through treatment of the recipient as an object. Even private giving of presents has degenerated to a social function exercised with rational bad grace, careful adherence to the prescribed budget, sceptical appraisal of the other and the least possible effort. Real giving had its joy in imagining the joy of the receiver. It means choosing, expending time, going out of one's way, thinking of the other as a subject: the opposite of distraction. Just this hardly anyone is now able to do. At the best they give what they would have liked themselves, only a few degrees worse. The decay of giving is mirrored in the distressing invention of gift-articles, based on the assumption that one does not know what to give because one really does not want to. This merchandise is unrelated like its buyers. It was a drug in the market from the first day. Likewise, the right to exchange the article, which signifies to the recipient: take this, it's all yours, do what you like with it; if you don't want it, that's all the same to me, get something else instead. Moreover, by comparison with the embarrassment

42

caused by ordinary presents this pure fungibility represents the more human alternative, because it at least allows the receiver to give himself a present, which is admittedly in absolute contradiction to the gift.

Beside the greater abundance of goods within reach even of the poor, the decline of present-giving might seem immaterial, reflection on it sentimental. However, even if amidst superfluity the gift were superflous – and this is a lie, privately as much as socially, for there is no-one today for whom imagination could not discover what would delight him utterly – people who no longer gave would still be in need of giving. In them wither the irreplaceable faculties which cannot flourish in the isolated cell of pure inwardness, but only in live contact with the warmth of things. A chill descends on all they do, the kind word that remains unspoken, the consideration unexercised. This chill finally recoils on those from whom it emanates. Every undistorted relationship, perhaps indeed the conciliation that is part of organic life itself, is a gift. He who through consequential logic becomes incapable of it, makes himself a thing and freezes.

22

Baby with the bath-water. – Among the motifs of cultural criticism one of the most long-established and central is that of the lie: that culture creates the illusion of a society worthy of man which does not exist; that it conceals the material conditions upon which all human works rise, and that, comforting and lulling, it serves to keep alive the bad economic determination of existence. This is the notion of culture as ideology, which appears at first sight common to both the bourgeois doctrine of violence and its adversary, both to Nietzsche and to Marx. But precisely this notion, like all expostulation about lies, has a suspicious tendency to become itself ideology. This can be seen on the private level. Inexorably, the thought of money and all its attendant conflicts extends into the most tender erotic, the most sublime spiritual relationships. With the logic of coherence and the pathos of truth, cultural criticism could therefore demand that relationships be entirely reduced to their material origin, ruthlessly and openly formed according to the interests of the participants. For meaning, as we know, is not independent of genesis, and it is easy to discern, in everything that cloaks or mediates the material, the trace of insincerity, sentimentality, indeed, precisely a concealed and doubly poisonous interest. But to act radically in accordance with this principle would be to extirpate, with the false, all that was true also, all that, however impotently, strives to escape the confines of universal practice, every chimerical anticipation of a nobler condition, and so to bring about directly the barbarism that culture is reproached with furthering indirectly. In the cultural critics after Nietzsche this reversal of position has always been obvious: Spengler endorsed it enthusiastically. But Marxists are not proof against it either. Cured of the Social-Democratic belief in cultural progress and confronted with growing barbarism, they are under constant temptation to advocate the latter in the interests of the 'objective tendency', and, in an act of desperation, to await salvation from their mortal enemy who, as the 'antithesis', is supposed in blind and mysterious fashion to help prepare the good end. Apart from this, emphasis on the material element, as against the spirit as a lie, gives rise to a kind of dubious affinity with that political economy which is subjected to an immanent criticism, comparable with the complicity between police and underworld. Since Utopia was set aside and the unity of theory and practice demanded, we have become all too practical. Fear of the impotence of theory supplies a pretext for bowing to the almighty production process, and so fully admitting the impotence of theory. Traits of malice are not alien even to authentic Marxist language, and today there is a growing resemblance between the business mentality and sober critical judgement, between vulgar materialism and the other kind, so that it is at times difficult properly to distinguish subject and object. – To identify culture solely with lies is more fateful than ever, now that the former is really becoming totally absorbed by the latter, and eagerly invites such identification in order to compromise every opposing thought. If material reality is called the world of exchange value, and culture whatever refuses to accept the domination of that world, then it is true that such refusal is illusory as long as the existent exists. Since, however, free and honest exchange is itself a lie, to deny it is at the same time to speak for truth: in face of the lie of the commodity world, even the lie that denounces it becomes a corrective. That culture so far has failed is no justification for furthering its failure, by strewing the store of good flour on the spilt beer like the girl in the fairy-tale.

People who belong together ought neither to keep silent about their material interests, nor to sink to their level, but to assimilate them by reflection into their relationships and so surpass them.

23

Plurale tantum.[1] – If society, as a contemporary theory teaches, is really one of rackets, then its most faithful model is the precise opposite of the collective, namely the individual as monad. By tracing the absolutely particular interests of each individual, the nature of the collective in a false society can be most accurately studied, and it is by no means far-fetched to consider the organization of divergent drives under the primacy of an ego answering the reality principle as, from the first, an internalized robber band with leader, followers, ceremonies, oaths of allegiance, betrayals, conflicts of interests, intrigues and all its other appurtenances. One need only observe outbursts in which the individual asserts himself energetically against his environment, for instance rage. The enraged man always appears as the gang-leader of his own self, giving his unconscious the order to pull no punches, his eyes shining with the satisfaction of speaking for the many that he himself is. The more someone has espoused the cause of his own aggression, the more perfectly he represents the repressive principle of society. In this sense more than in any other, perhaps, the proposition is true that the most individual is the most general.

24

Tough baby. – There is a certain gesture of virility, be it one's own or someone else's, that calls for suspicion. It expresses independence, sureness of the power to command, the tacit complicity of all males. Earlier, this was called with awed respect the whim of the master; today it has been democratized, and film heroes show the most insignificant bank clerk how it is done. Its archetype is the handsome dinner-jacketed figure returning late to his bachelor flat, switching on the indirect lighting and mixing himself a whisky and soda: the carefully recorded hissing of the mineral water says what the arrogant mouth keeps to itself: that he despises anything that

1. 'Only in the plural.'

does not smell of smoke, leather and shaving cream, particularly women, which is why they, precisely, find him irresistible. For him the ideal form of human relations is the club, that arena of a respect founded on scrupulous unscrupulousness. The pleasures of such men, or rather of their models, which are seldom equalled in reality, for people are even now better than their culture, all have about them a latent violence. This violence seems a threat directed against others, of whom such a one, sprawling in his easy chair, has long ceased to have need. In fact it is past violence against himself. If all pleasure has, preserved within it, earlier pain, then here pain, as pride in bearing it, is raised directly, untransformed, as a stereotype, to pleasure: unlike wine, each glass of whisky, each inhalation of cigar smoke, still recalls the repugance that it cost the organism to become attuned to such strong stimuli, and this alone is registered as pleasure. He-men are thus, in their own constitution, what film-plots usually present them to be, masochists. At the root of their sadism is a lie, and only as liars do they truly become sadists, agents of repression. This lie, however, is nothing other than repressed homosexuality presenting itself as the only approved form of heterosexuality. In Oxford two sorts of student are distinguished, the tough guys and the intellectuals; the latter through this contrast alone, are almost automatically equated with the effeminate. There is much reason to believe that the ruling stratum, on its way to dictatorship, becomes polarized towards these two extremes. Such disintegration is the secret of its integration, the joy of being united in the lack of joy. In the end the tough guys are the truly effeminate ones, who need the weaklings as their victims in order not to admit that they are like them. Totalitarianism and homosexuality belong together. In its downfall the subject negates everything which is not of its own kind. The opposites of the strong man and the compliant youth merge in an order which asserts unalloyed the male principle of domination. In making all without exception, even supposed subjects, its objects, this principle becomes totally passive, virtually feminine.

25

To them shall no thoughts be turned. – The past life of emigrés is, as we know, annulled. Earlier it was the warrant of arrest, today it is intellectual experience, that is declared non-transferable and un-naturalizable. Anything that is not reified, cannot be counted and measured, ceases to exist. Not satisfied with this, however, reification spreads to its own opposite, the life that cannot be directly actualized; anything that lives on merely as thought and recollection. For this a special rubric has been invented. It is called 'background' and appears on the questionnaire as an appendix, after sex, age and profession. To complete its violation, life is dragged along on the triumphal automobile of the united statisticians, and even the past is no longer safe from the present, whose remembrance of it consigns it a second time to oblivion.

26

English spoken. – In my childhood, some elderly English ladies with whom my parents kept up relations often gave me books as presents: richly illustrated works for the young, also a small green bible bound in morocco leather. All were in the language of the donors: whether I could read it none of them paused to reflect. The peculiar inaccessibility of the books, with their glaring pictures, titles and vignettes, and their indecipherable text, filled me with the belief that in general objects of this kind were not books at all, but advertisements, perhaps for machines like those my uncle produced in his London factory. Since I came to live in Anglo-Saxon countries and to understand English, this awareness has not been dispelled but strengthened. There is a song by Brahms, to a poem by Heyse,[1] with the lines: *O Herzeleid, du Ewigkeit!/Selbander nur ist Seligkeit.* In the most widely used American edition this is rendered as: 'O misery, eternity!/But two in one were ecstasy.' The archaic, passionate nouns of the original have been turned into catchwords for a hit song, designed to boost it. Illuminated in the neon-light switched on by these words, culture displays its character as advertising.

1. Paul Heyse (1830–1914): poet and novella-writer patronized by the Bavarian monarchy.

On parle français. – How intimately sex and language are inter-twined can be seen by reading pornography in a foreign language. When de Sade is read in the original no dictionary is needed. The most recondite expressions for the indecent, knowledge of which no school, no parental home, no literary experience transmits, are understood instinctively, just as in childhood the most tangential utterances and observations concerning the sexual crystallize into a true representation. It is as if the imprisoned passions, called by their name in these expressions, burst through the ramparts of blind language as through those of their own repression, and forced their way irresistibly into the innermost cell of meaning, which resembles them.

Paysage. – The shortcoming of the American landscape is not so much, as romantic illusion would have it, the absence of historical memories, as that it bears no traces of the human hand. This applies not only to the lack of arable land, the uncultivated woods often no higher than scrub, but above all to the roads. These are always in-serted directly in the landscape, and the more impressively smooth and broad they are, the more unrelated and violent their gleaming track appears against its wild, overgrown surroundings. They are expressionless. Just as they know no marks of foot or wheel, no soft paths along their edges as a transition to the vegetation, no trails leading off into the valley, so they are without the mild, soothing, un-angular quality of things that have felt the touch of hands or their immediate implements. It is as if no-one had ever passed their hand over the landscape's hair. It is uncomforted and comfortless. And it is perceived in a corresponding way. For what the hurrying eye has seen merely from the car it cannot retain, and the vanishing landscape leaves no more traces behind than it bears upon itself.

Dwarf fruit. – It is Proust's courtesy to spare the reader the embarrassment of believing himself cleverer than the author.

In the nineteenth century the Germans painted their dream and the outcome was invariably vegetable. The French needed only to paint a vegetable and it was already a dream.

In Anglo-Saxon countries the prostitutes look as if they purveyed, along with sin, the attendant pains of hell.

Beauty of the American landscape: that even the smallest of its segments is inscribed, as its expression, with the immensity of the whole country.

In the recollection of emigration each German venison roast tastes as if it had been felled with the charmed bullets of the *Freischütz*.[1]

In psycho-analysis nothing is true except the exaggerations.

We can tell whether we are happy by the sound of the wind. It warns the unhappy man of the fragility of his house, hounding him from shallow sleep and violent dreams. To the happy man it is the song of his protectedness: its furious howling concedes that it has power over him no longer.

The noiseless din that we have long known in dreams, booms at us in waking hours from newspaper headlines.

The mythical messenger of doom relives in radio. Important events announced peremptorily are always disasters. In English solemn means both ceremonious and menacing. The power of society behind the speaker turns of its own accord against the listeners.

The recent past always presents itself as if destroyed by catastrophes.

The expression of history in things is no other than that of past torment.

In Hegel self-consciousness was the truth of the certainty of one's self, in the words of the *Phenomenology*, the 'native realm of truth'.

1. Opera by the German romantic composer Carl Maria von Weber (1821).

When they had ceased to understand this, the bourgeois were self-conscious at least in their pride at owning wealth. Today self-consciousness no longer means anything but reflection on the ego as embarrassment, as realization of impotence: knowing that one is nothing.

In many people it is already an impertinence to say 'I'.

The splinter in your eye is the best magnifying-glass.

The basest person is capable of perceiving the weaknesses of the greatest, the most stupid, the errors in the thought of the most intelligent.

The first and only principle of sexual ethics: the accuser is always in the wrong.

The whole is the false.[1]

30

Pro domo nostra. – When during the last war, – which like all others, seems peaceful in comparison to its successor – the symphony orchestras of many countries had their vociferous mouths stopped, Stravinsky wrote the *Histoire du Soldat* for a sparse, shock-maimed chamber ensemble. It turned out to be his best score, the only convincing surrealist manifesto, its convulsive, dreamlike compulsion imparting to music an inkling of negative truth. The pre-condition of the piece was poverty: it dismantled official culture so drastically because, denied access to the latter's material goods, it also escaped the ostentation that is inimical to culture. There is here a pointer for intellectual production after the present war, which has left behind in Europe a measure of destruction undreamt of by even the voids in that music. Progress and barbarism are today so matted together in mass culture that only barbaric asceticism towards the latter, and towards progress in technical means, could restore an unbarbaric condition. No work of art, no thought, has a chance of survival, unless it bear within it repudiation of false riches and high-class

1. Inversion of Hegel's famous dictum: *Das Wahre ist das Ganze* – the whole is the true (*Phänomenologie des Geistes,* p. 24; *The Phenomenology of Mind,* p. 81).

production, of colour films and television, millionaire's magazines and Toscanini. The older media, not designed for mass-production, take on a new timeliness: that of exemption and of improvisation. They alone could outflank the united front of trusts and technology. In a world where books have long lost all likeness to books, the real book can no longer be one. If the invention of the printing press inaugurated the bourgeois era, the time is at hand for its repeal by the mimeograph, the only fitting, the unobtrusive means of dissemination.

31

Cat out of the bag. – Even solidarity, the most honourable mode of conduct of socialism, is sick. Solidarity was once intended to make the talk of brotherhood real, by lifting it out of generality, where it was an ideology, and reserving it for the particular, the Party, as the sole representative in an antagonistic world of generality. It was manifested by groups of people who together put their lives at stake, counting their own concerns as less important in face of a tangible possibility, so that, without being possessed by an abstract idea, but also without individual hope, they were ready to sacrifice themselves for each other. The prerequisites for this waiving of self-preservation were knowledge and freedom of decision: if they are lacking, blind particular interest immediately reasserts itself. In the course of time, however, solidarity has turned into confidence that the Party has a thousand eyes, into enrolment in workers' battalions – long since promoted into uniform – as the stronger side, into swimming with the tide of history. Any temporary security gained in this way is paid for by permanent fear, by toadying, manoeuvring and ventriloquism: the strength that might have been used to test the enemy's weakness is wasted in anticipating the whims of one's own leaders, who inspire more inner trembling than the old enemy; for one knows dimly that in the end the leaders on both sides will come to terms on the backs of those yoked beneath them. A reflection of this is discernible between individuals. Anyone who, by the stereotypes operative today, is categorized in advance as progressive, without having signed the imaginary declaration that seems to unite the true believers – who recognize each other by something imponderable in gesture and language, a kind of bluffly obedient resignation, as by a password – will repeatedly have the same experience. The orthodox, but also the deviationists all too like them, approach him expecting solidarity. They appeal explicitly and implicitly to the progressive pact. But the moment he looks for the slightest proof of the same solidarity from them, or mere sympathy for his own share of the social product of suffering, they give him the cold shoulder, which in the age of restored Pontiffs is all that remains of materialism and atheism. These organization men want the honest intellectual to expose himself for them, but as soon as they only remotely fear having to expose themselves, they see him as the capitalist, and the same honesty on which they were speculating, as ridiculous sentimentality and stupidity. Solidarity is polarized into the desperate loyalty of those who have no way back, and virtual blackmail practised on those who want nothing to do with gaolers, nor to fall foul of thieves.

32

Savages are not more noble. – There is to be found in African students of political economy, Siamese at Oxford, and more generally in diligent art-historians and musicologists of petty-bourgeois origins, a ready inclination to combine with the assimilation of new material, an inordinate respect for all that is established, accepted, acknowledged. An uncompromising mind is the very opposite of primitivism, neophytism, or the 'non-capitalist world'. It presupposes experience, a historical memory, a fastidious intellect and above all an ample measure of satiety. It has been observed time and again how those recruited young and innocent to radical groups have defected once they felt the force of tradition. One must have tradition in oneself, to hate it properly. That snobs show more aptitude than proletarians for *avant-garde* movements in art throws light on politics too. Late-comers and newcomers have an alarming affinity to positivism, from Carnap-worshippers in India to the stalwart defenders of the German masters Matthias Grünewald and Heinrich Schütz.[1] It would be poor psychology to assume that

1. Rudolf Carnap (1891–1970): leading philosopher of neo-positivism, who emigrated to the USA in 1936. Matthias Grünewald (c. 1470/80–1528): late Gothic painter, and Heinrich Schütz (1585–1672): early Baroque composer – both of intense religious inspiration.

exclusion arouses only hate and resentment; it arouses too a possessive, intolerant kind of love, and those whom repressive culture has held at a distance can easily enough become its most diehard defenders. There is even an echo of this in the sententious language of the worker who wants, as a Socialist, to 'learn something', to partake of the so-called heritage, and the philistinism of the Bebels[1] lies less in their incomprehension of culture than in the alacrity with which they accept it at face value, identify with it and in so doing, of course, reverse its meaning. Socialism is in general no more secure against this transformation than against lapsing theoretically into positivism. It can happen easily enough that in the Far East Marx is put in the place vacated by Driesch and Rickert.[2] There is some reason to fear that the involvement of non-Western peoples in the conflicts of industrial society, long overdue in itself, will be less to the benefit of the liberated peoples than to that of rationally improved production and communications, and a modestly raised standard of living. Instead of expecting miracles of the pre-capitalist peoples, older nations should be on their guard against their unimaginative, indolent taste for everything proven, and for the successes of the West.

33

Out of the firing-line. – Reports of air-attacks are seldom without the names of the firms which produced the planes: Focke-Wulff, Heinkel, Lancaster feature where once the talk was of cuirassiers, lancers and hussars. The mechanism for reproducing life, for dominating and for destroying it, is exactly the same, and accordingly industry, state and advertising are amalgamated. The old exaggeration of sceptical Liberals, that war was a business, has come true: state power has shed even the appearance of independence from particular interests in profit; always in their service really, it now also places itself there ideologically. Every laudatory mention of

1. August Bebel was co-founder and leader of the German Social-Democratic Party from the Franco-Prussian War to the eve of the First World War.
2. Hans Driesch (1867–1941): vitalist philosopher and biologist, author of 'The Science and Philosophy of the Organism'. Heinrich Rickert (1863–1936): Neo-Kantian philosopher and subjectivist exponent of a value-oriented epistemology.

the chief contractor in the destruction of cities, helps to earn it the good name that will secure it the best commissions in their rebuilding.

Like the Thirty Years' War, this too – a war whose beginning no-one will remember when it comes to an end – falls into discontinuous campaigns separated by empty pauses, the Polish campaign, the Norwegian, the Russian, the Tunisian, the Invasion. Its rhythm, the alternation of jerky action and total standstill for lack of geographically attainable enemies, has the same mechanical quality which characterizes individual military instruments and which too is doubtless what has resurrected the pre-Liberal form of the campaign. But this mechanical rhythm completely determines the human relation to the war, not only in the disproportion between individual bodily strength and the energy of machines, but in the most hidden cells of experience. Even in the previous conflict the body's incongruity with mechanical warfare made real experience impossible. No-one could have recounted it as even the Artillery-General Napoleon's battles could be recalled. The long interval between the war memoirs and the conclusion of peace is not fortuitous: it testifies to the painful reconstruction of memory, which in all the books conveys a sense of impotence and even falseness, no matter what terrors the writers have passed through. But the Second War is as totally divorced from experience as is the functioning of a machine from the movements of the body, which only begins to resemble it in pathological states. Just as the war lacks continuity, history, an 'epic' element, but seems rather to start anew from the beginning in each phase, so it will leave behind no permanent, unconsciously preserved image in the memory. Everywhere, with each explosion, it has breached the barrier against stimuli beneath which experience, the lag between healing oblivion and healing recollection, forms. Life has changed into a timeless succession of shocks, interspaced with empty, paralysed intervals. But nothing, perhaps, is more ominous for the future than the fact that, quite literally, these things will soon be past thinking on, for each trauma of the returning combatants, each shock not inwardly absorbed, is a ferment of future destruction. Karl Kraus was right to call his play *The Last Days of Mankind*. What is being enacted now ought to bear the title: 'After Doomsday'.

The total obliteration of the war by information, propaganda, commentaries, with camera-men in the first tanks and war reporters dying heroic deaths, the mish-mash of enlightened manipulation of public opinion and oblivious activity: all this is another expression for the withering of experience, the vacuum between men and their fate, in which their real fate lies. It is as if the reified, hardened plaster-cast of events takes the place of events themselves. Men are reduced to walk-on parts in a monster documentary film which has no spectators, since the least of them has his bit to do on the screen. It is just this aspect that underlies the much-maligned designation 'phoney war'. Certainly, the term has its origin in the Fascist inclination to dismiss the reality of horror as 'mere propaganda' in order to perpetrate it unopposed. But like all Fascist tendencies, this too has its source in elements of reality, which assert themselves only by virtue of the Fascist attitude malignantly insinuating them. The war is really phoney, but with a phoneyness more horrifying than all the horrors, and those who mock at it are principal contributors to disaster.

Had Hegel's philosophy of history embraced this age, Hitler's robot-bombs would have found their place beside the early death of Alexander and similar images, as one of the selected empirical facts by which the state of the world-spirit manifests itself directly in symbols. Like Fascism itself, the robots career without a subject. Like it they combine utmost technical perfection with total blindness. And like it they arouse mortal terror and are wholly futile. 'I have seen the world spirit', not on horseback, but on wings and without a head, and that refutes, at the same stroke, Hegel's philosophy of history.

The idea that after this war life will continue 'normally' or even that culture might be 'rebuilt' – as if the rebuilding of culture were not already its negation – is idiotic. Millions of Jews have been murdered, and this is to be seen as an interlude and not the catastrophe itself. What more is this culture waiting for? And even if countless people still have time to wait, is it conceivable that what happened in Europe will have no consequences, that the quantity of victims will not be transformed into a new quality of society at large, barbarism? As long as blow is followed by counter-blow, catastrophe is perpetuated. One need only think of revenge for the murdered. If as many of the others are killed, horror will be institutionalized and the pre-capitalist pattern of vendettas, confined from time immemorial to remote mountainous regions, will be re-introduced in extended form, with whole nations as the subjectless subjects. If, however, the dead are not avenged and mercy is exercised, Fascism will despite everything get away with its victory scot-free, and, having once been shown so easy, will be continued elsewhere. The logic of history is as destructive as the people that it brings to prominence: wherever its momentum carries it, it reproduces equivalents of past calamity. Normality is death.

To the question what is to be done with defeated Germany, I could say only two things in reply. Firstly: at no price, on no conditions, would I wish to be an executioner or to supply legitimations for executioners. Secondly: I should not wish, least of all with legal machinery, to stay the hand of anyone who was avenging past misdeeds. This is a thoroughly unsatisfactory, contradictory answer, one that makes a mockery of both principle and practice. But perhaps the fault lies in the question and not only in me.

Cinema newsreel: the invasion of the Marianas, including Guam. The impression is not of battles, but of civil engineering and blasting operations undertaken with immeasurably intensified vehemence, also of 'fumigation', insect-extermination on a terrestrial scale. Works are put in hand, until no grass grows. The enemy acts as patient and corpse. Like the Jews under Fascism, he features now as merely the object of technical and administrative measures, and should he defend himself, his own action immediately takes on the same character. Satanically, indeed, more initiative is in a sense demanded here than in old-style war: it seems to cost the subject his whole energy to achieve subjectlessness. Consummate inhumanity is the realization of Edward Grey's humane dream, war without hatred.

Autumn 1944

34

Johnny-Head-in-Air. – The relation of knowledge to power is one not only of servility but of truth. Much knowledge, if out of proportion to the disposition of forces, is invalid, however formally correct it may be. If an émigré doctor says: 'For me, Adolf Hitler is a pathological case', his pronouncement may ultimately be confirmed by clinical findings, but its incongruity with the objective calamity visited on the world in the name of that paranoiac renders the diagnosis ridiculous, mere professional preening. Perhaps Hitler is 'in-himself' a pathological case, but certainly not 'for-him'. The vanity and poverty of many of the declarations against Fascism by émigrés is connected with this. People thinking in the forms of free, detached, disinterested appraisal were unable to accommodate within those forms the experience of violence which in reality annuls such thinking. The almost insoluble task is to let neither the power of others, nor our own powerlessness, stupefy us.

35

Back to culture. – The claim that Hitler has destroyed German culture is no more than an advertising stunt of those who want to rebuild it from their telephone desks. Such art and thought as were exterminated by Hitler had long been leading a severed and apocryphal existence, whose last hideouts Fascism swept out. Anyone who did not play the game was forced into inner emigration years before the Third Reich broke out: at the latest with the stabilization of the German currency, coinciding with the end of Expressionism, German culture stabilized itself in the spirit of the Berlin illustrated magazines, which yielded little to that of the Nazis' 'Strength through Joy', Reich autobahns, and jaunty exhibition-hall Classicism. The whole span of German culture was languishing, precisely where it was most liberal, for its Hitler, and it is an injustice to the editors of Mosse and Ullstein[1] or to the reorganizers of the *Frankfurter Zeitung*, to reproach them with time-serving under Nazism. They were always like that, and their line of least resistance to the intellectual wares they produced was continued undeflected in the line of least resistance to a political regime among whose ideological methods, as the Führer himself declared, comprehensibility to the most stupid ranked highest. This has led to fatal confusion. Hitler eradicated culture, Hitler drove Mr X into exile, therefore Mr X is culture. He is indeed. A glance at the literary output of

1. Mosse-Verlag and Ullstein-Verlag were the two largest press combines of German-Jewish capital in the Weimar Republic, controlling newspapers, magazines and publishing houses. Both were taken over by the Nazis.

those émigrés who, by discipline and a sharp separation of spheres of influence, performed the feat of representing the German mind, shows what is to be expected of a happy reconstruction: the introduction of Broadway methods on the Kurfürstendamm, which differed from the former in the Twenties only through its lesser means, not its better intentions. Those who oppose cultural Fascism should start with Weimar, the 'Bombs on Monte Carlo' and the Press Ball, if they do not wish to finish by discovering that equivocal figures like Fallada[1] spoke more truth under Hitler than the unambiguous celebrities who successfully transplanted their prestige.

36

The Health unto Death.[2] – If such a thing as a psycho-analysis of today's prototypical culture were possible; if the absolute predominance of the economy did not beggar all attempts at explaining conditions by the psychic life of their victims; and if the psychoanalysts had not long since sworn allegiance to those conditions – such an investigation would needs show the sickness proper to the time to consist precisely in normality. The libidinal achievements demanded of an individual behaving as healthy in body and mind, are such as can be performed only at the cost of the profoundest mutilation, of internalized castration in extroverts, beside which the old renunciation of identification with the father is the child's play as which it was first rehearsed. The regular guy, the popular girl, have to repress not only their desires and insights, but even the symptoms that in bourgeois times resulted from repression. Just as the old injustice is not changed by a lavish display of light, air and hygiene, but is in fact concealed by the gleaming transparency of rationalized big business, the inner health of our time has been secured by blocking flight into illness without in the slightest altering its aetiology. The dark closets have been abolished as a troublesome waste of space, and incorporated in the bathroom. What psycho-analysis suspected, before it became itself a part of

1. Hans Fallada (1893–1947): social novelist of reportorial realism, whose works enjoyed great popular success in the last years of the Weimar period, and who continued to write novels in Germany under the Nazi regime.
2. Inversion of the title of Kierkegaard's work *The Sickness unto Death.*

hygiene, has been confirmed. The brightest rooms are the secret domain of faeces. The verses: 'Wretchedness remains. When all is said, / It cannot be uprooted, live or dead. / So it is made invisible instead', are still more true of the psychic economy than of the sphere where abundance of goods may temporarily obscure constantly increasing material inequalities. No science has yet explored the inferno in which were forged the deformations that later emerge to daylight as cheerfulness, openness, sociability, successful adaptation to the inevitable, an equable, practical frame of mind. There is reason to suppose that these characteristics are laid down at even earlier phases of childhood development than are neuroses: if the latter result from a conflict in which instinct is defeated, the former condition, as normal as the damaged society it resembles, stems from what might be called a prehistoric surgical intervention, which incapacitates the opposing forces before they have come to grips with each other, so that the subsequent absence of conflicts reflects a predetermined outcome, the *a priori* triumph of collective authority, not a cure effected by knowledge. Unruffled calm, already a prerequisite for applicants receiving highly-paid posts, is an image of the stifled silence that the employers of the personnel manager only later impose politically. The only objective way of diagnosing the sickness of the healthy is by the incongruity between their rational existence and the possible course their lives might be given by reason. All the same, the traces of illness give them away: their skin seems covered by a rash printed in regular patterns, like a camouflage of the inorganic. The very people who burst with proofs of exuberant vitality could easily be taken for prepared corpses, from whom the news of their not-quite-successful decease has been withheld for reasons of population policy. Underlying the prevalent health is death. All the movements of health resemble the reflex-movements of beings whose hearts have stopped beating. Scarcely ever does an unhappily furrowed brow, bearing witness to terrible and long-forgotten exertions, or a moment of pathic stupidity disrupting smooth logic, or an awkward gesture, embarrassingly preserve a trace of vanished life. For socially ordained sacrifice is indeed so universal as to be manifest only in society as a whole, and not in the individual. Society has, as it were, assumed the sickness of all individuals, and in it, in the pent-up lunacy of Fascist acts and all their innumerable precursors and mediators, the subjective fate buried deep in the individual is integrated with its visible objective counterpart. And how comfortless is the thought that the sickness of the normal does not necessarily imply as its opposite the health of the sick, but that the latter usually only present, in a different way, the same disastrous pattern.

37

This side of the pleasure principle. – The repressive traits in Freud have nothing to do with the want of human warmth that business-like revisionists point to in the strict theory of sexuality. Professional warmth, for the sake of profit, fabricates closeness and immediacy where people are worlds apart. It deceives its victim by affirming in his weakness the way of the world which made him so, and it wrongs him in the degree that it deviates from truth. If Freud was deficient in such human sympathy, he would in this at least be in the company of the critics of political economy, which is better than that of Tagore or Werfel.[1] The fatality was rather that, in the teeth of bourgeois ideology, he tracked down conscious actions materialistically to their unconscious instinctual basis, but at the same time concurred with the bourgeois contempt of instinct which is itself a product of precisely the rationalizations that he dismantled. He explicitly aligns himself, in the words of the *Introductory Lectures*, with 'the general evaluation . . . which places social goals higher than the fundamentally selfish sexual ones'. As a specialist in psychology, he takes over the antithesis of social and egoistic, statically, without testing it. He no more discerns in it the work of repressive society than the trace of the disastrous mechanisms that he has himself described. Or rather, he vacillates, devoid of theory and swaying with prejudice, between negating the renunciation of instinct as repression contrary to reality, and applauding it as sublimation beneficial to culture. In this contradiction something of the Janus-character of culture exists objectively, and no amount of praise for healthy sensuality can wish it away. In Freud, however, it leads to a devaluation of the critical standard that decides the goal of analysis. Freud's unenlightened enlightenment plays into the hands of bourgeois disillusion. As a late opponent of

1. Rabindranath Tagore (1861–1941): Bengali poet and philosopher of mystical populist inclinations. Franz Werfel (1890–1945): Austrian writer of religious-humanitarian pathos.

hypocrisy, he stands ambivalently between desire for the open emancipation of the oppressed, and apology for open oppression. Reason is for him a mere superstructure, not – as official philosophy maintains – on account of his psychologism, which has penetrated deeply enough into the historical moment of truth, but rather because he rejects the end, remote to meaning, impervious to reason, which alone could prove the means, reason, to be reasonable: pleasure. Once this has been disparagingly consigned to the repertoire of tricks for preserving the species, and so itself exposed as a cunning form of reason, without consideration of that moment in pleasure which transcends subservience to nature, *ratio* is degraded to rationalization. Truth is abandoned to relativity and people to power. He alone who could situate utopia in blind somatic pleasure, which, satisfying the ultimate intention, is intentionless, has a stable and valid idea of truth. In Freud's work, however, the dual hostility towards mind and pleasure, whose common root psycho-analysis has given us the means for discovering, is unintentionally reproduced. The place in the *Future of an Illusion* where, with the worthless wisdom of a hard-boiled old gentleman, he quotes the commercial-traveller's dictum about leaving heaven to the angels and the sparrows,[1] should be set beside the passage in the *Lectures* where he damns in pious horror the perverse practices of pleasure-loving society. Those who feel equal revulsion for pleasure and paradise are indeed best suited to serve as objects: the empty, mechanized quality observable in so many who have undergone successful analysis is to be entered to the account not only of their illness but also of their cure, which dislocates what it liberates. The therapeutically much-lauded transference, the breaking of which is not for nothing the crux of analytic treatment, the artificially contrived situation where the subject performs, voluntarily and calamitously, the annulment of the self which was once brought about involuntarily and beneficially by erotic self-abandonment, is already the pattern of the reflex-dominated, follow-my-leader behaviour which liquidates, together with all intellect, the analysts who have betrayed it.

1. Allusion to Heine's poem *Deutschland. Ein Wintermärchen*, see *The Future of an Illusion* (London, 1970, p. 46).

Invitation to the dance.[1] – Psycho-analysis prides itself on restoring the capacity for pleasure, which is impaired by neurotic illness. As if the mere concept of a capacity for pleasure did not suffice gravely to devalue such a thing, if it exists. As if a happiness gained through speculation on happiness were not the opposite, a further enroachment of institutionally planned behaviour-patterns on the ever-diminishing sphere of experience. What a state the dominant consciousness must have reached, when the resolute proclamation of compulsive extravagance and champagne jollity, formerly reserved to attachés in Hungarian operettas, is elevated in deadly earnest to a maxim of right living. Prescribed happiness looks exactly what it is; to have a part in it, the neurotic thus made happy must forfeit the last vestige of reason left to him by repression and regression, and to oblige the analyst, display indiscriminate enthusiasm for the trashy film, the expensive but bad meal in the French restaurant, the serious drink and the love-making taken like medicine as 'sex'. Schiller's dictum that 'Life's good, in spite of all', *papier-mâché* from the start, has become idiocy now that it is blown into the same trumpet as omnipresent advertising, with psycho-analysis, despite its better possibilities, adding its fuel to the flames. As people have altogether too few inhibitions and not too many, without being a whit the healthier for it, a cathartic method with a standard other than successful adaptation and economic success would have to aim at bringing people to a consciousness of unhappiness both general and – inseparable from it – personal, and at depriving them of the illusory gratifications by which the abominable order keeps a second hold on life inside them, as if it did not already have them firmly enough in its power from outside. Only when sated with false pleasure, disgusted with the goods offered, dimly aware of the inadequacy of happiness even when it is that – to say nothing of cases where it is bought by abandoning allegedly morbid resistance to its positive surrogate – can men gain an idea of what experience might be. The admonitions to be happy, voiced in concert by the scientifically epicurean sanatorium-director and the highly-strung propaganda chiefs of the entertainment-

1. *Aufforderung zum Tanz*: title of the piano-solo that was the first modern dance-music of the post-Napoleonic epoch, composed by Carl Maria von Weber in 1819.

industry, have about them the fury of the father berating his children for not rushing joyously downstairs when he comes home irritable from his office. It is part of the mechanism of domination to forbid recognition of the suffering it produces, and there is a straight line of development between the gospel of happiness and the construction of camps of extermination so far off in Poland that each of our own countrymen can convince himself that he cannot hear the screams of pain. That is the model of an unhampered capacity for happiness. He who calls it by its name will be told gloatingly by psycho-analysis that it is just his Oedipus complex.

39

Ego is Id. – A connection is commonly drawn between the development of psychology and the rise of the bourgeois individual, both in Antiquity and since the Renaissance. This ought not to obscure the contrary tendency also common to psychology and the bourgeois class, and which today has developed to the point of excluding all others: the suppression and dissolution of the very individual in whose service knowledge was related back to its subject. If all psychology since that of Protagoras has elevated man by conceiving him as the measure of all things, it has thereby also treated him from the first as an object, as material for analysis, and transferred to him, once he was included among them, the nullity of things. The denial of objective truth by recourse to the subject implies the negation of the latter: no measure remains for the measure of all things; lapsing into contingency, he becomes untruth. But this points back to the real life-process of society. The principle of human domination, in becoming absolute, has turned its point against man as the absolute object, and psychology has collaborated in sharpening that point. The self, its guiding idea and its *a priori* object, has always, under its scrutiny, been rendered at the same time non-existent. In appealing to the fact that in an exchange society the subject was not one, but in fact a social object, psychology provided society with weapons for ensuring that this was and remained the case. The dissection of man into his faculties is a projection of the division of labour onto its pretended subjects, inseparable from the interest in deploying and manipulating them to greater advantage. Psycho-technics is not merely a form of psychology's decay, but is inherent in its principle. Hume, whose work bears witness in every sentence to his real humanism, yet who dismisses the self as a prejudice, expresses in this contradiction the nature of psychology as such. In this he even has truth on his side, for that which posits itself as 'I' is indeed mere prejudice, an ideological hypostasization of the abstract centres of domination, criticism of which demands the removal of the ideology of 'personality'. But its removal also makes the residue all the easier to dominate. This is flagrantly apparent in psycho-analysis. It incorporates personality as a lie needed for living, as the supreme rationalization holding together the innumerable rationalizations by which the individual achieves his instinctual renunciation, and accommodates himself to the reality principle. But precisely in demonstrating this, it confirms man's non-being. Alienating him from himself, denouncing his autonomy with his unity, psycho-analysis subjugates him totally to the mechanism of rationalization, of adaptation. The ego's unflinching self-criticism gives way to the demand that the ego of the other capitulate. The psycho-analyst's wisdom finally becomes what the Fascist unconscious of the horror magazines takes it for: a technique by which one particular racket among others binds suffering and helpless people irrevocably to itself, in order to command and exploit them. Suggestion and hypnosis, rejected by psycho-analysis as apocryphal, the charlatan magician masquerading before a fairground booth, reappear within its grandiose system as the silent film does in the Hollywood epic. What was formerly help through greater knowledge has become the humiliation of others by dogmatic privilege. All that remains of the criticism of bourgeois consciousness is the shrug with which doctors have always signalled their secret complicity with death. – In psychology, in the bottomless fraud of mere inwardness, which is not by accident concerned with the 'properties' of men, is reflected what bourgeois society has practised for all time with outward property. The latter, as a result of social exchange, has been increased, but with a proviso dimly present to every bourgeois. The individual has been, as it were, merely invested with property by the class, and those in control are ready to take it back as soon as universalization of property seems likely to endanger its principle, which is precisely that of withholding. Psychology repeats in the case of properties what was done to property. It expropriates the individual by allocating him its happiness.

Always speak of it, never think of it.[1] – Now that depth-psychology, with the help of films, soap operas and Horney, has delved into the deepest recesses, people's last possibility of experiencing themselves has been cut off by organized culture. Ready-made enlightenment turns not only spontaneous reflection but also analytical insights – whose power equals the energy and suffering that it cost to gain them – into mass-produced articles, and the painful secrets of the individual history, which the orthodox method is already inclined to reduce to formulae, into commonplace conventions. Dispelling rationalizations becomes itself rationalization. Instead of working to gain self-awareness, the initiates become adept at subsuming all instinctual conflicts under such concepts as inferiority complex, mother-fixation, extroversion and introversion, to which they are in reality inaccessible. Terror before the abyss of the self is removed by the consciousness of being concerned with nothing so very different from arthritis or sinus trouble. Thus conflicts lose their menace. They are accepted, but by no means cured, being merely fitted as an unavoidable component into the surface of standardized life. At the same time they are absorbed, as a general evil, by the mechanism directly identifying the individual with social authority, which has long since encompassed all supposedly normal modes of behaviour. Catharsis, unsure of success in any case, is supplanted by pleasure at being, in one's own weakness, a specimen of the majority; and rather than gaining, like inmates of a sanatorium in former days, the prestige of an interesting pathological case, one proves on the strength of one's very defects that one belongs, thereby transferring to oneself the power and vastness of the collective. Narcissism, deprived of its libidinal object by the decay of the self, is replaced by the masochistic satisfaction of no longer being a self, and the rising generation guards few of its goods so jealously as its selflessness, its communal and lasting possession. The realm of reification and standardization is thus extended to include its ultimate contradiction, the ostensibly abnormal and chaotic. The incommensurable is made, precisely as such, commensurable, and the individual is now scarcely capable of any impulse that he could

1. *Immer davon reden, nie daran denken*: inversion of the pro-Anschluss slogan in pre-war Austria, *Nie davon reden, immer daran denken* (never speak of it, always think of it).

not classify as an example of this or that publicly recognized con-stellation. However, this outwardly assumed identification, accom-plished, as it were, beyond one's own dynamic, finally abolishes not only genuine consciousness of the impulse but the impulse itself. The latter becomes the reflex of stereotyped atoms to stereo-typed stimuli, switched on or off at will. Moreover, psycho-analysis itself is castrated by its conventionalization: sexual motives, partly disavowed and partly approved, are made totally harmless but also totally insignificant. With the fear they instil vanishes the joy they might procure. Thus psycho-analysis falls victim to the very replacement of the appropriate super-ego by a stubbornly adopted, unrelated, external one, that it taught us itself to understand. The last grandly-conceived theorem of bourgeois self-criticism has become a means of making bourgeois self-alienation, in its final phase, absolute, and of rendering ineffectual the lingering awareness of the ancient wound, in which lies hope of a better future.

41

Inside and outside. – Piety, indolence and calculation allow philo-sophy to keep muddling along within an ever narrower academic groove, and even there steadily increasing efforts are made to replace it by organized tautology. Those who throw in their lot with salaried profundity are compelled, as a hundred years ago, to be at each moment as naive as the colleagues on whom their careers depend. But extra-academic thinking, which seeks to escape such compulsion, with its contradiction between high-flown subject matter and petty-minded treatment, faces a scarcely lesser threat: the economic pressure of the market, from which in Europe the professors at least were protected. The philosopher who wishes to earn his living as a writer is obliged at each moment to have some-thing choice, ultra-select to offer, and to counter the monopoly of office with that of rarity. The repulsive notion of the intellectual titbit, conceived by pedants, finally proves humiliatingly applicable to their opponents. The hack journalist groaning under his editor's demands for continuous brilliance,[1] openly gives voice to the law that lurks tacitly behind all the works on the Cosmogonic Eros and

1. Reference to the archetypal character Schmock in Gustav Freytag's comedy *Die Journalisten* (1854).

kindred mysteries,[1] the metamorphoses of the gods and the secret of the Gospel according to St John. The life-style of belated bohemianism forced on the non-academic philosopher is itself enough to give him a fatal affinity to the world of arts-and-crafts, crackpot religion and half-educated sectarianism. Munich before the First World War was a hotbed of that spirituality whose protest against the rationalism of the schools led, by way of the cults of fancy-dress festivities, more swiftly to Fascism than possibly even the spiritless system of old Rickert. So great is the power of the advancing organization of thought, that those who want to keep outside it are driven to resentful vanity, babbling self-advertisement and finally, in their defeat, to imposture. If the academics uphold the principle of *sum ergo cogito* and fall victim, in the open system, to agoraphobia, and in the existential exposure of Being-in-the-world, to the racial community, their opponents stray, unless exceptionally vigilant, into the region of graphology and rhythmic gymnastics.[2] The compulsive type there corresponds to the paranoiac here. Ardent opposition to factual investigations, and a legitimate consciousness that scientism overlooks what is most valuable, aggravates by its naivety the split from which it suffers. Instead of comprehending the facts behind which the others are entrenched, it snatches those it can reach in its haste and makes off to play so uncritically with apocryphal knowledge, with a few isolated and hypostasized categories, and with itself, that simple reference to unyielding facts is enough to defeat it. It is precisely the critical element that is wanting in ostensibly independent thought. Insistence on the cosmic secret hidden beneath the outer shell, in reverently omitting to establish the relation between the two, often enough confirms by just this omission that the shell has its good reasons that must be accepted without asking questions. Between delight in emptiness and the lie of fullness, the prevailing intellectual situation allows no third way.

Yet a gaze averted from the beaten track, a hatred of brutality, a search for fresh concepts not yet encompassed by the general

1. Ludwig Klages (1872–1956), conservative and irrationalist philosopher who was a *Privatgelehrter* in Munich, was the author of *Vom Kosmogonischen Eros* (1922).

2. Respective allusions to Heidegger's concept of *Geworfenheit* (existential exposure), and to Klages's ventures into graphology and eurhythmics (*Vom Wesen des Rhythmus*, 1933). Both Heidegger and Klages were compromised by Fascism.

pattern, is the last hope for thought. In an intellectual hierarchy which constantly makes everyone answerable, unanswerability alone can call the hierachy directly by its name. The circulation sphere, whose stigmata are borne by intellectual outsiders, opens a last refuge to the mind that it barters away, at the very moment when refuge really no longer exists. He who offers for sale something unique that no-one wants to buy, represents, even against his will, freedom from exchange.

42

Freedom of thought.[1] – The displacement of philosophy by science has led, as we know, to a separation of the two elements whose unity, according to Hegel, constitutes the life of philosophy: reflection and speculation. The land of truth is handed over in dis-illusion to reflection, and speculation is tolerated ungraciously within it merely for the purpose of formulating hypotheses, which must be conceived outside working hours and yield results as quickly as possible. To believe, however, that the speculative realm has been preserved unscathed in its extra-scientific form, left in peace by the bustle of universal statistics, would be to err grievously. First, severance from reflection costs speculation itself dear enough. It is either degraded to a docile echo of traditional philosophical schemes, or, in its aloofness from blinded facts, perverted to the non-committal chatter of a private *Weltanschauung*. Not satisfied with this, however, science assimilates speculation to its own operations. Among the public functions of psycho-analysis, this is not the least. Its medium is free association. The way into the patient's unconscious is laid open by persuading him to forgo the responsibility of reflection, and the formation of analytic theory follows the same track, whether it allows its findings to be traced by the progress and the falterings of these associations, or whether the analysts – and I mean precisely the most gifted of them, like Groddeck[2] – trust to their own associations. We are presented on

1. *Gedankenfreiheit*: a play on the two meanings of the German expression, which can be used both for the liberty of thought of a citizen in the political sense, and for the free association of a patient in the psychoanalytic sense.

2. Georg Groddeck: author of *Der Seelensucher* (1921), a work sufficiently un-puritan in tone for Freud to have to defend it against colleagues by asking them how they would have reacted, had they been contemporaries, to Rabelais.

the couch with a relaxed performance of what was once enacted, with the utmost exertion of thought, by Schelling and Hegel on the lecturer's podium: the deciphering of the phenomenon. But this drop in tension affects the quality of the thought: the difference is hardly less than that between the philosophy of revelation[1] and the random gossip of a mother-in-law. The same movement of mind which was once to elevate its 'material' to a concept, is itself reduced to mere material for conceptual ordering. The ideas one has are just good enough to allow experts to decide whether their originator is a compulsive character, an oral type, or a hysteric. Thanks to the diminished responsibility that lies in its severance from reflection, from rational control, speculation is itself handed over as an object to science, whose subjectivity is extinguished with it. Thought, in allowing itself to be reminded of its unconscious origins by the administrative structure of analysis, forgets to be thought. From true judgement it becomes neutral stuff. Instead of mastering itself by performing the task of conceptualization, it entrusts itself impotently to processing by the doctor, who in any case knows everything beforehand. Thus speculation is definitively crushed, becoming itself a fact to be included in one of the departments of classification as proof that nothing changes.

43

Unfair intimidation. – What truth may objectively be is difficult enough to determine, but we should not, in our dealings with people, let this fact terrorize us. To this end criteria are used that at first sight seem convincing. One of the most dependable is the reproach that a statement is 'too subjective'. If this is brought to bear, with an indignation in which rings the furious harmony of all reasonable people, one has grounds, for a few seconds, to feel self-satisfied. The notions of subjective and objective have been completely reversed. Objective means the non-controversial aspect of things, their unquestioned impression, the façade made up of classified data, that is, the subjective; and they call subjective anything which breaches that façade, engages the specific experience of a matter, casts off all ready-made judgements and substitutes relatedness to the object for the majority consensus of those who do not

1. *Der Philosophie der Offenbarung*: the system of the late Schelling.

even look at it, let alone think about it – that is, the objective. Just how vacuous the formal objection to subjective relativity is, can be seen in the particular field of the latter, that of aesthetic judgements. Anyone who, drawing on the strength of his precise reaction to a work of art, has ever subjected himself in earnest to its discipline, to its immanent formal law, the compulsion of its structure, will find that objections to the merely subjective quality of his experience vanish like a pitiful illusion: and every step that he takes, by virtue of his highly subjective innervation, towards the heart of the matter, has incomparably greater force than the comprehensive and fully backed-up analyses of such things as 'style', whose claims to scientific status are made at the expense of such experience. This is doubly true in the era of positivism and the culture industry, where objectivity is calculated by the subjects managing it. In face of this, reason has retreated entirely behind a windowless wall of idiosyncrasies, which the holders of power arbitrarily reproach with arbitrariness, since they want subjects impotent, for fear of the objectivity that is preserved in these subjects alone.

44

For Post-Socratics. – Nothing is more unfitting for an intellectual resolved on practising what was earlier called philosophy, than to wish, in discussion, and one might almost say in argumentation, to be right. The very wish to be right, down to its subtlest form of logical reflection, is an expression of that spirit of self-preservation which philosophy is precisely concerned to break down. I knew someone who invited all the celebrities in epistemology, science and the humanities one after the other, discussed his own system with each of them from first to last, and when none of them dared raise any further arguments against its formalism, believed his position totally impregnable. Such naivety is at work wherever philosophy has even a distant resemblance to the gestures of persuasion. These are founded on the presupposition of a *universitas literarum*, an *a priori* agreement between minds able to communicate with each other, and thus on complete conformism. When philosophers, who are well known to have difficulty in keeping silent, engage in conversation, they should try always to lose the argument, but in such a way as to convict their opponent of untruth. The point should not be to have absolutely correct, irrefutable, watertight cognitions – for they inevitably boil down to tautologies, but insights which cause the question of their justness to judge itself. – To say this is not, however, to advocate irrationalism, the postulation of arbitrary theses justified by an intuitive faith in revelation, but the abolition of the distinction between thesis and argument. Dialectical thinking, from this point of view, means that an argument should take on the pungency of a thesis and a thesis contain within itself the fullness of its reasoning. All bridging concepts, all links and logical auxiliary operations that are not a part of the matter itself, all secondary developments not saturated with the experience of the object, should be discarded. In a philosophical text all the propositions ought to be equally close to the centre. Without Hegel's ever having said so explicitly, his whole procedure bears witness to such an intention. Because it acknowledges no first principle, it ought, strictly speaking, to know of nothing secondary or deduced; and it transfers the concept of mediation from formal connections to the substance of the object itself, thereby attempting to overcome the difference between the latter and an external thought that mediates it. The limits to the success of such an intention in Hegelian philosophy are also those of its truth, that is to say, the remnants of *prima philosophia*, the supposition of the subject as something which is, in spite of everything, 'primary'. One of the tasks of dialectical logic is to eliminate the last traces of a deductive system, together with the last advocatory gestures of thought.

45

'*How sickly seem all growing things*'.[1] – Dialectical thought opposes reification in the further sense that it refuses to affirm individual things in their isolation and separateness: it designates isolation as precisely a product of the universal. Thus it acts as a corrective both to manic fixity and to the unresisting and empty drift of the paranoid mind, which pays for its absolute judgements by loss of the experience of the matter judged. But the dialectic is not for this reason what it became in the English Hegelian school and, still more

1. *Wie scheint doch alles Werdende so krank*: line from Georg Trakl's poem *Heiterer Frühling*.

completely, in Dewey's strenuous pragmatism: a sense of proportion, a way of putting things in their correct perspective, plain but obdurate common sense. If Hegel seemed himself, in his conversation with Goethe, to come close to such a view, when he defended his philosophy against Goethe's platonism on the grounds that it was 'basically no more than the spirit of opposition innate in each human being, regulated and methodically developed, a gift which proves its worth in distinguishing truth from falsehood',[1] the veiled meaning of his formulation mischievously includes in the praise of what is 'innate in each human being' a denunciation of common sense, since man's innermost characteristic is defined as precisely a refusal to be guided by common sense, indeed, as opposition to it. Common sense, the correct assessment of situations, the worldly eye schooled by the market, shares with the dialectic a freedom from dogma, narrow-mindedness and prejudice. Its sobriety undeniably constitutes a moment of critical thinking. But its lack of passionate commitment makes it, all the same, the sworn enemy of such thinking. For opinion in its generality, accepted directly as that of society as it is, necessarily has agreement as its concrete content. It is no coincidence that in the nineteenth century it was stale dogmatism, given a bad conscience by the Enlightenment, that appealed to common sense, so that an archpositivist like Mill had to inveigh against the latter. The sense of proportion entails a total obligation to think in terms of the established measures and values. One need only have once heard a diehard representative of a ruling clique say: 'That is of no consequence', or note at what times the bourgeois talk of exaggeration, hysteria, folly, to know that the appeal to reason invariably occurs most promptly in apologies for unreason. Hegel stressed the healthy spirit of contradiction with the obstinacy of the peasant who has learned over the centuries to endure the hunts and ground-rent of mighty feudal lords. It is the concern of dialectics to cock a snook at the sound views held by later powers-that-be on the immutability of the course of the world, and to decipher in their 'proportions' the faithful and reduced mirror-image of inordinately enlarged disproportions. Dialectical reason is, when set against the dominant mode of reason, unreason: only in encompassing and

1. Johann-Peter Eckermann, *Gespräche mit Goethe*, in Goethe, *Werke* Vol. 24, Zurich 1948, pp. 669–70 (Eckermann, *Conversations with Goethe*, London 1946, p. 244).

cancelling this mode does it become itself reasonable. Was it not bigoted and talmudic to insist, in the midst of the exchange economy, on the difference between the labour-time expended by the worker and that needed for the reproduction of his life? Did not Nietzsche put the cart before all the horses on which he rode his charges? Did not Karl Kraus, Kafka, even Proust prejudice and falsify the image of the world in order to shake off falsehood and prejudice? The dialectic cannot stop short before the concepts of health and sickness, nor indeed before their siblings reason and unreason. Once it has recognized the ruling universal order and its proportions as sick — and marked in the most literal sense with paranoia, with 'pathic projection' — then it can see as healing cells only what appears, by the standards of that order, as itself sick, eccentric, paranoia — indeed, 'mad'; and it is true today as in the Middle Ages that only fools tell their masters the truth. The dialectician's duty is thus to help this fool's truth to attain its own reasons, without which it will certainly succumb to the abyss of the sickness implacably dictated by the healthy common sense of the rest.

46

On the morality of thinking. — Naivety and sophistication are concepts so endlessly intertwined that no good can come of playing one off against the other. The defence of the ingenuous, as practised by irrationalists and intellectual-baiters of all kinds, is ignoble. Reflection that takes sides with naivety condemns itself: cunning and obscurantism remain what they always were. Mediately to affirm immediacy, instead of comprehending it as mediated within itself, is to pervert thought into an apologia of its antithesis, into the immediate lie. This perversion serves all bad purposes, from the private pigheadedness of 'life's-like-that' to the justification of social injustice as a law of nature. However, to wish on these grounds to erect the opposite as a principle, and to call philosophy — as I once did myself — the binding obligation to be sophisticated, is hardly better. It is not only that sophistication, in the sense of worldly-wise, hard-boiled shrewdness, is a dubious medium of knowledge, forever liable, through its affinity to the practical orders of life and its general mental distrust of theory, itself to revert to a naivety engrossed with utilitarian goals. Even when sophistication is understood in the theoretically acceptable sense of that which widens horizons, passes beyond the isolated phenomenon, considers the whole, there is still a cloud in the sky. It is just this passing-on and being unable to linger, this tacit assent to the primacy of the general over the particular, which constitutes not only the deception of idealism in hypostasizing concepts, but also its inhumanity, that has no sooner grasped the particular than it reduces it to a through-station, and finally comes all too quickly to terms with suffering and death for the sake of a reconciliation occurring merely in reflection – in the last analysis, the bourgeois coldness that is only too willing to underwrite the inevitable. Knowledge can only widen horizons by abiding so insistently with the particular that its isolation is dispelled. This admittedly presupposes a relation to the general, though not one of subsumption, but rather almost the reverse. Dialectical mediation is not a recourse to the more abstract, but a process of resolution of the concrete in itself. Nietzsche, who too often thought in over-wide horizons himself, was nevertheless aware of this: 'He who seeks to mediate between two bold thinkers', he writes in the *Gay Science*, 'stamps himself as mediocre: he has not the eyes to see uniqueness: to perceive resemblances everywhere, making everything alike, is a sign of weak eyesight.'[1] The morality of thought lies in a procedure that is neither entrenched nor detached, neither blind nor empty, neither atomistic nor consequential. The double-edged method which has earned Hegel's *Phenomenology* the reputation among reasonable people of unfathomable difficulty, that is, its simultaneous demands that phenomena be allowed to speak as such – in a 'pure looking-on' – and yet that their relation to consciousness as the subject, reflection, be at every moment maintained, expresses this morality most directly and in all its depth of contradiction. But how much more difficult has it become to conform to such morality now that it is no longer possible to convince oneself of the identity of subject and object, the ultimate assumption of which still enabled Hegel to conceal the antagonistic demands of observation and interpretation. Nothing less is asked of the thinker today than that he should be at every moment both within things and outside them – Münchhausen pulling himself out of the bog by his pig-tail becomes the pattern of knowledge which wishes to be more than either verification or speculation. And then the salaried

1. Nietzsche, *Werke*, Vol. II, pp. 152–3 (*The Joyful Wisdom*, p. 201).

philosophers come along and reproach us with having no definite point of view.

47

De gustibus est disputandum. — Even someone believing himself convinced of the non-comparability of works of art will find himself repeatedly involved in debates where works of art, and precisely those of highest and therefore incommensurable rank, are compared and evaluated one against the other. The objection that such considerations, which come about in a peculiarly compulsive way, have their source in mercenary instincts that would measure everything by the ell, usually signifies no more than that solid citizens, for whom art can never be irrational enough, want to keep serious reflection and the claims of truth far from the works. This compulsion to evaluate is located, however, in the works of art themselves. So much is true: they refuse to be compared. They want to annihilate one another. Not without cause did the ancients reserve the pantheon of the compatible to Gods or Ideas, but obliged works of art to enter the *agon*, each the mortal enemy of each. The notion of a 'pantheon of classicity', as still entertained by Kierkegaard, is a fiction of neutralized culture. For if the Idea of Beauty appears only in dispersed form among many works, each one nevertheless aims uncompromisingly to express the whole of beauty, claims it in its singularity and can never admit its dispersal without annulling itself. Beauty, as single, true and liberated from appearance and individuation, manifests itself not in the synthesis of all works, in the unity of the arts and of art, but only as a physical reality: in the downfall of art itself. This downfall is the goal of every work of art, in that it seeks to bring death to all others. That all art aims to end art, is another way of saying the same thing. It is this impulse to self-destruction inherent in works of art, their innermost striving towards an image of beauty free of appearance, that is constantly stirring up the aesthetic disputes that are apparently so futile. While obstinately seeking to establish aesthetic truth, and trapping themselves thereby in an irresoluble dialectic, they stumble on the real truth, for by making the works of art their own and elevating them to concepts, they limit them all, and so contribute to the destruction of art which is its salvation. Aesthetic tolerance that simply acknowledges works of art in their limitation, without breaking it, leads them only to a false downfall, that of a juxtaposition which denies their claims to indivisible truth.

48

For Anatole France. – Even virtues like openness to life, the capacity to find and enjoy beauty in the most trivial and insignificant places, begin to show a questionable aspect. Once, in the age of overflowing subjective abundance, aesthetic indifference to the choice of object, together with the power to derive meaning from all experience, expressed a relatedness to the objective world, which even in its fragments confronted the subject, antagonistically it is true, yet immediately and significantly. In a phase when the subject is capitulating before the alienated predominance of things, his readiness to discover value or beauty everywhere shows the resignation both of his critical faculties and of the interpreting imagination insepar-able from them. Those who find everything beautiful are now in danger of finding nothing beautiful. The universality of beauty can communicate itself to the subject in no other way than in obsession with the particular. No gaze attains beauty that is not accompanied by indifference, indeed almost by contempt, for all that lies outside the object contemplated. And it is only infatuation, the unjust dis-regard for the claims of every existing thing, that does justice to what exists. In so far as the existent is accepted, in its one-sidedness, for what it is, its one-sidedness is comprehended as its being, and reconciled. The eyes that lose themselves to the one and only beauty are sabbath eyes. They save in their object something of the calm of its day of creation. But if one-sidedness is cancelled by the introduction from outside of awareness of universality, if the par-ticular is startled from its rapture, interchanged and weighed up, the just overall view makes its own the universal injustice that lies in exchangeability and substitution. Such justice executes the sen-tence passed by myth on creation. Doubtless, no thought is dis-pensed from such associations; none may be permanently blinkered. But everything depends on the manner of transition. Perdition comes from thought as violence, as a short cut that breaches the impenetrable to attain the universal, which has content in impene-trability alone, not in abstracted correspondences between different objects. One might almost say that truth itself depends on the tempo, the patience and perseverance of lingering with the particular: what passes beyond it without having first entirely lost itself, what proceeds to judge without having first been guilty of the injustice of contemplation, loses itself at last in emptiness. Liberality that accords men their rights indiscriminately, terminates in annihilation, as does the will of the majority that ill uses a minority, and so makes a mockery of democracy while acting in accordance with its principles. Indiscriminate kindness towards all carries the constant threat of indifference and remoteness to each, attitudes communicated in their turn to the whole. Injustice is the medium of true justice. Unrestricted benevolence becomes affirmation of all the bad that exists, in that it minimizes its difference from the traces of good and levels it to that generality which prompts the hopeless conclusion of bourgeois-mephistophelian wisdom, that all that sees the light of day deserves to go the selfsame way.[1] The salving of beauty even in the insipid and indifferent appears all the more noble than obstinate persistence in criticizing and specifying, because it shows itself in fact more compliant to the orders of life.

Such argument is countered by pointing to the holiness of life that shines forth precisely in what is ugliest and most distorted. However, this light does not come to us directly, but only refracted: something that must be thought beautiful solely because it exists, is for that very reason ugly. The concept of life in its abstraction, that is resorted to here, is inseparable from what is repressive and ruthless, truly deadly and destructive. The cult of life for its own sake always boiled down to the cult of these powers. Things commonly called expressions of life, from burgeoning fertility and the boisterous activity of children to the industry of those who achieve something worthwhile, and the impulsiveness of woman, who is idolized because appetite shows in her so unalloyed; all this, understood absolutely, takes away the light from the other possibility in blind self-assertion. Exuberant health is always, as such, sickness also. Its antidote is a sickness aware of what it is, a curbing of life itself. Beauty is such a curative sickness. It arrests life, and therefore its decay. If, however, sickness is rejected for the sake of life, then hypostasized life, in its blind separation from its other moment,

1. Citation of Mephistopheles's dictum: *Alles was entsteht, ist wert, dass es zugrunde geht*, in Goethe's *Faust*, Part One.

becomes the latter, destructiveness and evil, insolence and braggadocio. To hate destructiveness, one must hate life as well: only death is an image of undistorted life. Anatole France, in his enlightened way, was well aware of this contradiction. 'No', says none other than the mild M. Bergeret,[1] 'I would rather think that organic life is an illness peculiar to our unlovely planet. It would be intolerable to believe that throughout the infinite universe there was nothing but eating and being eaten.' The nihilistic revulsion in his words is not merely the psychological, but the objective condition of humanism as utopia.

49

Morality and temporal sequence. – While literature has treated all the psychological species of erotic conflict, the simplest external source of conflict has remained unnoticed because of its obviousness. It is the phenomenon of prior engagement: a loved person refuses herself to us not through inner antagonisms and inhibitions, too much coldness or repressed warmth, but because a relationship already exists that excludes another. Abstract temporal sequence plays in reality the part one would like to ascribe to the hierarchy of feelings. In being previously engaged there is, apart from the freedom of choice and decision, also an accidental element that seems in flat contradiction to the claims of freedom. Even, and precisely, in a society cured of the anarchy of commodity production, there could scarcely be rules governing the order in which one met people. Such an arrangement would amount to the most intolerable interference with freedom. Thus the priority of the fortuitous has powerful arguments on its side: someone ousted by a newcomer is always misused, a shared past life annulled, experience itself deleted. The irreversibility of time constitutes an objective moral criterion. But it is one intimately related to myth, like abstract time itself. The exclusiveness implicit in time gives rise, by its inherent law, to the exclusive domination of hermetically sealed groups, finally to that of big business. Nothing is more touching than a loving woman's anxiety lest love and tenderness, her best possession just because they cannot be possessed, be stolen

1. Hero of Anatole France's four-volume novel cycle *Histoire Contemporaine* (1897–1901).

away by a newcomer, simply because of her newness, itself conferred by the prerogative of the older. But from this touching feeling, without which all warmth and protection would pass away, an irresistible path leads, by way of the little boy's aversion for his younger brother and the fraternity-student's contempt for his 'fag', to the immigration laws that exclude all non-Caucasians from Social-Democratic Australia, and right up to the Fascist eradication of the racial minority, in which, indeed, all warmth and shelter explode into nothingness. Not only were all good things, as Nietzsche knew, once bad things: the gentlest, left to follow their own momentum, have a tendency to culminate in unimaginable brutality.

It would serve no purpose to try to point to a way out of this entanglement. Yet it is undoubtedly possible to name the fatal moment that brings the whole dialectic into play. It lies in the exclusive character of what comes first. The original relationship, in its mere immediacy, already presupposes abstract temporal sequence. Historically, the notion of time is itself formed on the basis of the order of ownership. But the desire to possess reflects time as a fear of losing, of the irrecoverable. Whatever is, is experienced in relation to its possible non-being. This alone makes it fully a possession and, thus petrified, something functional that can be exchanged for other, equivalent possessions. Once wholly a possession, the loved person is no longer really looked at. Abstraction in love is the complement of exclusiveness, which manifests itself deceptively as the opposite of abstract, a clinging to this one unique being. But such possessiveness loses its hold on its object precisely through turning it into an object, and forfeits the person whom it debases to 'mine'. If people were no longer possessions, they could no longer be exchanged. True affection would be one that speaks specifically to the other, and becomes attached to beloved features and not to the idol of personality, the reflected image of possession. The specific is not exclusive: it lacks the aspiration to totality. But in another sense it is exclusive, nevertheless: the experience indissolubly bound up with it does not, indeed, forbid replacement, but by its very essence precludes it. The protection of anything quite definite is that it cannot be repeated, which is just why it tolerates what is different. Underlying the property relation to human beings, the exclusive right of priority, is the following piece of wisdom: After all, they are all only people, which one it is does not really matter. Affection which knows nothing of such wisdom need not fear infidelity, since it is proof against faithlessness.

50

Gaps. – The injunction to practise intellectual honesty usually amounts to sabotage of thought. The writer is urged to show explicitly all the steps that have led him to his conclusion, so enabling every reader to follow the process through and, where possible – in the academic industry – to duplicate it. This demand not only invokes the liberal fiction of the universal communicability of each and every thought and so inhibits their objectively appropriate expression, but is also wrong in itself as a principle of representation. For the value of a thought is measured by its distance from the continuity of the familiar. It is objectively devalued as this distance is reduced; the more it approximates to the pre-existing standard, the further its antithetical function is diminished, and only in this, in its manifest relation to its opposite, not in its isolated existence, are the claims of thought founded. Texts which anxiously undertake to record every step without omission inevitably succumb to banality, and to a monotony related not only to the tension induced in the reader, but to their own substance. Simmel's writings, for example, are all vitiated by the incompatibility of their out-of-the-ordinary subject matter with its painfully lucid treatment.[1] They show the recondite to be the true complement of mediocrity, which Simmel wrongly believed Goethe's secret. But quite apart from this, the demand for intellectual honesty is itself dishonest. Even if we were for once to comply with the questionable directive that the exposition should exactly reproduce the process of thought, this process would be no more a discursive progression from stage to stage than, conversely, knowledge falls from Heaven. Rather, knowledge comes to us through a network of prejudices, opinions, innervations, self-corrections, presuppositions and exaggerations, in short through the dense, firmly-founded but by no means uniformly transparent medium of experience. Of this the Cartesian rule that we must address ourselves only to objects, 'to gain clear and indubitable knowledge of which

1. Georg Simmel: vitalist philosopher and sociologist (1858–1918) of the Wilhelmine period.

our minds seem sufficient', with all the order and disposition to which the rule refers, gives as false a picture as the opposed but deeply related doctrine of the intuition of essences.[1] If the latter denies logic its rights, which in spite of everything assert themselves in every thought, the former takes logic in its immediacy, in relation to each single intellectual act, and not as mediated by the whole flow of conscious life in the knowing subject. But in this lies also an admission of profound inadequacy. For if honest ideas unfailingly boil down to mere repetition, whether of what was there beforehand or of categorical forms, then the thought which, for the sake of the relation to its object, forgoes the full transparency of its logical genesis, will always incur a certain guilt. It breaks the promise presupposed by the very form of judgement. This inadequacy resembles that of life, which describes a wavering, deviating line, disappointing by comparison with its premisses, and yet which only in this actual course, always less than it should be, is able, under given conditions of existence, to represent an unregimented one. If a life fulfilled its vocation directly, it would miss it. Anyone who died old and in the consciousness of seemingly blameless success, would secretly be the model schoolboy who reels off all life's stages without gaps or omissions, an invisible satchel on his back. Every thought which is not idle, however, bears branded on it the impossibility of its full legitimation, as we know in dreams that there are mathematics lessons, missed for the sake of a blissful morning in bed, which can never be made up. Thought waits to be woken one day by the memory of what has been missed, and to be transformed into teaching.

1. *Wesensschau*: allusion to the phenomenology of Husserl and Scheler.

Minima Moralia

1945

*Where everything is bad
it must be good to know the worst*

F. H. Bradley

Memento. – A first precaution for writers: in every text, every piece, every paragraph to check whether the central motif stands out clearly enough. Anyone wishing to express something is so carried away by it that he ceases to reflect on it. Too close to his intention, 'in his thoughts', he forgets to say what he wants to say.

No improvement is too small or trivial to be worthwhile. Of a hundred alterations each may seem trifling or pedantic by itself; together they can raise the text to a new level.

One should never begrudge deletions. The length of a work is irrelevant, and the fear that not enough is on paper, childish. Nothing should be thought worthy to exist simply because it exists, has been written down. When several sentences seem like variations on the same idea, they often only represent different attempts to grasp something the author has not yet mastered. Then the best formulation should be chosen and developed further. It is part of the technique of writing to be able to discard ideas, even fertile ones, if the construction demands it. Their richness and vigour will benefit other ideas at present repressed. Just as, at table, one ought not eat the last crumbs, drink the lees. Otherwise, one is suspected of poverty.

The desire to avoid clichés should not, on pain of falling into vulgar coquetry, be confined to single words. The great French prose of the nineteenth century was particularly sensitive to such vulgarity. A word is seldom banal on its own: in music too the single note is immune to triteness. The most abominable clichés are combinations of words, such as Karl Kraus skewered for inspection: utterly and completely, for better or for worse, implemented and effected. For in them the brackish stream of stale language swills aimlessly, instead of being dammed up, thrown into relief, by the precision of the writer's expressions. This applies not only to combinations of words, but to the construction of whole forms. If a dialectician, for example, marked the turning-point of his advancing ideas by starting with a 'But' at each caesura, the literary scheme would give the lie to the unschematic intention of his thought.

The thicket is no sacred grove. There is a duty to clarify all difficulties that result merely from esoteric complacency. Between the desire for a compact style adequate to the depth of its subject matter, and the temptation to recondite and pretentious slovenliness, there is no obvious distinction: suspicious probing is always salutary. Precisely the writer most unwilling to make concessions to drab common sense must guard against draping ideas, in themselves banal, in the appurtenances of style. Locke's platitudes are no justification for Hamann's obscurities.

Should the finished text, no matter of what length, arouse even the slightest misgivings, these should be taken inordinately seriously, to a degree out of all proportion to their apparent importance. Affective involvement in the text, and vanity, tend to diminish all scruples. What is let pass as a minute doubt may indicate the objective worthlessness of the whole.

The Echternach dancing procession is not the march of the World Spirit;[1] limitation and reservation are no way to represent the dialectic. Rather, the dialectic advances by way of extremes, driving thoughts with the utmost consequentiality to the point where they turn back on themselves, instead of qualifying them. The prudence that restrains us from venturing too far ahead in a sentence, is usually only an agent of social control, and so of stupefaction.

Scepticism is called for in face of the frequently raised objection that a text, a formulation, are 'too beautiful'. Respect for the matter expressed, or even for suffering, can easily rationalize mere resentment against a writer unable to bear the traces, in the reified form of language, of the degradation inflicted on humanity. The dream of an existence without shame, which the passion for language clings to even though forbidden to depict it as content, is to be maliciously strangled. The writer ought not acknowledge any distinction between beautiful and adequate expression. He should neither suppose such a distinction in the solicitous mind of the critic, nor tolerate it in his own. If he succeeds in saying entirely what he means, it is beautiful. Beauty of expression for its own sake is not at all 'too beautiful', but ornamental, arty-crafty, ugly. But he

1. Echternach is a town in Luxemburg, whose dance procession at Whitsun advances in a movement of three steps forward, and two steps backward.

who, on the pretext of unselfishly serving only the matter in hand, neglects purity of expression, always betrays the matter as well.

Properly written texts are like spiders' webs: tight, concentric, transparent, well-spun and firm. They draw into themselves all the creatures of the air. Metaphors flitting hastily through them become their nourishing prey. Subject matter comes winging towards them. The soundness of a conception can be judged by whether it causes one quotation to summon another. Where thought has opened up one cell of reality, it should, without violence by the subject, penetrate the next. It proves its relation to the object as soon as other objects crystallize around it. In the light that it casts on its chosen substance, others begin to glow.

In his text, the writer sets up house. Just as he trundles papers, books, pencils, documents untidily from room to room, he creates the same disorder in his thoughts. They become pieces of furniture that he sinks into, content or irritable. He strokes them affectionately, wears them out, mixes them up, re-arranges, ruins them. For a man who no longer has a homeland, writing becomes a place to live. In it he inevitably produces, as his family once did, refuse and lumber. But now he lacks a store-room, and it is hard in any case to part from left-overs. So he pushes them along in front of him, in danger finally of filling his pages with them. The demand that one harden oneself against self-pity implies the technical necessity to counter any slackening of intellectual tension with the utmost alertness, and to eliminate anything that has begun to encrust the work or to drift along idly, which may at an earlier stage have served, as gossip, to generate the warm atmosphere conducive to growth, but is now left behind, flat and stale. In the end, the writer is not even allowed to live in his writing.

52

Where the stork brings babies from. – For every person there is an original in a fairy-tale, one need only look long enough. A beauty asks the mirror whether she is the fairest of all, like the Queen in Snow-White.[1] She who is fretful and fastidious even unto death,

1. The successive allusions below are all to figures from *Grimms' Fairy Tales*.

was created after the goat which repeats the verse: 'I've had enough, can't eat the stuff, bleat, bleat.' A care-worn but unembittered man is like the little bent old lady gathering wood, who meets the Good Lord without recognizing him, and is blessed with all her own, because she helped Him. Another went out into the world as a lad to seek his fortune, got the better of numerous giants, but had to die all the same in New York. A girl braves the wilderness of the city like Little Red Riding Hood to bring her grandmother a piece of cake and a bottle of wine, yet another undresses for love-making with the same childlike immodesty as the girl with the starry silver pieces. The clever man finds out he has a strong animal spirit, dislikes the idea of meeting a bad end with his friends, forms the group of Bremen city musicians, leads them to the robbers' cave, outwits the swindlers there, but then wants to go back home. With yearning eyes the Frog King, an incorrigible snob, looks up to the Princess and cannot leave off hoping that she will set him free.

53

Folly of the wise. – Schiller's verbal demeanour calls to mind the young man of low origins who, embarrassed in good society, starts shouting to make himself heard: power and insolence mixed. German tirading and sententiousness are modelled on the French, but rehearsed in the beer-hall. In his limitless and implacable demands the petty-bourgeois sticks his chest out, identifying himself with a power that he does not have, outdoing it in his arrogance to the point of absolute spirit and absolute horror. Between the grandiose sublimity embracing the whole of humanity that all idealists have in common – a sublimity ever ready to trample inhumanly on anything small as mere existence – and the coarse ostentation of bourgeois men of violence, there is an intimate collusion. The dignity of spiritual giants is prone to hollow booming laughter, exploding, smashing. When they say Creation, they mean the compulsive will-power with which they puff themselves up and intimidate all questions: from the primacy of practical reason it was always only a step to hatred of theory. Such a dynamic inheres in all idealistic movement of thought: even Hegel's immeasurable effort to remedy the dynamic with itself, fell victim to it. The attempt to deduce the world in words from a principle, is the behaviour of someone who would like to usurp power instead of resisting it. Schiller, accordingly, was primarily concerned with usurpers. In the classical apotheosis of the sovereignty over nature, the vulgar and inferior mirrors itself by assiduous negation. Close behind the ideal stands life. The rose-scents of Elysium, much too voluble to be credited with the experience of a single rose, smell of the tobacco-smoke in a magistrate's office, and the soulful moon on the backdrop was fashioned after the miserable oil-lamp by whose meagre light the student swots for his exam. Weakness posing as strength betrayed the thought of the allegedly rising bourgeoisie to ideology, even when the class was thundering against tyranny. In the innermost recesses of humanism, as its very soul, there rages a frantic prisoner who, as a Fascist, turns the world into a prison.

54

The Robbers. – Schiller, the Kantian, is as much more insensible than Goethe as he is more sensual: as much more abstract, as he is a plaything of sexuality. Sex, as an immediate craving, makes everything an object of action and therewith equal. 'Amalia for the robbers' – which is why Louise remains insipid as lemonade.[1] Casanova's women, not for nothing often called by letters instead of names, are hardly distinguishable from one another, as too are the figurines forming complex pyramids to the strain of de Sade's mechanical organ. Something of this sexual crudity, this inability to make distinctions, animates the great speculative systems of Idealism, defying all the imperatives and yoking German mind to German barbarism. Peasant greed, only with difficulty held in check by the threats of priests, asserts in metaphysics its autonomous right to reduce everything in its path as unceremoniously to its basic essence as do soldiers the women of a captured town. The pure unreflective act[2] is violation projected on to the starry sky above. But in the long, contemplative look that fully discloses people and things, the urge towards the object is always deflected, reflected. Contemplation without violence, the source of all the

1. Amalia and Louise are, respectively, the leading female characters in Schiller's plays *Die Räuber* and *Kabale und Liebe*.
2. *Die reine Tathandlung*: an expression of Fichte.

joy of truth, presupposes that he who contemplates does not absorb the object into himself: a distanced nearness. Only because Tasso, whom psycho-analysts would call a destructive character, is afraid of the princess, and falls a civilized victim to the impossibility of immediate contact, can Adelheid, Klärchen and Gretchen speak the limpid, unforced language that makes of them an image of a pristine world.[1] The sense of life radiated by Goethe's women was bought with withdrawal, evasion; and there is more in this than mere resignation before the victorious order. The absolute opposite, symbolizing the unity of sensuality and abstraction, is Don Juan. When Kierkegaard says that in him sensuality is comprehended as a principle, he touches on the secret of sensuality itself. In the fixity of its gaze, until self-reflection dawns, is the very anonymity, the unhappy generality, that is fatefully reproduced in its negative, the unfettered sovereignty of thought.

55

May I be so bold? – When the poet in Schnitzler's *Merry-go-Round*[2] tenderly approaches the agreeably unpuritanical wench, she says: 'Be off, why don't you play the piano?' She can neither be unaware of the purpose of the arrangement, nor does she actually resist. Her impulse goes deeper than conventional or psychological prohibitions. It voices an archaic frigidity, the female animal's fear of copulation, which brings her nothing but pain. Pleasure is a late acquisition, scarcely older than consciousness. Observing how compulsively, as if spell-bound, animals couple, one recognizes the saying that 'bliss was given to the worm' as a piece of idealistic lying, at least as regards the females, who undergo love in unfreedom, as objects of violence. Women have retained a consciousness of this, particularly among the petty bourgeoisie, down to the late industrial era. The memory of the old injury persists, though the physical pain and the immediate fear have been removed by civilization. Society constantly casts woman's self-abandon back into the sacrificial situation from which it freed her. No man, cajoling some

1. Adelheid, Klärchen and Gretchen are the leading female characters in Goethe's plays *Götz von Berlichingen*, *Egmont* and *Faust*, respectively.
2. Artur Schnitzler (1862–1931): Austrian playwright and novelist, concerned with erotic themes in the setting of Viennese upper-bourgeois society.

poor girl to go with him, can mistake, unless he be wholly insensitive, the faint moment of rightness in her resistance, the only prerogative left by patriarchal society to woman, who, once persuaded, after the brief triumph of refusal, must immediately pay the bill. She knows that, as the giver, she has from time immemorial also been the dupe. But if she begrudges herself, she is only duped the more. This can be seen in the advice to a novice that Wedekind puts into the mouth of a brothel-keeper: 'There is only one way to be happy in this world: to do everything to make others as happy as possible.'[1] The experience of pleasure presupposes a limitless readiness to throw oneself away, which is as much beyond women in their fear as men in their arrogance. Not merely the objective possibility, but also the subjective capacity for happiness, can only be achieved in freedom.

56

Genealogical research. – Between Ibsen and *Struwwelpeter* there exists a deep affinity. It is of the same kind as the frozen likeness between all family members in the flashlight photographs of nineteenth-century albums.[2] Is not Fidgety Philip truly what *Ghosts* claims to be, a family drama? Do not the lines 'And at table Mother's glare/silently at all did stare' describe the expression of Mrs Borkman, the bank director's wife? What can be the cause of Augustus's wasting disease, if not the sins of his fathers and the inherited memory of guilt? Furious Frederick is prescribed bitter but effective medicine by the enemy of the people, that Dr Stockman who in return lets the dog have his liver-sausage. Little dancing Harriet with the matches is a touched-up photo of little Hilde Wangel from the time when her mother, the lady of the sea, left her alone in the house, and Flying Robert, high over the church steeple, is her master-builder in person. What does Johnny Head-in-Air want except the sun? Who else lured him into the water, but little Eyolf's Rat-Wife, akin to the red legg'd Scissor-Man? The

1. Frank Wedekind (1864–1918): radical expressionist playwright of pre-First World War Germany, whose work later influenced Brecht.
2. The successive allusions below are to characters in Ibsen's plays: *Ghosts, John Gabriel Borkman, An Enemy of the People, The Lady from the Sea, The Master-Builder, Brand* and *Little Eyolf.*

stern poet, however, follows the example of tall Agrippa, who dips the modern children's pictures into his great ink-pot, blackens them out as agitated marionettes and so sits in judgement over himself.

57

Excavation. – No sooner is a name like Ibsen's mentioned, than he and his themes are condemned as old-fashioned and outdated. Sixty years ago the same voices were raised in indignation against the modernistic decadence and immoral extravagance of the *Doll's House* and *Ghosts*. Ibsen, the truculent bourgeois, vented his spleen on the society from whose very principle his implacability and his ideals were derived. He portrayed in a declamatory but durable monument, a deputation of the solid majority shouting down the enemy of the people, and they still do not find the portrayal flattering. And so they pass on to the pressing business of the day. Where reasonable people are in agreement over the unreasonable behaviour of others, we can always be sure to find something unresolved that has been deferred, painful scars. This is how things stand with the question of the condition of women. Through the distortion of the 'masculine' liberal competitive economy, through the participation of women in salaried employment, where they have as much or as little independence as men, through the stripping away of the magic aura of the family and the relaxation of sexual taboos, this problem is indeed, on the surface, no longer 'acute'. Yet, equally the continued existence of traditional society has warped the emancipation of women. Few things are as symptomatic of the decay of the workers' movement as its failure to notice this. The admittance of women to every conceivable supervised activity conceals continuing dehumanization. In big business they remain what they were in the family, objects. We should think not only of their miserable working-day, and of their home-life senselessly clinging to self-contained conditions of domestic labour in the midst of an industrial world, but also of themselves. Willingly, without any countervailing impulse, they reflect and identify themselves with domination. Instead of solving the question of women's oppression, male society has so extended its own principle that the victims are no longer able even to pose the question. Provided only a certain abundance of commodities are granted them, they enthusiastically assent to their fate, leave thinking to the men, defame all reflection as an offence against the feminine ideal propagated by the culture industry, and are altogether at their ease in the unfreedom they take as the fulfilment of their sex. The defects with which they pay for it, neurotic stupidity heading the list, help to perpetuate this state of affairs. Even in Ibsen's time most of the women who had gained some standing in bourgeois society were ready to turn and rend their hysterical sisters who undertook, in their stead, the hopeless attempt to break out of the social prison which so emphatically turned its four walls to them all. Their grand-daughters, however, would smile indulgently over these hysterics, without even feeling implicated, and hand them over to the benevolent treatment of social welfare. The hysteric who wanted the miraculous has thus given way to the furiously efficient imbecile who cannot wait for the triumph of doom. – But perhaps this is the way of all outdatedness. It is to be explained not only by mere temporal distance, but by the verdict of history. Its expression in things is the shame that overcomes the descendant in face of an earlier possibility that he has neglected to bring to fruition. What was accomplished can be forgotten, and preserved in the present. Only what failed is outdated, the broken promise of a new beginning. It is not without reason that Ibsen's women are called 'modern'. Hatred of modernity and of outdatedness are identical.

58

The truth about Hedda Gabler. – The aestheticism of the nineteenth century cannot be understood internally in terms of intellectual history, but only in relation to its real basis in social conflicts. Underlying amorality was a bad conscience. Critics confronted bourgeois society not only economically but morally with its own norms. This left the ruling stratum, in so far as it was unwilling simply to lapse into apologetic and impotent lying like the court poets and the novelist upholders of the state, with no other defence than to reject the very principle by which society was judged, its own morality. The new position which radical bourgeois thought took up to parry the thrusts against it went further, however, than merely replacing ideological illusion by a truth proclaimed in a fury of self-destruction, defiant protest, and capitulation. The uprising of beauty against bourgeois good was an uprising against 'goodness'. Goodness is itself a deformation of good. By severing the moral principle from the social and displacing it into the realm of private conscience, goodness limits it in two senses. It dispenses with the realization of a condition worthy of men that is implicit in the principle of morality. Each of its actions has inscribed in it a certain resignation and solace: it aims at alleviation, not cure, and consciousness of incurability finally sides with the latter. In this way goodness becomes limited within itself as well. Its guilt is intimacy. It creates a mirage of direct relations between people and ignores the distance that is the individual's only protection against the infringements of the universal. It is precisely in the closest contact that he feels the unabolished difference most painfully. Retention of strangeness is the only antidote to estrangement. The ephemeral image of harmony in which goodness basks only emphasizes more cruelly the pain of irreconcilability that it foolishly denies. The offence against taste and consideration from which no act of goodness is exempt, completes the levelling that the impotent utopia of beauty opposes. In this way the creed of evil has been, since the beginnings of highly industrialized society, not only a precursor of barbarism but a mask of good. The worth of the latter was transferred to the evil that drew to itself all the hatred and resentment of an order which drummed good into its adherents so that it could with impunity be evil. When Hedda Gabler mortally offends the utterly well-meaning Aunt Julle; when she deliberately pretends the abominable hat which the aunt has got herself in honour of the general's daughter belongs to the maid, the frustrated woman not only sadistically vents her hatred of her obnoxious marriage on a defenceless victim. She sins against what is best in her own life, because she sees the best as a desecration of the good. Unconsciously and absurdly she represents, against the old woman who adores her bungling nephew, the absolute. Hedda is the victim and not Julle. Beauty, Hedda's *idée fixe*, opposes morality even before mocking it. For it baulks at anything general, and posits as absolute the differences determined by mere existence, the accident that has favoured one thing and not another. In beauty, opaque particularity asserts itself as the norm, as alone general, normal generality having become too transparent. So it challenges the latter, the equality of everything unfree. But in so doing it becomes guilty itself, by cutting off, with the general, all possibility of transcending that mere existence whose opacity only reflects the untruth of bad generality. So beauty finds itself in the wrong against right, while yet being right against it. In beauty the frail future offers its sacrifice to the Moloch of the present: because, in the latter's realm, there can be no good, it makes itself bad, in order in its defeat to convict the judge. Beauty's protestation against good is the bourgeois, secularized form of the delusion of the tragic hero. In the immanence of society, consciousness of its negative essence is blocked, and only abstract negation acts as a substitute for truth. Anti-morality, in rejecting what is immoral in morality, repression, inherits morality's deepest concern: that with all limitations all violence too should be abolished. This is why the motives of intransigent bourgeois self-criticism coincide in fact with those of materialism, through which the former attain self-awareness.

59

Since I set eyes on him.[1] – The feminine character, and the ideal of femininity on which it is modelled, are products of masculine society. The image of undistorted nature arises only in distortion, as its opposite. Where it claims to be humane, masculine society imperiously breeds in woman its own corrective, and shows itself through this limitation implacably the master. The feminine character is a negative imprint of domination. But therefore equally bad. Whatever is in the context of bourgeois delusion called nature, is merely the scar of social mutilation. If the psychoanalytical theory is correct that women experience their physical constitution as a consequence of castration, their neurosis gives them an inkling of the truth. The woman who feels herself a wound when she bleeds knows more about herself than the one who imagines herself a flower because that suits her husband. The lie consists not only in the claim that nature exists where it has been tolerated and adapted, but what passes for nature in civilization is by its very substance

1. Allusion to the lines *Seit ich ihn gesehen | glaub'ich blind zu sein* (since I set eyes on him / I seem to have gone blind), from a poem by Adelbert von Chamisso, in his cycle *Frauen-Liebe und-Leben*, later set to music by Schumann. Von Chamisso (1781–1838) was an émigré French noble who became one of the first German romantic poets.

furthest from all nature, its own self-chosen object. The femininity which appeals to instinct, is always exactly what every woman has to force herself by violence – masculine violence – to be: a she-man. One need only have perceived, as a jealous male, how such feminine women have their femininity at their finger-tips – deploying it just where needed, flashing their eyes, using their impulsiveness – to know how things stand with the sheltered unconscious, unmarred by intellect. Just this unscathed purity is the product of the ego, of censorship, of intellect, which is why it submits so unresistingly to the reality principle of the rational order. Without a single exception feminine natures are conformist. The fact that Nietzsche's scrutiny stopped short of them, that he took over a second-hand and unverified image of feminine nature from the Christian civilization that he otherwise so thoroughly mistrusted, finally brought his thought under the sway, after all, of bourgeois society. He fell for the fraud of saying 'the feminine' when talking of women. Hence the perfidious advice not to forget the whip: femininity itself is already the effect of the whip. The liberation of nature would be to abolish its self-fabrication. Glorification of the feminine character implies the humiliation of all who bear it.

60

A word for morality. – Amoralism, with which Nietzsche chastised the old untruth, is itself now subject to the verdict of history. With the decay of religion and its palpable philosophical secularizations, restrictive prohibitions lost their inherent authority, their substantiality. At first, however, material production was still so undeveloped that it could be proclaimed with some reason that there was not enough to go round. Anyone who did not criticize political economy as such, had to cling to the limiting principle which was then articulated as unrationalized appropriation at the expense of the weak. The objective preconditions of this have changed. It is not only the social non-conformist or even the narrow-minded bourgeois who must see restriction as superfluous in face of the immediate possibility of superfluity. The implied meaning of the master-morality, that he who wants to live must fend for himself, has in the meantime become a still more miserable lie than it was when a nineteenth-century piece of pulpit-wisdom. If in Germany the common citizen has proved himself a blond beast, this has nothing to do with national peculiarities, but with the fact that blond bestiality itself, social rapine, has become in face of manifest abundance the attitude of the backwoodsman, the deluded philistine, that same 'hard-done-by' mentality which the master-morality was invented to combat. If Cesare Borgia were resurrected today, he would look like David Friedrich Strauss[1] and his name would be Adolf Hitler. The cause of amorality has been espoused by the same Darwinists whom Nietzsche despised, and who proclaim as their maxim the barbaric struggle for existence with such vehemence, just because it is no longer needed. True distinction has long ceased to consist in taking the best for oneself, and has become instead a satiety with taking, that practises in reality the virtue of giving, which in Nietzsche occurs only in the mind. Ascetic ideals constitute today a more solid bulwark against the madness of the profit-economy than did the hedonistic life sixty years ago against liberal repression. The amoralist may now at last permit himself to be as kind, gentle, unegoistic and open-hearted as Nietzsche already was then. As a guarantee of his undiminished resistance, he is still as alone in this as in the days when he turned the mask of evil upon the normal world, to teach the norm to fear its own perversity.

61

Court of appeal. – Nietzsche in the *Antichrist* voiced the strongest argument not merely against theology but against metaphysics, that hope is mistaken for truth; that the impossibility of living happily, or even living at all, without the thought of an absolute, does not vouch for the legitimacy of that thought. He refutes the Christian 'proof by efficacy', that faith is true because it brings felicity. For 'could happiness – or, more technically speaking, pleasure – ever be a proof of truth? So far from this, it almost proves the converse, at any rate it gives the strongest grounds for suspecting 'truth' whenever feelings of pleasure have had a say in the matter. The proof of pleasure is proof of: pleasure – nothing more; why in the world should true judgements cause more enjoyment

1. David-Friedrich Strauss (1808–74): biblical critic and ideologist who rallied to Bismarck after 1866, and advocated evolutionism as a philosophical substitute for Christianity in *Der alte und der neue Glaube* (1872).

than false ones and, in accordance with a preordained harmony, necessarily bring pleasant feelings in their train.'[1] But Nietzsche himself taught *amor fati:* 'thou shalt love thy fate'. This, he says in the *Epilogue* to the *Twilight of the Idols*, was his innermost nature. We might well ask whether we have more reason to love what happens to us, to affirm what is because it is, than to believe true what we hope. Is it not the same false inference that leads from the existence of stubborn facts to their erection as the highest value, as he criticizes in the leap from hope to truth? If he consigns 'happiness through an *idée fixe*' to the lunatic asylum, the origin of *amor fati* might be sought in a prison. Love of stone walls and barred windows is the last resort of someone who sees and has nothing else to love. Both are cases of the same ignominious adaptation which, in order to endure the world's horror, attributes reality to wishes and meaning to senseless compulsion. No less than in the *credo quia absurdum*, resignation bows down in the *amor fati*, the glorification of the absurdest of all things, before the powers that be. In the end hope, wrested from reality by negating it, is the only form in which truth appears. Without hope, the idea of truth would be scarcely even thinkable, and it is the cardinal untruth, having recognized existence to be bad, to present it as truth simply because it has been recognized. Here, rather than in the opposite, lies the crime of theology that Nietzsche arraigned without ever reaching the final court. In one of the most powerful passages of his critique he charges Christianity with mythology: 'The guilt sacrifice, in its most repulsive and most barbaric form: the sacrifice of the innocent for the sins of the guilty! What appalling paganism!'[2] Nothing other, however, is love of fate, the absolute sanctioning of an infinity of such sacrifice. Myth debars Nietzsche's critique of myth from truth.

62

Briefer expositions. – On re-reading one of Anatole France's meditative books, such as the *Jardin d' Épicure*, one cannot help feeling, despite gratitude for enlightenment dispensed, an uneasiness that is

1. Nietzsche, *Werke*, Vol. II, p. 1215 (*The Twilight of the Gods / The Antichrist*, Edinburgh–London 1911, pp. 201–2).

2. Nietzsche, *Werke*, Vol. II, p. 1203 (*The Twilight of the Gods / The Antichrist*, p. 183).

sufficiently explained neither by the old-fashioned pose so eagerly adopted by renegade French irrationalists, nor by the personal vanity. But when this latter serves as a pretext for envy – all intellect necessarily revealing a moment of vanity as soon as it represents itself – the reason for the uneasiness becomes clear. It stems from the contemplative leisureliness, the sermonizing, however sporadic, the indulgently raised forefinger. The critical content of the thought is belied by that air of having all the time in the world, familiar from professorial pillars of the status quo, and the irony with which this impersonator of Voltaire admits on his title pages to membership of the Académie Française rebounds on its witty author. His mode of delivery contains, beneath the poised humanity, a hidden violence: he can afford to talk in this way because no-one interrupts the master. The element of usurpation inherent in all holding-forth, and even in all reading aloud, has seeped into the lucid construction of his periods, which reserve so much repose for the most disquieting things. The unmistakable sign of latent contempt for mankind in this last advocate of human dignity is the imperturbable enunciation of platitudes, as if no-one may dare to notice their triteness: '*L'artiste doit aimer la vie et nous montrer qu'elle est belle. Sans lui, nous en douterions.*' [The artist ought to love life and show us that it is beautiful. Without him, we should doubt it.] But what is so obtrusive in France's archaically stylized meditations is more subtly present in any reflection that claims exemption from immediate purposes. Serenity is becoming, as such, the same lie that purposive haste already is. While a thought in terms of its content may oppose the irresistibly rising tide of horror, the nerves, the sensitive feelers of historical consciousness, detect in its form, indeed in its very willingness still to be a thought, a trace of connivance at the world, to which a concession has already been made the moment one steps back sufficiently from it to make it an object of philosophy. In the detachment necessary to all thought is flaunted the privilege that permits immunity. The aversion aroused by this is now the most serious obstacle to theory: if one gives way to it, one keeps quiet; if not, one is coarsened and debased by confiding in one's own culture. Even the odious division of talk into professional conversations and strictly conventional ones, hints at our sense of the impossibility of uttering thoughts without arrogance, without trespassing on the time of others. The most urgent need of exposition, if it is to be in the least serviceable, is to keep such experiences always in view, and by its tempo, compactness, density, yet also its tentativeness, to give them expression.

63

Death of immortality. – Flaubert, said to have claimed to despise the fame on which he staked his life, was still as snug in the consciousness of such contradictions as the comfortably-off bourgeois who wrote *Madame Bovary.* Faced by corrupt public opinion and the press, to which he reacted in the same way as Kraus, he thought he could rely on posterity, a bourgeoisie delivered from stupidity, to give due honour to its authentic critic. But he underestimated stupidity: the society he represents cannot speak its own name, and as it has become total, so stupidity, like intelligence, has become absolute. This attacks the vital centres of the intellectual. He can no longer pin his hopes even on posterity without sinking into conformity, even if this were only agreement with great minds. But as soon as he abandons such hope, something blind and dogmatic comes into his work, prone to swing over to the other extreme of cynical capitulation. Fame resulting from objective processes in a market society, always fortuitous and often unsought, yet with an aura of justice and free choice, has been liquidated. It has become wholly a function of paid propagandists and is measured in terms of the investment risked by the bearer of a name or the interests behind him. The hired applauder, considered by someone as recent as Daumier as an excrescence, has now attained respectability as an official agent of the cultural system. Writers bent on a career talk of their agents as naturally as their predecessors of their publishers, who even then had a foot in the advertising business. They assume personal responsibility for becoming famous, and thus in a sense for their after-life – for what, in totally organized society, can hope to be remembered if it is not already known? – and purchase from the lackeys of the trusts, as in former times from the Church, an expectation of immortality. But no blessing goes with it. Just as voluntary memory and utter oblivion always belonged together, organized fame and remembrance lead ineluctably to nothingness, the foretaste of which is perceptible in the hectic doings of all celebrities. The famous are not happy in their lot. They become brand-name commodities, alien and incomprehensible to themselves, and, as their own living images, they are as if dead. In their pretentious concern for their aureoles they squander the disinterested energy that is alone capable of permanence. The inhuman indifference and contempt instantaneously visited on the fallen idols of the culture industry reveals the truth about their fame, though without granting those disdainful of it any better hopes of posterity. The intellectual, then, discovering his secret motive to be illegitimate, has no other remedy than to record his discovery.

64

Morality and style. – A writer will find that the more precisely, conscientiously, appropriately he expresses himself, the more obscure the literary result is thought, whereas a loose and irresponsible formulation is at once rewarded with certain understanding. It avails nothing ascetically to avoid all technical expressions, all allusions to spheres of culture that no longer exist. Rigour and purity in assembling words, however simple the result, create a vacuum. Shoddiness that drifts with the flow of familiar speech is taken as a sign of relevance and contact: people know what they want because they know what other people want. Regard for the object, rather than for communication, is suspect in any expression: anything specific, not taken from pre-existent patterns, appears inconsiderate, a symptom of eccentricity, almost of confusion. The logic of the day, which makes so much of its clarity, has naively adopted this perverted notion of everyday speech. Vague expression permits the hearer to imagine whatever suits him and what he already thinks in any case. Rigorous formulation demands unequivocal comprehension, conceptual effort, to which people are deliberately disencouraged, and imposes on them in advance of any content a suspension of all received opinions, and thus an isolation, that they violently resist. Only what they do not need first to understand, they consider understandable; only the word coined by commerce, and really alienated, touches them as familiar. Few things contribute so much to the demoralization of intellectuals. Those who would escape it must recognize the advocates of communicability as traitors to what they communicate.

Not half hungry. – To play off workers' dialects against the written language is reactionary. Leisure, even pride and arrogance, have given the language of the upper classes a certain independence and self-discipline. It is thus brought into opposition to its own social sphere. It turns against the masters, who misuse it to command, by seeking to command them, and refuses to serve their interests. The language of the subjected, on the other hand, domination alone has stamped, so robbing them further of the justice promised by the unmutilated, autonomous word to all those free enough to pronounce it without rancour. Proletarian language is dictated by hunger. The poor chew words to fill their bellies. From the objective spirit of language they expect the sustenance refused them by society; those whose mouths are full of words have nothing else between their teeth. So they take revenge on language. Being forbidden to love it, they maim the body of language, and so repeat in impotent strength the disfigurement inflicted on them. Even the best qualities of the North Berlin or Cockney dialects, the ready repartee and the mother wit, are marred by the need, in order to endure desperate situations without despair, to mock themselves along with the enemy, and so to acknowledge the way of the world. If the written language codifies the estrangement of classes, redress cannot lie in regression to the spoken, but only in the consistent exercise of strictest linguistic objectivity. Only a speaking that transcends writing by absorbing it, can deliver human speech from the lie that it is already human.

Mélange. – The familiar argument of tolerance, that all people and all races are equal, is a boomerang. It lays itself open to the simple refutation of the senses, and the most compelling anthropological proofs that the Jews are not a race will, in the event of a pogrom, scarcely alter the fact that the totalitarians know full well whom they do and whom they do not intend to murder. If the equality of all who have human shape were demanded as an ideal instead of being assumed as a fact, it would not greatly help. Abstract utopia is all too compatible with the most insidious tendencies of society. That all men are alike is exactly what society would like to hear. It considers actual or imagined differences as stigmas indicating that not enough has yet been done; that something has still been left outside its machinery, not quite determined by its totality. The technique of the concentration camp is to make the prisoners like their guards, the murdered, murderers. The racial difference is raised to an absolute so that it can be abolished absolutely, if only in the sense that nothing that is different survives. An emancipated society, on the other hand, would not be a unitary state, but the realization of universality in the reconciliation of differences. Politics that are still seriously concerned with such a society ought not, therefore, propound the abstract equality of men even as an idea. Instead, they should point to the bad equality today, the identity of those with interests in films and in weapons, and conceive the better state as one in which people could be different without fear. To assure the black that he is exactly like the white man, while he obviously is not, is secretly to wrong him still further. He is benevolently humiliated by the application of a standard by which, under the pressure of the system, he must necessarily be found wanting, and to satisfy which would in any case be a doubtful achievement. The spokesmen of unitary tolerance are, accordingly, always ready to turn intolerantly on any group that remains refractory: intransigent enthusiasm for blacks does not exclude outrage at Jewish uncouthness. The melting-pot was introduced by unbridled industrial capitalism. The thought of being cast into it conjures up martyrdom, not democracy.

67

Unmeasure for unmeasure. – What the Germans have done passes understanding, particularly by psychology, just as, indeed, their horrors seem to have been committed rather as measures of blind planning and alienated terrorization than for spontaneous gratification. According to eye-witness reports, the torturing and murdering was done without pleasure, and perhaps for that reason so utterly without measure. Nevertheless, a consciousness that wishes to withstand the unspeakable finds itself again and again thrown back on the attempt to understand, if it is not to succumb subjectively to the madness that prevails objectively. The thought obtrudes that the German horror is a kind of anticipated revenge. The credit system, in which everything, even world conquest, can be advanced, also determines the actions which will put an end to it and the whole market economy, including the suicide of dictatorship. In the concentration camps and the gas-chambers the ruin of Germany is being, as it were, discounted. No-one who observed the first months of National Socialism in Berlin in 1933 could fail to perceive the moment of mortal sadness, of half-knowing self-surrender to perdition, that accompanied the manipulated intoxication, the torchlight processions and the drum-beating. How disconsolate sounded the favourite German song of those months, 'Nation to Arms', along the Unter den Linden. The saving of the Fatherland, fixed from one day to the next, bore from the first moment the expression of catastrophe that was rehearsed in the concentration camps while the triumph in the streets drowned all forebodings. This premonition of catastrophe need not be explained by the collective unconscious, though this may clearly have had a voice in the matter. Germany's position in the competition between imperialist powers was, in terms of the available raw materials and of her industrial potential, hopeless in peace and war. Everybody, and nobody, was stupid enough to overlook this. To commit Germany to the final struggle in this competition was to leap into the abyss, so the others were pushed into it first, in the belief that Germany might thereby be spared. The chances of the National Socialist enterprise compensating, by record-breaking terror and temporal priority, for its disadvantage in total volume of production, were minute. It was the others who had believed in such a possibility, rather than the Germans, whom even the conquest of Paris brought no joy. While they were winning everything, they were already frenzied like those with nothing to lose. At the beginning of German imperialism stands Wagner's *Twilight of the Gods*, that inflamed prophecy of the nation's own doom, the composition of which was undertaken at the same time as the victorious campaign of 1870. In the same spirit, two years before the Second World War, the German people were shown on film the crash of their Zeppelin at Lakehurst. Calmly, unerringly, the ship went on its way, then suddenly dropped like a stone. When no way out is left, the destructive drive becomes entirely indifferent to the question it never posed quite clearly: whether it is directed against others or against its own subject.

68

People are looking at you.[1] – Indignation over cruelty diminishes in proportion as the victims are less like normal readers, the more they are swarthy, 'dirty', dago-like. This throws as much light on the crimes as on the spectators. Perhaps the social schematization of perception in anti-Semites is such that they do not see Jews as human beings at all. The constantly encountered assertion that savages, blacks, Japanese are like animals, monkeys for example, is the key to the pogrom. The possibility of pogroms is decided in the moment when the gaze of a fatally-wounded animal falls on a human being. The defiance with which he repels this gaze –'after all, it's only an animal' – reappears irresistibly in cruelties done to human beings, the perpetrators having again and again to reassure themselves that it is 'only an animal', because they could never fully believe this even of animals. In repressive society the concept of man is itself a parody of divine likeness. The mechanism of 'pathic projection' determines that those in power perceive as human only their own reflected image, instead of reflecting back the human as precisely what is different. Murder is thus the repeated attempt, by yet greater madness, to distort the madness of such false perception into reason: what was not seen as human and yet is human, is made a thing, so that its stirrings can no longer refute the manic gaze.

69

Little folk. – Those who deny objective historic forces find a ready-made argument in the outcome of the war. The Germans should really have won: that they did not was due to the stupidity of their leaders. Now Hitler's decisive moments of 'stupidity', his refusal, in the thick of war, to make war on England, his attacks on Russia and America, have a precise social meaning, which developed according to its own dialectic ineluctably from one reasonable step to the next and to catastrophe. But even if it had been stupidity, it would have been historically comprehensible; stupidity is not a

1. Modification of the title of a book by Paul Eipper (1891–1964), an author of animal stories, *Tiere siehen dich an* (Animals are looking at you).

natural quality, but one socially produced and reinforced. The German ruling clique drove towards war because they were excluded from a position of imperial power. But in their exclusion lay the reason for the blind and clumsy provincialism that made Hitler's and Ribbentropp's policies uncompetitive and their war a gamble. That they were as badly informed about the Tory balance between general class interests and British special interests, and about the strength of the Red Army, as were their own masses behind the cordon of the Third Reich, is inseparable from the historical causes of National Socialism and almost from its strength. The sole chance of success for their reckless adventure lay in their knowing no better, and this was also the reason for its failure. Germany's industrial backwardness forced its politicians – anxious to regain lost ground and, as have-nots, specially qualified for the role – to fall back on their immediate, narrow experience, that of the political façade. They saw nothing before them except cheering assemblies and frightened negotiators: this blocked their view of the objective power of a greater mass of capital. It was immanent revenge on Hitler that he, the executioner of liberal society, was yet in his own state of consciousness too 'liberal' to perceive how industrial potential outside Germany was establishing, under the veil of liberalism, its irresistible domination. He, who recognized the untruth in liberalism as did no other bourgeois, could yet not recognize the power behind him, the social tendency for which Hitler was really no more than drummer. His consciousness regressed to the standpoint of his weaker short-sighted opponents, that he had first adopted in order to make shorter work of them. Germany's hour necessarily accorded with such stupidity. For only leaders who resembled the people of the country in their ignorance of the world and global economics could harness them to war and their pig-headedness to an enterprise wholly unhampered by reflection. Hitler's stupidity was a ruse of reason.

70

Uninformed opinion. – The Third Reich failed to produce a single work of art, a single mental structure capable of satisfying even the meagre liberalistic requirement of 'quality'. The demolition of humanity, and the conservation of works of the mind, were as incompatible as air-raid shelter and stork's nest, and the regenerated, martial culture looked, on its first day, like the cities on their last, a heap of rubble. To this culture at least, the population practised passive resistance. But the cultural energies allegedly released by National Socialism were in no way absorbed by the technical, political or military spheres. The whole thing is truly barbarism, and triumphs as such even over its own barbaric spirit. This can be seen in the sphere of strategy. The Fascist era has not brought about a flowering of strategy, but abolished it. The great military conceptions were inseparable from cunning, imagination: almost from private astuteness and initiative. They were part of a discipline relatively independent of the production process. The object was to derive decisive advantages from specialized innovations, such as diagonal battle lines or the accuracy of artillery. There was something of the bourgeois virtue of self-reliant enterprise in all this. Hannibal was a scion of merchants, not of heroes, and Napoleon of a democratic revolution. The element of bourgeois competition in the conduct of war has blown up in the face of Fascism. The Fascists raised to an absolute the basic idea of strategy: to exploit the temporary discrepancy between one nation with a leadership organized for murder, and the total potential of the rest. Yet by taking this idea to its logical conclusion in inventing total war, and by erasing the distinction between army and industry, they themselves liquidated strategy. Today it is as antiquated as the sound of military bands and paintings of battleships. Hitler sought world dominion through concentrated terror. The means he used, however, were unstrategic – the accumulation of overwhelming forces at particular points, the crude frontal breakthrough, the mechanical encirclement of the enemy stranded by armoured spearheads. This principle, wholly quantitive, positivistic, without surprises, thus everywhere 'public' and merging with publicity, no longer sufficed. The Allies, infinitely wealthier in economic resources, needed only to outdo the Germans in their own tactics to crush Hitler. The torpor and apathy of the war, the general defeatism which helped to protract its catastrophes, were conditioned by the decay of strategy. When all actions are mathematically calculated, they also take on a stupid quality. As if in mockery of the idea that anybody ought to be able to run the state, this war is conducted, despite the radar and the artificial harbours, as if by a schoolboy sticking flags into a chart. Spengler saw in the downfall of the West the promise of a golden age of engineers. The prospect coming into view, however, is the downfall of technology itself.

71

Pseudomenos.[1] – The magnetic power exerted by patently threadbare ideologies is to be explained, beyond psychology, by the objectively determined decay of logical evidence as such. Things have come to a pass where lying sounds like truth, truth like lying. Each statement, each piece of news, each thought has been preformed by the centres of the culture industry. Whatever lacks the familiar trace of such pre-formation lacks credibility, the more so because the institutions of public opinion accompany what they send forth by a thousand factual proofs and all the plausibility that total power can lay hands on. Truth that opposes these pressures not only appears improbable, but is in addition too feeble to make any headway in competition with their highly-concentrated machinery of dissemination. The extreme case of Germany is instructive of the general mechanism. When the National Socialists began to torture, they not only terrorized the peoples inside and outside Germany, but were the more secure from exposure the more wildly the horror increased. The implausibility of their actions made it easy to disbelieve what nobody, for the sake of precious peace, wanted to believe, while at the same time capitulating to it. Trembling voices persuade themselves that, after all, there is much exaggeration: even after the outbreak of the war, details about the concentration camps were unwanted in the English press. Every horror necessarily becomes, in the enlightened world, a horrific fairy-tale. For the untruth of truth has a core which finds an avid response in the unconscious. It is not only that the unconscious wishes horrors to come about; Fascism is itself less 'ideological', in so far as it openly proclaims the principle of domination that is elsewhere concealed. Whatever humane values the democracies can oppose it with, it can effortlessly refute by pointing out that they represent not the whole of humanity but a mere illusory image that Fascism has had the courage to discard. So desperate have people

1. The Greek term for 'liar', which gave its name to the logical puzzle invented by Eubulides, often known as the Cretan paradox, of he who says: 'All men are liars'.

become in civilization, however, that they are forever ready to abandon their frail better qualities as soon as the world does their worse ones the obligation of confessing how evil it is. The political forces of opposition, however, are compelled to make constant use of lies if they are not themselves to be completely wiped out as destructive. The deeper the divergence of an opposition from the established order, which at least affords it refuge from a blacker future, the more easily Fascists can pin it down to untruths. Only the absolute lie now has any freedom to speak the truth. The confounding of truth and lies, making it almost impossible to maintain a distinction, and a labour of Sisyphus to hold on to the simplest piece of knowledge, marks the victory in the field of logical organization of the principle that lies crushed on that of battle. Lies have long legs: they are ahead of their time. The conversion of all questions of truth into questions of power, a process that truth itself cannot escape if it is not to be annihilated by power, not only suppresses truth as in earlier despotic orders, but has attacked the very heart of the distinction between true and false, which the hirelings of logic were in any case diligently working to abolish. So Hitler, of whom no-one can say whether he died or escaped, survives.

72

Second harvest. – Talent is perhaps nothing other than successfully sublimated rage, the capacity to convert energies once intensified beyond measure to destroy recalcitrant objects, into the concentration of patient observation, so keeping as tight a hold on the secret of things, as one had earlier when finding no peace until the quavering voice had been wrenched from the mutilated toy. Who has not seen on the face of a man sunk in thought, far removed from practical objects, traits of the same aggression which is otherwise exerted practically? Does not the artist feel himself, amid the transports of creation, brutalized, 'working furiously'? Indeed, is not such fury necessary to free oneself from confinement and the fury of confinement? Might not the very conciliatoriness of art have been only bullied out of its destructiveness?

Nowadays most people kick with the pricks.

How some things have gestures, and so modes of behaviour, inscribed in them. Slippers are designed to be slipped into without help from the hand. They are monuments to the hatred of bending down.

That in repressive society freedom comes to the same thing as insolence is demonstrated by the nonchalant gestures of teenagers, who 'don't care a cent' for the world as long as they do not sell it their labour. To show that they are dependent on no-one and so owe no-one respect, they put their hands in their trouser pockets. But their elbows, stuck outwards, are ready to barge anyone who gets in their way.

A German is someone who cannot tell a lie without believing it himself.

The phrase *'Kommt überhaupt gar nicht in Frage'* ['it's completely and utterly out of the question'] which probably came into use in Berlin in the twenties, is already potentially Hitler's seizure of power. For it pretends that private will, founded sometimes on real rights but usually on mere affrontery, directly represents an objective necessity that admits no disagreement. At bottom, it is the refusal of a bankrupt negotiator to pay the other a farthing, in the proud awareness that there is nothing more to be got out of him. The crooked lawyer's dodge is brazenly inflated to heroic steadfastness: the linguistic formula for usurpation. This bluff defines equally the success and the collapse of National Socialism.

The existence of bread factories, turning the prayer that we be given our daily bread into a mere metaphor and an avowal of desperation, argues more strongly against the possibility of Christianity than all the enlightened critiques of the life of Jesus.

Anti-Semitism is the rumour about the Jews.

German words of foreign derivation are the Jews of language.

One evening, in a mood of helpless sadness, I caught myself using a ridiculously wrong subjunctive form of a verb that was itself not entirely correct German, being part of the dialect of my native town. I had not heard, let alone used, the endearing misconstruction since my first years at school. Melancholy, drawing me irresistibly into the abyss of childhood, awakened this old, impotently yearning sound in its depths. Language sent back to me like an echo the humiliation which unhappiness had inflicted on me in forgetting what I am.

The second part of *Faust*, decried as obscure and allegorical, is more crammed with commonly-used quotations than any play except *William Tell*. The transparency and simplicity of a text bears no direct relation to its capacity to enter tradition. It may be its very impenetrability, demanding constantly renewed interpretation, that confers on a sentence or a work the authority which dedicates it to posterity.

Every work of art is an uncommitted crime.

Tragedies which, by means of 'style', most strictly maintain a distance from mere existence, at the same time most faithfully preserve, with their communal processions, masks and sacrifices, the memory of the demonology of primitive man.

The poverty of the sunrise in Richard Strauss' 'Alpine Symphony' results not only from its banal sequences but from its very splendour. For no sunrise, even in mountains, is pompous, triumphal, imperial; each one is faint and timorous, like a hope that all may yet be well, and it is this very unobtrusiveness of the mightiest light that is moving and overpowering.

The sound of any woman's voice on the telephone tells us whether the speaker is attractive. It reflects back as self-confidence, natural ease and self-attention all the admiring and desirous glances she has ever received. It expresses the double meaning of graciousness: gratitude and grace. The ear perceives what is for the eye, because both live on the experience of a single beauty. It is recognized on first hearing: a familiar quotation from a book never read.

Waking in the middle of a dream, even the worst, one feels disappointed, cheated of the best in life. But pleasant, fulfilled dreams are actually as rare, to use Schubert's words, as happy music. Even the loveliest dream bears like a blemish its difference from reality, the awareness that what it grants is mere illusion. This is why precisely the loveliest dreams are as if blighted. Such an impression is captured superlatively in the description of the nature theatre of Oklahoma in Kafka's *America*.

To happiness the same applies as to truth: one does not have it, but is in it. Indeed, happiness is nothing other than being encompassed, an after-image of the original shelter within the mother. But for this reason no-one who is happy can know that he is so. To see happiness, he would have to pass out of it: to be as if already born. He who says he is happy lies, and in invoking happiness, sins against it. He alone keeps faith who says: I was happy. The only relation of consciousness to happiness is gratitude: in which lies its incomparable dignity.

To a child returning from a holiday, home seems new, fresh, festive. Yet nothing has changed there since he left. Only because duty has now been forgotten, of which each piece of furniture, window, lamp, was otherwise a reminder, is the house given back this sabbath peace, and for minutes one is at home in a never-returning world of rooms, nooks and corridors in a way that makes the rest of life there a lie. No differently will the world one day appear, almost unchanged, in its constant feast-day light, when it stands no longer under the law of labour, and when for home-comers duty has the lightness of holiday play.

Now that we can no longer pluck flowers to adorn our beloved – a sacrifice that adoration for the one atones by freely taking on itself the wrong it does all others – picking flowers has become something evil. It serves only to perpetuate the transient by fixing it. But nothing is more ruinous: the scentless bouquet, the institutionalized remembrance, kills what still lingers by the very act of preserving it. The fleeting moment can live in the murmur of forgetfulness, that the ray will one day touch to brightness; the moment we want to possess is lost already. The luxurious blooms that the child struggles home with at the mother's command, might be stuck behind the mirror as artificial ones were sixty years ago, and in the end they become the greedily seized holiday snapshot, in which the landscape is littered with those who saw nothing of it, and who grab as a souvenir something that sank unremembered into nothingness. But he who in rapture sends flowers, will reach instinctively for the ones that look mortal.

We owe our life to the difference between the economic framework of late capitalism, and its political façade. To theoretical criticism the discrepancy is slight: everywhere the sham character of supposed public opinion, the primacy of the economy in real decisions, can be demonstrated. For countless individuals, however, the thin, ephemeral veil is the basis of their entire existence. Precisely those on whose thought and action change, alone essential, depends, are indebted for their existence to the inessential, illusion; indeed to what, measured by the great laws of historical development, amounts to mere chance. But is not the whole construction of essence and appearance thereby affected? Measured by its concept, the individual has indeed become as null and void as Hegel's philosophy anticipated: seen *sub specie individuationis*, however, absolute contingency, permitted to persist as a seemingly abnormal state, is itself the essential. The world is systematized horror, but therefore it is to do the world too much honour to think of it entirely as a system; for its unifying principle is division, and it reconciles by asserting unimpaired the irreconcilability of the general and the particular. Its essence is abomination; but its appearance, the lie by virtue of which it persists, is a stand-in for truth.

73

Deviation. – The decay of the workers' movement is corroborated by the official optimism of its adherents. This seems to grow with the immovable consolidation of the capitalist world. The founders of the movement never regarded success as guaranteed, and therefore throughout their lives said dire things to the workers' organizations. Today, when the enemy's power and control over the consciousness of the masses has been immeasurably strengthened, the attempt radically to alter this consciousness by withholding assent to it is considered reactionary. Suspicion falls on anyone who combines criticism of capitalism with that of the proletariat, which is more and more becoming a mere reflection of the tendencies of capitalist development. Once it crosses class boundaries, the negative element of thought is frowned upon. Kaiser Wilhelm's words of wisdom, 'I tolerate no Jeremiahs', have penetrated the ranks of those he wanted to crush. Anyone who pointed, for example, to the lack of any spontaneous resistance by the German workers was told in reply that things were so much in a state of flux that such judgements were impossible; anyone who was not on the spot, right among the poor German victims of aerial warfare – victims, however, who had few objections to air-raids as long as they were directed at the other side – had no right to open his mouth, and in any case agrarian reforms were imminent in Rumania and Yugoslavia. Yet the further the rational expectation diminishes that society's doom can really be averted, the more reverently they repeat the old prayers: masses, solidarity, Party, class struggle. While not a single idea in the critique of political economy is firmly believed any longer by the adherents of the left-wing platform; while their newspapers daily and witlessly trumpet forth theses that outdo all revisionism yet signify nothing, and can be replaced at will tomorrow by the opposite, the ears of the faithful party-liners show a musician's sensitivity to the faintest disrespect for the slogans that have jettisoned theory. Hurrah-optimism has a fitting counterpart in international patriotism. The staunch supporter must swear allegiance to a people, no matter which. In the dogmatic concept of the people, however, the acceptance of an alleged common destiny between men as the authority for action, the idea of a society liberated from the compulsion of nature, is implicitly denied.

Even this frantic optimism is the perversion of a motif that has seen better days: the refusal to wait. Confidence in the state of technology made people see change as imminent, a palpable possibility. Conceptions entailing long intervals of time, precautions, elaborate measures for public enlightenment, were suspected of abandoning the goal they claimed to pursue. At that time optimism, amounting to a disregard for death, expressed an autonomous will. All that is left is its shell, belief in the power and greatness of the organization as such, devoid of any willingness for individual action, indeed, imbued with the destructive conviction that while spontaneity is no longer possible, the Red Army will win in the end. The constantly enforced insistence that everybody should admit that everything will turn out well, places those who do not under suspicion of being defeatists and deserters. In the fairy-tale, the toads who came from the depths were messengers of great joy. Today, when the abandonment of utopia looks as much like its realization as the Antichrist resembles the paraclete, toad has become a term of abuse among those who are themselves in the depths. The optimism of the left repeats the insidious bourgeois superstition that one should not talk of the devil but look on the bright side. 'The gentleman does not find the world to his liking? Then

let him go and look for a better one' – such is the popular parlance
of socialist realism.

74

Mammoth. – Some years ago American newspapers announced the
discovery of a well-preserved dinosaur in the state of Utah. It was
stressed that the specimen had survived its kind and was millions
of years younger than those previously known. Such pieces of news,
like the repulsive humoristic craze for the Loch Ness Monster and
the King Kong film, are collective projections of the monstrous
total State. People prepare themselves for its terrors by familiarizing
themselves with gigantic images. In its absurd readiness to accept
these, impotently prostrate humanity tries desperately to assimilate
to experience what defies all experience. But the imagining of primeval animals still living or only extinct for a few million years is
not explained solely by these attempts. The desire for the presence
of the most ancient is a hope that animal creation might survive the
wrong that man has done it, if not man himself, and give rise to a
better species, one that finally makes a success of life. Zoological
gardens stem from the same hope. They are laid out on the pattern
of Noah's Ark, for since their inception the bourgeois class has
been waiting for the flood. The use of zoos for entertainment and
instruction seems a thin pretext. They are allegories of the specimen
or the pair who defy the disaster that befalls the species *qua* species.
This is why the over-richly stocked zoos of large European cities
seem like forms of decadence: more than two elephants, two
giraffes, one hippopotamus, are a bad sign. Nor can any good come
of Hagenbeck's layout,[1] with trenches instead of cages, betraying
the Ark by simulating the rescue that only Ararat can promise.
They deny the animals' freedom only the more completely by
keeping the boundaries invisible, the sight of which would inflame
the longing for open spaces. They are to self-respecting zoos what
botanical gardens are to palm courts. The more purely nature is
preserved and transplanted by civilization, the more implacably it
is dominated. We can now afford to encompass ever larger natural
units, and leave them apparently intact within our grasp, whereas

1. Karl Hagenbeck (1844–1913): an animal-dealer who created an open zoo
or *Tierpark* near Hamburg in 1907.

previously the selecting and taming of particular items bore witness to the difficulty we still had in coping with nature. The tiger endlessly pacing back and forth in his cage reflects back negatively, through his bewilderment, something of humanity, but not the one frolicking behind the pit too wide to leap. The anticipated beauty of Brehm's *Animal Life* stems from its way of describing animals as they are seen through the bars of a zoological garden, even, and above all, when quoting reports by fanciful explorers on life in the wilds.[1] The fact, however, that animals really suffer more in cages than in the open range, that Hagenbeck does in fact represent a step forward in humanity, reflects on the inescapability of imprisonment. It is a consequence of history. The zoological gardens in their authentic form are products of nineteenth-century colonial imperialism. They flourished since the opening-up of wild regions of Africa and Central Asia, which paid symbolic tribute in the shape of animals. The value of the tributes was measured by their exoticism, their inaccessibility. The development of technology has put an end to this and abolished the exotic. The farm-bred lion is as fully tamed as the horse long since subjected to birth-control. But the millennium has not dawned. Only in the irrationality of civilization itself, in the nooks and crannies of the cities, to which the walls, towers and bastions of the zoos wedged among them are merely an addition, can nature be conserved. The rationalization of culture, in opening its doors to nature, thereby completely absorbs it, and eliminates with difference the principle of culture, the possibility of reconciliation.

75

Chilly hospitality. – With deep premonition, Schubert's romanticism of disillusion, in the cycle at whose centre stand the words 'I have done with all my dreams', reserves for the graveyard alone the name of hostel.[2] The *fata morgana* of the life of idleness has been seized by *rigor mortis*. Guests and host are as if spellbound. The former are in a rush. They would prefer to keep their hats on. On uncomfortable seats they are induced by the outheld bills and the

1. Alfred Brehm (1829–84): a prominent zoologist and explorer of the later nineteenth century.
2. The song is *Das Wirtshaus*, from the cycle *Winterreise* (1827).

moral pressure of the waiting queues behind them to leave the place, still called with mockery a café, at all possible speed. The host, however, with all his colleagues, is not himself at all, but an employee. Probably the decline of the hotel dates back to the dissolution of the ancient unity of inn and brothel, nostalgia for which lives on in every glance directed at the displayed waitress and the tell-tale gestures of the chamber-maids. But now that the innkeeper's trade, the most honourable of the professions in the sphere of circulation, has been purged of its last ambiguities, such as still cling to the word 'intercourse', things have become very bad. Step by step, and always for irrefutable reasons, the means are destroying the ends. The division of labour, the system of auto-matized facilities, has the result that no-one is concerned for the client's comfort. No-one can divine from his expression what might take his fancy, for the waiter no longer knows the menu, and if he makes suggestions of his own he must be prepared to face rebuke for having overstepped his limits. No-one hastens to serve the guest, however long he has to wait, if the person responsible for him is busy: concern for the institution, a concern that reaches its culmination in prisons, takes precedence, as in a clinic, over that for the subject, who is administered as an object. That the 'Restaurant' is divided by gulfs of antagonism from the Hotel, an empty husk of rooms, is a matter of course, as are the time-limits on eating and on insufferable 'room service', from which one flees to the drugstore, blatantly a shop, behind whose inhospitable counter a juggler with fried-eggs, crispy bacon and ice-cubes proves himself the last solicitous host. But in the hotel every unforeseen question is disposed of by the porter with an irate nod to another counter, usually closed. The objection that all this is no more than a caterwauling *laudatio temporis acti* does not hold water. Who would not prefer the 'Blauer Stern' in Prague or the 'Österreichischer Hof' in Salzburg, even if he had to cross the landing to reach the bathroom, and was no longer woken in the small hours by unfailing central heating? The nearer the sphere of immediate, physical existence is approached, the more questionable progress becomes, a Pyrrhic victory of fetishized production. Sometimes such progress horrifies itself, and strives to reunite even if only symbolically the labour functions that calculation has disjoined. This gives rise to figures like the hostess, a synthetic landlady. Just as in reality she looks after nothing, has no real powers to hold together the severed, cold facilities, but confines herself to the vacuous gesture of welcome and, certainly, the supervision of the personnel, so also she appears: peevishly pretty, a slimly upright, strenuously youthful, faded woman. Her true function is to see to it that the incoming guest does not even choose for himself the table at which he is to be processed. Her graciousness is the reverse-side of the dignity of the bouncer.

76

Gala dinner. – How far progress and regression are intertwined today can be seen in the notion of technical possibilities. Mechanical processes of reproduction have developed independently of what they reproduce, and become autonomous. They are considered progressive, and anything that has no part in them, reactionary and quaint. Such beliefs are promoted all the more thoroughly because super-machines, once they are to the slightest degree unused, threaten to become bad investments. Since, however, their development is essentially concerned with what, under liberalism, was known as 'getting up' goods for sale, while at the same time crushing the goods themselves under its own weight, as an apparatus external to them, the adaptation of needs to this apparatus results in the death of objectively appropriate demands. The fascinated eagerness to consume the latest process of the day not only leads to indifference towards the matter transmitted by the process, but encourages stationary rubbish and calculated idiocy. It confirms the old kitsch in ever new paraphrases as *haute nouveauté*. The concomitant of technical progress is the narrow-minded determination at all costs to buy nothing that is not in demand, not to fall behind the careering production process, never mind what the purpose of the product might be. Keeping up, crowding and queuing everywhere take the place of what were to some extent rational needs. Scarcely less than the hatred for a radical, overly modern composition is that for a film already three months old, to which the latest, though in no way differing from it, it relentlessly preferred. Just as the customers of mass society have to be on the scene at once, they cannot leave anything out. If the nineteenth-century connoisseur only stayed for one act of an opera, partly for the barbaric reason that he would allow no spectacle to shorten his dinner, barbarism has now reached a point, the possibility of escape to a dinner being cut off, where it cannot stuff itself full enough of culture. Every programme must be sat through to the end, every best-seller read, every film seen in its first flush in the top Odeon. The abundance of commodities indiscriminately consumed is becoming calamitous. It makes it impossible to find one's way, and just as in a gigantic department store one looks out for a guide, the population wedged between wares await their leader.

77

Auction. – Rampant technology eliminates luxury, but not by declaring privilege a human right; rather, it does so by both raising the general standard of living and cutting off the possibility of fulfilment. The express train that in three nights and two days hurtles across the continent is a miracle, but travelling in it has nothing of the faded splendour of the *train bleu*. What made up the voluptuousness of travel, beginning with the goodbye-waving through the open window, the solicitude of amiable accepters of tips, the ceremonial of mealtimes, the constant feeling of receiving favours that take nothing from anyone else, has passed away, together with the elegant people who were wont to promenade along the platforms before the departure, and who will by now be sought in vain even in the foyers of the most prestigious hotels. That the steps of railway carriages have to be retracted intimates to the passenger of even the most expensive express that he must obey the company's terse regulations like a prisoner. Certainly, the company gives him the exactly calculated value of his fare, but this includes nothing that research has not proved an average demand. Who, aware of such conditions, could depart on impulse on a voyage with his mistress as once from Paris to Nice? But one cannot be rid of the suspicion that even luxury that deviates from the norm, announcing itself ostentatiously as such, is mingled with an increasing element of premeditation, artificial show. It is meant, in keeping with Veblen's theory, to permit the wealthy to demonstrate their status to themselves and others, rather than to satisfy their needs, which in any case are becoming increasingly undifferentiated. While a Cadillac undoubtedly excels a Chevrolet by the amount that it costs more, this superiority, unlike that of the old Rolls

Royce, nevertheless itself proceeds from an overall plan which artfully equips the former with better, the latter with worse cylinders, bolts, accessories, without anything being altered in the basic pattern of the mass-produced article: only minor rearrangements in production would be needed to turn the Chevrolet into a Cadillac. So luxury is sapped. For amid universal fungibility happiness attaches without exception to the non-fungible. No humane exertions, no formal reasoning, can sever happiness from the fact that the ravishing dress is worn by only one, and not by twenty thousand. The utopia of the qualitative – the things which through their difference and uniqueness cannot be absorbed into the prevalent exchange relationships – takes refuge under capitalism in the traits of fetishism. But this promise of happiness in luxury in turn pre-supposes privilege, economic inequality, a society based on fungibility. Thus the qualitative itself becomes a special case of quantification, the non-fungible becomes fungible, luxury turns into comfort and finally into a senseless gadget. This vicious circle would put an end to luxury even without the levelling tendency of mass society, over which reactionaries wax sentimentally indignant. The inner constitution of luxury is not unaffected by what happens to the useless in its total incorporation into the realm of use. Its remnants, even objects of the highest quality, already look like junk. The valuables cramming the homes of the very rich cry out helplessly for the museum; yet there the meaning of sculpture and paintings, as Valéry perceived, is destroyed, only architecture, their mother, showing them their rightful place. But kept by force in the houses of people with whom they have no ties, they are an open affront to the mode of existence which private property has now adopted. If there was still some excuse for the antiques with which millionaires surrounded themselves up to the First War, in that they heightened the idea of the bourgeois home to a dream – a nightmare – without disintegrating it, the *chinoiseries* subsequently adopted merely tolerate sullenly the private owner who only feels at ease in light and air that are barricaded by luxury. Modern, practical luxury is a contradiction in terms that may just provide a living for false Russian princes hired by Hollywood people as interior decorators. The lines of advanced taste converge in asceticism. The child reading the *Arabian Nights*, intoxicated by the rubies and emeralds, wondered why possession of the stones should cause such ecstasy, when they are described, after all, not as means of exchange, but as a hoard. In this question is involved the whole dialectic of enlightenment. It is as reasonable as it is unreasonable: reasonable in recognizing idolization; unreasonable in turning against its own goal, which is present only where it need be justified to no authority, indeed to no intention: no happiness without fetishism. Gradually, however, the child's sceptical question has spread to every kind of luxury, and even naked sensual pleasure is not proof against it. To the aesthetic eye, which sides with the useless against utility, the aesthetic, when severed violently from purpose, becomes anti-aesthetic, because it expresses violence: luxury becomes brutality. Finally it is swallowed up in drudgery or conserved in caricature. What beauty still flourishes under terror is a mockery and ugliness to itself. Yet its fleeting shape attests to the avoidability of terror. Something of this paradox is fundamental to all art; today it appears in the fact that art still exists at all. The captive idea of beauty strives at once to reject happiness and to assert it.

78

Over the hills. – More perfectly than any other fairy-tale, Snow-White expresses melancholy. The pure image of this mood is the queen looking out into the snow through her window and wishing for her daughter, after the lifelessly living beauty of the flakes, the black mourning of the window-frame, the stab of bleeding; and then dying in childbirth. The happy end takes away nothing of this. As the granting of her wish is death, so the saving remains illusion. For deeper knowledge cannot believe that she was awakened who lies as if asleep in the glass coffin. Is not the poisoned bite of apple which the journey shakes from her throat, rather than a means of murder, the rest of her unlived, banished life, from which only now she truly recovers, since she is lured by no more false messengers? And how inadequate happiness sounds: 'Snow-White felt kindly towards him and went with him.' How it is revoked by the wicked triumph over wickedness. So, when we are hoping for rescue, a voice tells us that hope is in vain, yet it is powerless hope alone that allows us to draw a single breath. All contemplation can do no more than patiently trace the ambiguity of melancholy in ever new configurations. Truth is inseparable from the illusory belief that from the figures of the unreal one day, in spite of all, real deliverance will come.

79

Intellectus sacrificium intellectus.[1] – The assumption that thought profits from the decay of the emotions, or even that it remains unaffected, is itself an expression of the process of stupefaction. The social division of labour recoils on man, however much it may expedite the task exacted from him. The faculties, having developed through interaction, atrophy once they are severed from each other. Nietzsche's aphorism, that 'the degree and kind of a man's sexuality extends to the highest pinnacle of his spirit', has a more than merely psychological application. Because even its remotest objectifications are nourished by impulses, thought destroys in the latter the condition of its own existence. Is not memory inseparable from love, which seeks to preserve what yet must pass away? Is not each stirring of fantasy engendered by desire which, in displacing the elements of what exists, transcends it without betrayal? Is not indeed the simplest perception shaped by fear of the thing perceived, or desire for it? It is true that the objective meaning of knowledge has, with the objectification of the world, become progressively detached from the underlying impulses; it is equally true that knowledge breaks down where its effort of objectification remains under the sway of desire. But if the impulses are not at once preserved and surpassed in the thought which has escaped their sway, then there will be no knowledge at all, and the thought that murders the wish that fathered it will be overtaken by the revenge of stupidity. Memory is tabooed as unpredictable, unreliable, irrational. The resulting intellectual asthma, which culminates in the dissolution of the historical dimension of consciousness, leads directly to a depreciation of the synthetic apperception which, according to Kant, cannot be divorced from 'reproduction in imagination', from recollection. Fantasy alone, today consigned to the realm of the unconscious and proscribed from knowledge as a childish, injudicious rudiment, can establish that relation between objects which is the irrevocable source of all judgement: should

1. Play on the Jesuit maxim *Dei sacrificium intellectus*, expressed by Loyola: 'To subordinate the intellect to obedience is to offer the highest sacrifice to God.'

fantasy be driven out, judgement too, the real act of knowledge, is exorcised. But the castration of perception by a court of control that denies it any anticipatory desire, forces it thereby into a pattern of helplessly reiterating what is already known. When nothing more may actually be seen, the intellect is sacrificed. Just as, under the primacy of the autonomous production process, the purpose of reason dwindles away until it sinks into the fetishism of itself and of external power, so reason itself is reduced to an instrument and assimilated to its functionaries, whose power of thought serves only the purpose of preventing thought. Once the last trace of emotion has been eradicated, nothing remains of thought but absolute tautology. The utterly pure reason of those who have divested themselves entirely of the ability 'to conceive of an object even in its absence', converges with pure unconsciousness, with feeble-mindedness in the most literal sense, for measured against the extravagantly realistic ideal of a datum freed of any categories, all knowledge is false, and true only where the question of truth or falsity cannot be applied. That such tendencies are far advanced can be seen at every turn in the activities of science, which is on the point of bringing the last remnants of the world, defenceless ruins, under its yoke.

80

Diagnosis. – That the world has by now become the system that National Socialist vilification mistakenly took the lax Weimar Republic to be, is evident in the pre-established harmony between institutions and those they serve. A breed of men has secretly grown up that hungers for the compulsion and restriction imposed by the absurd persistence of domination. These people, however, aided and abetted by the objective social framework, have by degrees themselves taken over the functions which ought by right, against the pre-established harmony, to represent dissonance. Among the many that have been quashed is the saying 'Pressure produces counter-pressure': if the former increases sufficiently, the latter disappears, and society seems intent, by a deathly elimination of tensions, on making a noteworthy contribution to entropy. The scientific industry has its exact counterpart in the kind of minds it harnesses: they no longer need to do themselves any violence in becoming their own voluntary and zealous overseers. Even if they show themselves, outside their official capacity, to be quite human and sensible beings, they are paralysed by pathic stupidity the moment they begin to think professionally. But far from finding anything inimical in the prohibitions on thinking, the candidates – and all scientists are candidates for posts – feel relieved. Because thinking burdens them with a subjective responsibility which their objective position in the productive process does not allow them to meet, they renounce it, shiver a bit, and run to join their opponents. Dislike of thinking rapidly becomes incapacity for it: people who can effortlessly discover the most sophisticated statistical objections when it is a question of sabotaging a piece of knowledge, are unable to make *ex cathedra* the simplest predictions. They hit out at speculation and in it kill common sense. The more intelligent of them suspect the sickness of their intellectual powers, since it first appears not universally but in the organs whose services they sell. Many wait in fear and shame for their defect to be discovered. But they all find it publicly acclaimed as a moral achievement, and see themselves recognized for a scientific asceticism which to them is none, but the secret contour of their weakness. Their rancour is socially rationalized with the argument: thinking is unscientific. At the same time, their mental power has, in a number of dimensions, been prodigiously increased by control mechanisms. The collective stupidity of research technicians is not simply an absence or regression of intellectual faculties, but a proliferation of the thinking faculty itself, which consumes thought with its own strength. The masochistic malice of young intellectuals springs from the malignance of their disease.

81

Great and small. – One of the disastrous transferences from the field of economic planning to that of theory, which is no longer really distinguished from the ground-plan of the whole, is the belief that intellectual work can be administered according to the criterion whether an occupation is necessary and reasonable. Priorities of urgency are established. But to deprive thought of the moment of spontaneity is to annul precisely its necessity. It is reduced to replaceable, exchangeable dispositions. As in war economies orders of precedence are decided for the distribution of raw materials, for the production of this or that type of weapon, a hierarchy of importance is creeping into theory-formation which gives preference to either particularly topical or particularly relevant themes, and discriminates against, or indulgently tolerates, anything non-essential, letting it pass as ornamentation of the basic facts, finesse. The concept of relevance is determined by organizational considerations, that of topicality measured by the most powerful objective tendency of the moment. This schematization into important and subsidiary categories follows the scale of values of prevalent practice with regard to form, even if contradicting it in content. In the origins of progressive philosophy, in Bacon and Descartes, the cult of the important is already contained. Yet in the end this cult shows an unfree, regressive quality. Importance is represented by the dog out on a walk: at some unexplained spot he stands and sniffs, tense, unyielding, earnestly displeased – and then relieves himself, scrapes the ground with his feet and trots on his way in unconcern. In primitive times life and death may have depended on such things; after thousands of years of domestication they have become an unreal ritual. Who can help being reminded of them when observing a serious committee weighing the urgency of problems before turning over the carefully defined and time-tabled tasks to the attentions of their colleagues? There is something of this anachronistic doggedness in all importance, and to use it as a criterion of thought is to impose on thought a spellbound fixity, and a loss of self-reflection. The great themes are nothing other than primeval rumblings which cause the animal to pause and try to bring them forth once again. This does not mean that the hierarchy of importance should be ignored. Just as its narrow-mindedness reflects that of the system, so it is saturated with all the latter's force and stringency. Thought ought not, however, to repeat this hierarchy, but by completing, end it. The division of the world into important and unimportant matters, which has always served to neutralize the key phenomena of social injustice as mere exceptions, should be followed up to the point where it is convicted of its own untruth. The division which makes everything objects must itself become an object of thought, instead of guiding it. The large themes will then also make their appearance, though hardly in the traditional 'thematic' sense, but refractedly and eccentrically. 'Philosophy retained the barbarism of immediate quantity as a legacy from its earlier alliance with administrators and mathematicians: whatever does not bear the stamp of the inflated, world-historical bustle is handed over to the procedures of the positive sciences. In this, philosophy behaves like bad painting, which imagines that the dignity of a work and the fame it earns depends on the gravity of the subject matter; a picture of the Battle of Leipzig is worth more than a chair in oblique perspective. The distinction between the conceptual and the artistic media makes no difference to this bad naivety. If the process of abstraction marks all its thinking with the illusion of greatness, it also harbours, in its distance from the object of action, in its reflection and transparency, the antidote: the self-criticism of reason is its truest morality. The opposite, in the most recent phase of self-governing thought, is nothing other than the abolition of the subject. The gesture of theoretical work, passing judgement on themes according to their importance, neglects the theoretical worker. The development of an ever-diminishing number of technical faculties is supposed to equip him adequately to deal with every specified task. Thinking subjectivity, however, is precisely what cannot be fitted into a set of tasks imposed heteronomously from above: it is adequate to them only in the sense that it is no part of them, so that its existence is a pre-condition of any objectively binding truth. The overbearing matter-of-factness which sacrifices the subject to the ascertainment of the truth, rejects at once truth and objectivity.

82

Keeping one's distance. – Positivism reduces the detachment of thought to a reality, that reality itself no longer tolerates. Cowed into wanting to be no more than a mere provisional abbreviation for the factual matter beneath it, thought loses not only its autonomy in face of reality, but with it the power to penetrate reality. Only at a remove from life can the mental life exist, and truly engage the empirical. While thought relates to facts and moves by criticizing them, its movement depends no less on the maintenance of distance. It expresses exactly what is, precisely because what is is never quite as thought expresses it. Essential to it is an element of exaggeration, of over-shooting the object, of self-detachment from the weight of the factual, so that instead of merely reproducing being it can, at once rigorous and free, determine it. Thus every thought resembles play, with which Hegel no less than Nietzsche compared the work of the mind. The unbarbaric side of philosophy is its tacit awareness of the element of irresponsibility, of blitheness springing from the volatility of thought, which forever escapes what it judges. Such licence is resented by the positivistic spirit and put down to mental disorder. Divergence from the facts becomes mere wrongness, the moment of play a luxury in a world where the intellectual functions have to account for their every moment with a stop-watch. But as soon as thought repudiates its inviolable distance and tries with a thousand subtle arguments to prove its literal correctness, it founders. If it leaves behind the medium of virtuality, of anticipation that cannot be wholly fulfilled by any single piece of actuality; in short, if instead of interpretation it seeks to become mere statement, everything it states becomes, in fact, untrue. Its apologetics, inspired by uncertainty and a bad conscience, can be refuted at every step by demonstrating the non-identity which it will not acknowledge, yet which alone makes it thought. If, on the other hand, it tried to claim its distance as a privilege, it would act no better, but would proclaim two kinds of truth, that of the facts and that of ideas. That would be to decompose truth itself, and truly to denigrate thought. Distance is not a safety-zone but a field of tension. It is manifested not in relaxing the claim of ideas to truth, but in delicacy and fragility of thinking. Vis-à-vis positivism it is fitting neither to insist on being right nor to put on airs of distinction, but rather to prove, by criticism of knowledge, the impossibility of a coincidence between the idea and what fulfils it. The passion for equating the non-synonymous is not the ever-striving toil that at last attains redemption,[1] but naive and inexperienced. Thought has known and forgotten the reproaches of positivism a thousand times, and only through such knowing and forgetting did it first become thought. The distance of thought from reality is itself nothing other than the precipitate of history in concepts. To use them without distance is, despite all the resignation it implies or perhaps because of it, a child's affair. For thought must aim beyond its target just because it never quite reaches it, and positivism is uncritical in its confidence of doing so,

1. Allusion to the lines of the last scene of Goethe's *Faust*, Part Two, sung by angels: *Wer immer strebend sich bemüht, / den können wir erlösen* (He who strives with ceaseless toil / can we redeem).

imagining its tergiversations to be due to mere conscientiousness. A transcending thought takes its own inadequacy more thoroughly into account than does one guided by the control mechanisms of science. It extrapolates in order, by the over-exertion of the too-much, to master, however hopelessly, the inevitable too-little. The illegitimate absolutism, the allegedly definitive stamp of its formulations, with which philosophy is reproached, derives precisely from the abyss of relativity. The exaggerations of speculative metaphysics are scars of reflecting reason, and the unproven alone unmasks proof as tautology. In contrast, the immediate proviso of relativity, the modesty that remains within whatever conceptual area has been marked off for it, denies itself by its very caution the experience of its limit, to think which is, according to Hegel's superb insight, the same thing as to cross it. Thus the relativists are the real – the bad – absolutists and, moreover, the bourgeois, who need to make sure of their knowledge as of a possession, only to lose it all the more thoroughly. The claim to the absolute that overleaps its own shadow alone does justice to the relative. By taking untruth upon itself, it leads to the threshold of truth in its concrete awareness of the conditionality of human knowledge.

83

Vice-President. – Advice to intellectuals: let no-one represent you. The fungibility of all services and people, and the resultant belief that everyone must be able to do everything, prove, in the existing order, fetters. The egalitarian ideal of interchangeability is a fraud when not backed by the principle of revocability and responsibility to the rank and file. The most powerful person is he who is able to do least himself and burden others most with the things for which he lends his name and pockets the credit. This seems like collectivism, yet amounts only to a feeling of superiority, of exemption from work by the power to control others. In material production, admittedly, interchangeability has an objective basis. The quantification of work processes tends to diminish the difference between the duties of managing director and petrol-pump attendant. It is a wretched ideology which postulates that more intelligence, experience, even training is needed to run a trust under present conditions than to read a pressure-gauge. But while this ideology is obstinately upheld in material production, the intellect is subjected to its opposite. This is the doctrine, now gone to the dogs, of the *universitas literarum*, of the equality of all in the republic of scholarship, which not only employs everybody as overseers of everybody, but is supposed to qualify everybody to do everybody else's work equally well. Interchangeability subjects ideas to the same procedure as exchange imposes on things. The incommensurable is eliminated. But while the first task of thought is to criticize the all-embracing commensurability that stems from exchange relationships, this commensurability constitutes the intellectual relations of production which turn against the forces of production. In the material realm interchangeability is what is already possible, and non-interchangeability the pretext for preventing it; in theory, which ought properly to see through this kind of *quid pro quo*, interchangeability serves to allow the mechanism to propagate itself even where its objective antithesis is to be found. Non-interchangeability alone could arrest the incorporation of mind into the ranks of employment. The demand, presented as obvious, that every intellectual achievement should be performable by every qualified member of an organization, makes the most blinkered academic technician the measure of intellect: where is this very man to find the ability to criticize his own technification? Thus the economy effects the levelling process that then calls after itself in anger 'Stop thief!' In the age of the individual's liquidation, the question of individuality must be raised anew. While the individual, like all individualistic processes of production, has fallen behind the state of technology and become historically obsolete, he becomes the custodian of truth, as the condemned against the victor. For the individual alone preserves, in however distorted a form, a trace of that which legitimizes all technification, and yet to which the latter blinds itself. Because unbridled progress exhibits no immediate identity with that of mankind, its antithesis can give true progress shelter. A pencil and rubber are of more use to thought than a battalion of assistants. Those who neither give themselves up wholly to the individualism of intellectual production nor are prepared to pitch themselves headlong into the collectivism of egalitarian interchangeability, with its inherent contempt for man, must fall back on free collaboration and solidarity, with shared responsibility. Anything else sells off the intellect to forms of business and therefore finally to the latter's interests.

Timetable. – Few things separate more profoundly the mode of life befitting an intellectual from that of the bourgeois than the fact that the former acknowledges no alternative between work and recreation. Work that need not, to satisfy reality, first inflict on the subject all the evil that it is afterwards to inflict on others, is pleasure even in its despairing effort. Its freedom is the same as that which bourgeois society reserves exclusively for relaxation and, by this regimentation, at once revokes. Conversely, anyone who knows freedom finds all the amusements tolerated by this society unbearable, and apart from his work, which admittedly includes what the bourgeois relegate to non-working hours as 'culture', has no taste for substitute pleasures. Work while you work, play while you play – this is a basic rule of repressive self-discipline. The parents for whom it was a matter of prestige that their children should bring home good reports, were the least disposed to let them read too long in the evening, or make what they took to be any kind of intellectual over-exertion. Through their folly spoke the genius of their class. The doctrine inculcated since Aristotle that moderation is the virtue appropriate to reasonable people, is among other things an attempt to found so securely the socially necessary division of man into functions independent of each other, that it occurs to none of these functions to cross over to the others and remind each other of man. But one could no more imagine Nietzsche in an office, with a secretary minding the telephone in an anteroom, at his desk until five o'clock, than playing golf after the day's work was done. Only a cunning intertwining of pleasure and work leaves real experience still open, under the pressure of society. Such experience is less and less tolerated. Even the so-called intellectual professions are being deprived, through their growing resemblance to business, of all joy. Atomization is advancing not only between men, but within each individual, between the spheres of his life. No fulfilment may be attached to work, which would otherwise lose its functional modesty in the totality of purposes, no spark of reflection is allowed to fall into leisure time, since it might otherwise leap across to the workaday world and set it on fire. While in their structure work and amusement are becoming increasingly alike, they are at the same time being divided ever more rigorously by invisible demarcation lines. Joy and mind have been expelled equally from both. In each, blank-faced seriousness and pseudo-activity hold sway.

85

Passing muster. – For the so-called man of affairs with interests to pursue, plans to realize, the people he comes into contact with are metamorphosed automatically into friends or enemies. In looking at them with a view to deciding how well they fit in with his intentions, he reduces them from the outset to objects: some are usable, others an obstacle. Every differing opinion appears on the system of co-ordinates provided by the pre-decided purposes without which the practical man is lost, as tiresome resistance, sabotage, intrigue; all agreement, though it may stem from the basest interests, becomes support, something of use, a testimony of alliance. Thus impoverishment of the relation to others sets in: the capacity for seeing them as such and not as functions of one's own will withers, as does that, above all, of fruitful contrast, the possibility of going beyond oneself by assimilating the contradictory. These are replaced by an appraising knowledge of people for which the best are in the end the lesser evil, and the worst not the greatest. This way of reacting, however, the pattern of all administration and 'personnel policy', tends of its own accord, and in advance of any education of the political will or commitment to exclusive programmes, towards Fascism. Anyone who has once made it his concern to judge people's suitability sees those judged, by a kind of technological necessity, as insiders or outsiders, as belonging or alien to the race, as accomplices or victims. The fixed, inspecting, hypnotic and hypnotized stare that is common to all the leaders of horror, has its model in the appraising look of the manager asking an interview candidate to sit down, and illuminating his face in such a way as to divide it pitilessly into bright, utilizable parts, and dark, disreputable areas of incompetence. The last stage is the medical examination to decide between capacity for work and liquidation. The New Testament words, 'He who is not for me is against me', lay bare the heart of anti-Semitism down the centuries. It is a basic feature of domination that everyone who does not identify with it is consigned for mere difference to the enemy camp: it is no accident that catholicism is the Greek word for the Latin totality, which the National Socialists have realized. It means the equation of the dissimilar, whether it be the 'deviationist' or the members of a different race, with the opponent. In this respect National Socialism has attained to historical consciousness of itself: Carl Schmitt defined the very essence of politics by the categories of friend and enemy.[1] Progress to such consciousness makes its own regression to the behaviour patterns of the child, which either likes things or fears them. The *a priori* reduction to the friend-enemy relationship is one of the primal phenomena of the new anthropology. Freedom would be not to choose between black and white but to abjure such prescribed choices.

86

Little Hans.[2] – The intellectual, particularly when philosophically inclined, is cut off from practical life: revulsion from it has driven him to concern himself with so-called things of the mind. But material practice is not only the pre-condition of his existence, it is basic to the world which he criticizes in his work. If he knows nothing of this basis, he shoots into thin air. He is confronted with the choice of informing himself or turning his back on what he hates. If he chooses the former, he does violence to himself, thinks against his impulses and in addition runs the risk of sinking to the level of what he is dealing with, for economics is no joke, and merely to understand it one has to 'think economically'. If, however, he has no truck with it, he hypostasizes as an absolute his intellect, which was only formed through contact with economic reality and abstract exchange relations, and which can become intellect solely by reflecting on its own conditions. The intellectual is thereby seduced into the vain and unrelated substitution of the reflection for the thing. The naive but dishonest importance accorded to intellectual products in the public culture industry, adds new stones to the wall barring knowledge from economic brutality. Intellectual business is helped, by the isolation of intellect from business, to

1. Carl Schmitt (born 1888): authoritarian legal theorist and philosopher of the State, who acquired official status during Nazi rule.
2. Allusion to a well-known German song that begins: *Hänschen klein / ging allein / in die weite Welt hinein* (Little Hans went out alone into the wide world).

become a comfortable ideology. This dilemma is communicated to intellectual behaviour even in its subtlest reactions. Only someone who keeps himself in some measure pure has hatred, nerves, freedom and mobility enough to oppose the world, but just because of the illusion of purity – for he lives as a 'third person' – he allows the world to triumph not merely externally, but in his innermost thoughts. Anyone, however, who knows the business too well forgets to know it for what it is; his capacity for differentiation deserts him, and as the others are threatened by a fetishism of culture, so is he by a lapse into barbarism. That intellectuals are at once beneficiaries of a bad society, and yet those on whose socially useless work it largely depends whether a society emancipated from utility is achieved – this is not a contradiction acceptable once and for all and therefore irrelevant. It gnaws incessantly at the objective quality of their work. Whatever the intellectual does, is wrong. He experiences drastically and vitally the ignominious choice that late capitalism secretly presents to all its dependants: to become one more grown-up, or to remain a child.

87

Wrestling club.[1] – There is a type of intellectual who is to be the more deeply distrusted the more appealing his honest endeavour, his 'intellectual seriousness' and often his modest objectivity may seem. These are the wrestlers with difficulties, permanently locked in a struggle with themselves, living amid decisions demanding the commitment of their whole person. But things are not so terrible as that. Their lives, put so radically at stake, have after all a reliable armoury at their disposal, and the ready use they make of it gives the lie to their struggle with the angel: one need only glance through the books published by Eugen Diederichs or those of a certain kind of cantingly emancipated theologian. The vigorous vocabulary makes one wonder about the fairness of these wrestling bouts arranged and contested by inwardness. The expressions are all taken from war, physical danger, real destruction, but they

1. *Ringverein*: the term has a double meaning, referring to the criminal gangs that haunted Berlin after the First World War, which were also euphemistically known as 'wrestling clubs'.

describe mere processes of reflection, which may indeed have been connected with a fatal outcome in the cases of Kierkegaard and Nietzsche, whom the wrestlers are fond of quoting, but certainly not in that of their unsolicited followers, who claim to be at risk. While they take the credit twice over for sublimating the struggle of existence – for their intellect, and for their courage, they neutralize the element of danger by internalization, reducing it to an ingredient in a complacently rooted, hale and hearty *Weltanschauung*. Their attitude to the outside world is one of superior indifference – beside the gravity of their decisions it shrinks to insignificance; and so they leave it as it is, finally acknowledging it after all. The wild expressions are arty-crafty adornment like the cowry-shells of the gymnastics girls, with whom the wrestlers are so fond of consorting. The sword dance is rigged. No matter whether it is the Categorical Imperative which triumphs or the Rights of the Individual – whether the candidate succeeds in freeing himself from faith in a personal God or in reconquering it, whether he confront the abyss of Being or the harrowing experience of the Senses, he falls on his feet. For the power which steers the conflicts, the ethos of responsibility and integrity, is always authoritarian, a mask of the State. If they choose acknowledged blessings, all's well in any case. If they come to rebellious conclusions, they go one better as the fine, independent men who are in demand. In either case they approve like good sons the authority which might call them to account, and in whose name the whole trial has really been fought out: the gaze under which they have been seemingly scrapping like two rowdy schoolboys is from the outset a frown. No wrestling match is without a referee: the whole brawl has been staged by society internalized in the individual, which both supervises the struggle and takes part in it. The triumph of society is all the more fatal the more oppositional the outcome: priests, senior schoolmasters whose conscience has exacted from them fundamental declarations of belief that brought them trouble with their authorities, have always sympathized with persecution and counter-revolution. Just as there is an element of delusion in any conflict that affirms itself, repression is at the bottom of the whole fake dynamic of self-torment. They only unroll the whole spiritual paraphernalia because they were not allowed to vent their frenzy and fury anywhere else, and they are ready to reconvert the struggle against the enemy within into a deed, believing as they do that the latter was there 'in the beginning' in any case.[1] Their prototype is Luther, the inventor of inwardness, throwing his ink-pot at the devil, who does not exist, and already meaning it for the peasants and the Jews. Only a crippled mind needs self-hatred in order to demonstrate its intellectual essence – untruth – by the size of its biceps.

88

Simple Simon. – To think that the individual is being liquidated without trace is over-optimistic. For his cursory negation, the abolition of the monad through solidarity, would at the same time prepare the ground for saving the single being, who only in relation to the general becomes particular. The present situation is very different. The disaster does not take the form of a radical elimination of what existed previously; rather the things that history has condemned are dragged along dead, neutralized and impotent as ignominious ballast. In the midst of standardized, organized human units the individual persists. He is even protected and gaining monopoly value. But he is in reality no more than the mere function of his own uniqueness, an exhibition piece, like the foetuses that once drew the wonderment and laughter of children. Since he no longer has an independent economic existence, his character begins to contradict his objective social role. Just because of this contradiction he is tended in nature reserves, enjoyed in idle contemplation. The individualities imported into America, and divested of individuality in the process, are called colourful personalities. Their eager, uninhibited impulsiveness, their sudden fancies, their 'originality', even if it be only a peculiar odiousness, even their garbled language, turn human qualities to account as a clown's costume. Succumbing to the universal mechanisms of competition and having no other means of adaptation to the market and making good than their petrified otherness, they plunge passionately into the privilege of their self and so exaggerate themselves that they completely eradicate what they are taken for. They shrewdly flaunt their naivety, a quality, as they soon find out, much prized by those in power. They sell themselves as heart-warmers

1. Reference to Faust's famous words in Goethe's play: *Im Anfang war die Tat* (In the beginning was the deed), from the second study scene in Part One.

in the commercial cold, ingratiate themselves with aggressive jibes masochistically enjoyed by their protectors, and confirm by their undignified ebullience the serious worth of the host nation. The *Graeculi* may have behaved similarly in the Roman Empire. Those who put their individuality on sale adopt voluntarily, as their own judges, the verdict pronounced on them by society. Thereby they justify objectively the injustice done to them. They undercut the general regression as private regressors, and even their noisy opposition is usually only a subtler means of adaptation from weakness.

89

Blackmail. – Those who won't take advice can't be helped, the bourgeois used to say, hoping, with advice that costs nothing, to buy themselves out of the obligation to help, and at the same time to gain power over the helpless person who had turned to them. But there was in this at least an appeal to reason, conceived in the same way by the suppliant and by the turner of the deaf ear, and remotely reminiscent of justice: by following shrewd advice one might even occasionally chance on a way out. That is past. Those who cannot help ought also not advise: in an order where every mousehole has been plugged, mere advice exactly equals condemnation. It invariably means telling the suppliant to do precisely what the last remaining vestige of his self most violently refuses. Taught wisdom by a thousand situations, he already knows all the advice he can be given, and only comes when wisdom has failed and action is needed. He is not improved in the process. He who once sought advice and finds no help, that is, the weaker party, appears from the outset as a blackmailer, a figure multiplying irresistibly with the growth of trusts. This tendency is seen most clearly in a certain kind of helper, who defends the interests of needy and impotent friends yet assumes in his zeal a sombre, threatening air. Even his ultimate virtue, selflessness, is ambiguous. While he rightly intercedes for those who must not perish, there is, behind the insistent 'You have to help', a tacit allusion to the superior power of collectives and groups, which no-one can afford to offend. By not excluding the hard-hearted from their ranks the compassionate become harbingers of hard-heartedness.

Institution for deaf-mutes. – While the schools drill people in speech as in first aid for road-accident victims and in glider-construction, the pupils become increasingly mute. They can give lectures; every sentence qualifies them for the microphone, before which they are placed as spokesmen for the average; but their capacity for speaking to each other is stifled. It presupposes experience worth communicating, freedom of expression, and at once independence and relatedness. In an all-embracing system conversation becomes ventriloquism. Everyone is his own Charlie McCarthy:[1] hence his popularity. Words in their entirety are coming to resemble the formulae which used to be reserved for greeting and leave-taking. A girl successfully brought up to comply with the most recent desiderata would have to say at every moment what is appropriate to it as a 'situation', and would have well-tried guide-lines at her disposal. But this determination of language through adaptation is its end: the relation between matter and expression is severed, and just as the concepts of positivists should be seen as mere counters, those of positivistic humanity have become literally coins. The voices of speakers are meeting the same fate as befell, according to psychology, that of conscience, from whose resonance all speech lives: they are being replaced, even in their finest intonations, by a socially prepared mechanism. As soon as this ceases to function and pauses occur that are not provided for in the unwritten law-books, panic ensues. For this reason people have taken recourse to elaborate games and other leisure-time activities intended to dispense them from the burden of conscience-ridden language. But the shadow of fear falls ominously on the speech that still remains. Spontaneity and objectivity in discussing matters are disappearing even in the most intimate circle, just as in politics debate has long since been supplanted by the assertion of power. Speaking takes on a malevolent set of gestures that bode no good. It is sportified. Speakers seek to pile up points: there is no conversation that is not infiltrated like a poison by an opportunity to compete. The emotions, which in conversation worthy of human beings were engaged in the subject discussed, are now harnessed to an obstinate insistence on being right, regardless of the relevance of what is said. But as pure means of power, disenchanted words acquire a magical sway

1. Popular American ventriloquist dummy of the forties.

over their users. It can be observed again and again that something once expressed, however absurd, fortuitous or wrong it may be, because it has been once said, so tyrannizes the sayer as his property that he can never have done with it. Words, figures, dates, once hatched and uttered, take on a life of their own, bringing woe on anyone who goes near them. They form a zone of paranoiac infection, and all the power of reason is needed to break their spell. The magic infusing all great and trivial political slogans is repeated privately, in the apparently most neutral objects: the *rigor mortis* of society is spreading at last to the cell of intimacy that thought itself secure. No harm comes to man from outside alone: dumbness is the objective spirit.

91

Vandals. – The haste, nervousness, restlessness observed since the rise of the big cities is now spreading in the manner of an epidemic, as did once the plague and cholera. In the process forces are being unleashed that were undreamed of by the scurrying passer-by of the nineteenth century. Everybody must have projects all the time. The maximum must be extracted from leisure. This is planned, used for undertakings, crammed with visits to every conceivable site or spectacle, or just with the fastest possible locomotion. The shadow of all this falls on intellectual work. It is done with a bad conscience, as if it had been poached from some urgent, even if only imaginary occupation. To justify itself in its own eyes it puts on a show of hectic activity performed under great pressure and shortage of time, which excludes all reflection, and therefore itself. It often seems as if intellectuals reserved for their actual production only those hours left over from obligations, excursions, appointments and unavoidable amusements. There is something repulsive, yet to a certain degree rational, about the prestige gained by those who can present themselves as such important people that they have to be on the spot everywhere. They stylize their lives with intentionally ham-acted discontent as a single *acte de présence*. The pleasure with which they turn down an invitation by reference to another previously accepted, signals a triumph between competitors. As here, so generally, the forms of the production process are repeated in private life, or in those areas of work exempted from these forms themselves. The whole of life must look like a job, and by this resemblance conceal what is not yet directly devoted to pecuniary gain. But the fear thus expressed only reflects a much deeper one. The unconscious innervations which, beyond thought processes, attune individual existence to historical rhythms, sense the approaching collectivization of the world. Yet since integral society does not so much take up individuals positively within itself as crush them to an amorphous and malleable mass, each individual dreads the process of absorption, which is felt as inevitable. Doing things and going places is an attempt by the sensorium to set up a kind of counter-irritant against a threatening collectivization, to get in training for it by using the hours apparently left to freedom to coach oneself as a member of the mass. The technique is to try to outdo the danger. One lives in a sense even worse, that is, with even less self, than one expects to have to live. At the same time one learns through this playful excess of self-loss that to live in earnest without a self could be easier, not more difficult. All this is done in great haste, for no warning bells will announce the earthquake. If one does not take part, and that means, if one does not swim bodily in the human stream, one fears, as when delaying too long to join a totalitarian party, missing the bus and bringing on oneself the vengeance of the collective. Pseudo-activity is an insurance, the expression of a readiness for self-surrender, in which one senses the only guarantee of self-preservation. Security is glimpsed in adaptation to the utmost insecurity. It is seen as a licence for flight that will take one somewhere else with the utmost speed. In the fanatical love of cars the feeling of physical homelessness plays a part. It is at the bottom of what the bourgeois were wont to call, mistakenly, the flight from oneself, from the inner void. Anyone who wants to move with the times is not allowed to be different. Psychological emptiness is itself only the result of the wrong kind of social absorption. The boredom that people are running away from merely mirrors the process of running away, that started long before. For this reason alone the monstrous machinery of amusement keeps alive and constantly grows bigger without a single person being amused by it. It channels the urge to be in on the act, which otherwise, indiscriminately, anarchically, as promiscuity or wild aggression, would throw itself on the collective, itself consisting of none other than those on the move. Most closely related to them are addicts. Their impulse reacts exactly to the dislocation of mankind that has led from the murky blurring of the difference between town and country, the abolition of the house, via the processions of millions of unemployed, to the deportations and uprooting of peoples on the devastated European continent. The nullity and lack of content of all collective rituals since the Youth Movement emerges retrospectively as a groping anticipation of stunning historical blows. The countless people who suddenly succumb to their own quantity and mobility, to the swarming getaway as to a drug, are recruits to the migration of nations, in whose desolated territories bourgeois history is preparing to meet its end.

92

Picture-book without pictures.[1] – The objective tendency of the Enlightenment, to wipe out the power of images over man, is not matched by any subjective progress on the part of enlightened thinking towards freedom from images. While the assault on images irresistibly demolishes, after metaphysical Ideas, those concepts once understood as rational and genuinely attained by thought, the thinking unleashed by the Enlightenment and immunized against thinking is now becoming a second figurativeness, though without images or spontaneity. Amid the network of now wholly abstract relations of people to each other and to things, the power of abstraction is vanishing. The estrangement of schemata and classifications from the data subsumed beneath them, indeed the sheer quantity of the material processed, which has become quite incommensurable with the horizons of individual experience, ceaselessly enforces an archaic retranslation into sensuous signs. The little silhouettes of men or houses that pervade statistics like hieroglyphics may appear in each particular case accidental, mere auxiliary means. But it is not by chance that they have such a resemblance to countless advertisements, newspaper stereotypes, toys. In them representation triumphs over what is represented. Their outsize, simplistic and therefore false comprehensibility corroborates the incomprehensibility of the intellectual processes themselves, from which their falseness – their blind, unthinking subsumption – is inseparable. The omnipresent images are none, because they present the wholly general, the average, the standard model, as something unique or

1. Title of a work by Hans Christian Andersen.

special, and so deride it. The abolition of the particular is turned insidiously into something particular. The desire for particularity has silted up while still at the stage of a need, and is reproduced on all sides by mass-culture, on the pattern of the comic strip. What was once called intellect is superseded by illustrations. It is not only that people are no longer able to imagine what is not shown and drilled into them in abbreviated form. Even the joke, in which once the freedom of the mind collided with the facts and exploded them, has gone over to illustration. The pictorial jokes filling magazines are for the most part pointless, devoid of meaning. They consist of nothing beyond a challenge to the eye to compete with the situation. One is supposed, schooled by countless precedents, to see what is 'going on' more quickly than the moments of significance in the situation can unfold. What is acted out by such pictures and then re-enacted by the well-versed onlooker, in the instantaneous sizing-up of the situation, the unresisting submission to the empty predominance of things, is the jettisoning of all meaning like ballast. The joke of our time is the suicide of intention. He who 'cracks' it is rewarded by admission to the collective of laughers, who have cruel things on their side. If one strove to understand such jokes by thinking, one would fall helplessly behind the runaway tempo of things, which tear along even in the simplest caricature as in the mad race at the end of a film cartoon. Cleverness turns straight into stupidity in face of regressive progress. The only comprehension left to thought is horror at the incomprehensible. Just as the reflective onlooker, meeting the laughing placard of a toothpaste beauty, discerns in her flashlight grin the grimace of torture, so from every joke, even from every pictorial representation, he is assailed by the death sentence on the subject, which is implicit in the universal triumph of subjective reason.

93

Intention and reproduction. – The pseudo-realism of the culture industry, its style, is in no need of fraudulent fabrication by film-magnates and their lackeys, but is dictated, under the prevailing conditions of production, by the stylistic principles of Naturalism itself. If the film were to give itself up to the blind representation of everyday life, following the precepts of, say, Zola, as would indeed be practicable with moving photography and sound-recording, the result would be a construction alien to the visual habits of the audience, diffuse, unarticulated outwards. Radical naturalism, to which the technique of film lends itself, would dissolve all surface coherence of meaning and finish up as the antithesis of familiar realism. The film would turn into an associative stream of images, deriving its form from their pure, immanent construction. Yet if, for commercial reasons, or even with some disinterested intention, it strives to choose words and gestures in a way that relates them to an idea conferring meaning, this perhaps inevitable attempt finds itself in equally inevitable contradiction with the presupposition of naturalism. The less dense reproduction of reality in naturalist literature left room for intentions: in the unbroken duplication achieved by the technical apparatus of film every intention, even that of truth, becomes a lie. The word that is intended to impress on the audience the character of the speaker or even the meaning of the whole, sounds, compared to the literal fidelity of its reproduction, 'unnatural'. It justifies the world as having been itself similarly meaningful, before the first deliberate fraud, the first real distortion was committed. No-one talks, no-one moves like this, whereas the film unceasingly urges that everyone does. One is trapped: conformism is produced *a priori* by meaning in itself, no matter what the concrete meaning may be, while it is only by meaning something that conformism, the respectful reiteration of the factual, could be shaken. True intentions would only be possible by renouncing intention. That this and realism are incompatible, that synthesis becomes a lie, stems from the concept of significance. It is ambiguous. It refers without distinction to the organization of the subject matter as such and to its communication to the audience. This ambiguity is, however, no accident. Significance designates the point of equilibrium between reason and communication. It is both right, in that the objective figure, the realized expression, turns outward from itself and speaks, and wrong, in that the figure is corrupted by counting in the interlocutor. Every artistic and even theoretical work must show itself able to meet the danger of such ambiguity. Significant form, however esoteric, makes concessions to consumption; lack of significance is dilettantism by its immanent criteria. Quality is decided by the depth at which the work incorporates the alternatives within itself, and so masters them.

All the world's not a stage. – The coming extinction of art is prefigured in the increasing impossibility of representing historical events. That there is no adequate drama about Fascism is not due to lack of talent; talent is withering through the insolubility of the writer's most urgent task. He has to choose between two principles, both equally inappropriate to the subject: psychology and infantilism. The former, now aesthetically obsolete, has been used by significant artists only as a trick and with a bad conscience, since modern drama came to see its object in politics. In his preface to *Fiesco* Schiller argues: 'If it is true that only emotion arouses emotion, the political hero must, it seems to me, be an unsuitable subject for the stage to the same extent that he is obliged to neglect the man in order to be the political hero. It was not my intention to give my plot the living glow which is the pure product of enthusiasm, but to spin the cold, sterile drama of state from the human heart, and so to connect it again to the human heart – to involve the man through his statesman's intelligence – and to draw human situations from an ingenious intrigue – that was my intention. Also, my relation to the ordinary world made me more familiar with the heart than with the council-chamber, and perhaps this very political weakness has become a poetic strength.' Perhaps not. The connection of alienated history to the human heart was already in Schiller's case a pretext for justifying the inhumanity of history as humanly comprehensible, and was given the lie whenever his technique equated the 'man' and the 'statesman's intelligence', as in the burlesque and fortuitous murder of Leonore by the betrayer of his own conspiracy. The tendency towards aesthetic re-privatization pulls the ground from under art in its attempt to conserve humanism. The cabals of Schiller's too-well constructed plays are impotent auxiliary constructions straddling the passions of the characters and a social and political reality already incommensurable with them, no longer comprehensible in terms of human motivations. Recently this has taken the form of a trashy biographical literature eager to bring the famous humanly closer to the humble reader. The same urge towards false humanization underlies the calculated re-introduction of plot, of action as a coherent meaning harmoniously performed. On the presuppositions of photographic realism this would not be tenable in film. In arbitrarily reinstating it, the cinema has disregarded the experience of the great novels on which it parasitically lives; they derived their meaning precisely from the dissolution of coherent meaning.

To clear all this aside, however, and to seek to portray the political scene as abstract and extra-human, excluding the deceptive mediations of the psychological, is to do no better. For it is just the essential abstractness of what really happens which rebuts the aesthetic image. To make this abstractness expressible at all, the writer is forced to translate it into a kind of children's language, into archetypes, and so a second time to 'bring it home', no longer to the emotions but to those check-points in comprehension which precede even the constitution of language, and cannot be side-stepped even by epic theatre. The appeal to these authorities is in itself a formal sanction of the subject's dissolution in collective society. The object, however, is scarcely less falsified by such trans-lation than would be a religious war by its deduction from the erotic needs of a queen. For as infantile as today's simplistic drama are the very people whose portrayal it abjures. Yet the political economy that it takes upon itself to portray instead, if it remains in principle unchanged, in each of its moments is so differentiated and advanced, as to exclude schematic parables. To present pro-cesses within large-scale industry as transactions between crooked vegetable dealers suffices for a momentary shock-effect, but not for dialectical theatre. The illustration of late capitalism by images from the agrarian or criminal registers does not permit the mons-trosity of modern society to emerge in full clarity from the complex phenomena masking it. Rather, the unconcern for the phenomena, which ought themselves to be derived visibly from their essence, distorts the essence. It harmlessly interprets the seizure of power on the highest level as the machination of rackets outside society, not as the coming-to-itself of society as such.[1] The impossibility of portraying Fascism springs from the fact that in it, as in its con-templation, subjective freedom no longer exists. Total unfreedom can be recognized, but not represented. Where freedom occurs as a motif in political narratives today, as in the praise of heroic resis-tance, it has the embarrassing quality of impotent reassurance. The outcome always appears decided in advance by high politics, and

1. This passage is a criticism of Brecht's play *The Resistible Rise of Arturo Ui*. Adorno later developed this critique of Brecht's theatre in his essay entitled *Engagement* in *Noten Zur Literatur III*, Frankfurt 1965, pp. 109–35.

freedom is manifested only ideologically, as talk about freedom, in stereotyped declamations, not in humanly commensurable actions. Art is least to be saved by stuffing the extinct subject like a museum piece, and the object, the purely inhuman, which alone is worthy of art today, escapes its reach at once by excess and inhumanity.

95

Damper and drum. – Taste is the most accurate seismograph of historical experience. Unlike almost all other faculties, it is even able to register its own behaviour. Reacting against itself, it recognizes its own lack of taste. Artists who repel or shock, spokesmen of unbridled cruelty, are governed, in their idiosyncrasy, by taste; the cultivation of a fine sensibility, the domain of nervous neo-romantics, is as patently coarse and unfeeling, even to its protagonists, as is Rilke's line: 'For poverty's a great glow from within. . . .' The delicate shudder, the pathos of being different, are now no more than stock masks in the cult of oppression. It is precisely the nerves most highly-developed aesthetically that now find self-righteous aestheticism intolerable. The individual is so thoroughly historical that he is able, with the fine filigree of his late bourgeois organization, to rebel against the fine filigree of late bourgeois organization. In repugnance for all artistic subjectivism, for expression and exaltation, the flesh creeps at the lack of historical tact, just as subjectivity itself earlier flinched from bourgeois conventions. Even the rejection of mimesis, the deepest concern of the new matter-of-factness in art, is mimetic. Judgement on subjective expression is not passed from outside, in political and social reflection, but within immediate impulses, every one of which, shamed in face of the culture industry, averts its eyes from its mirror image. Heading the list is the proscription of erotic pathos, evinced no less by the shift of lyrical accents than by the collective ban on sexuality in Kafka's works. In art since Expressionism the prostitute has become a key figure, though in reality she is dying out, since it is only by portrayal of figures devoid of shame that sex can now be handled without aesthetic embarrassment. Such displacements in the deepest levels of our reaction have brought about the decay of art in its individualistic form, without a collective form being possible. It is beyond the faith and independence of the individual artist to hold unwaveringly to the expressive sphere and to oppose the brutal compulsion of collectivization; rather he must feel this compulsion, even against his will, in the most secret cells of his isolation, if he is not, through anachronistic humanity, to fall untruthfully and helplessly behind the inhuman. Even intransigent literary Expressionism, Stramm's poetry, Kokoschka's dramas,[1] show as the reverse-side of their genuine radicalism a naive aspect of liberal trustfulness. Progress beyond them, however, is no less questionable. Works of art which attempt consciously to eliminate innocuous absolute subjectivity, raise in so doing the demand for a positive community, not present in themselves, but which they arbitrarily quote. This merely makes them mouthpieces of doom and victims of an ultimate naivety which cancels them out: that of still being art at all. The aporia of responsible work benefits the irresponsible. Should it once prove possible to do away with nerves entirely, then no herbicide will avail against the renascent springtime of song, and the national front extending all the way from barbaric Futurism to the ideology of the cinema, will go entirely unopposed.

96

Palace of Janus. – If one gave way to a need to place the system of the culture industry in a wide, world-historical perspective, it would have to be defined as the systematic exploitation of the ancient fissure between men and their culture. The dual nature of progress, which always developed the potential of freedom simultaneously with the reality of oppression, gave rise to a situation where peoples were more and more inducted into the control of nature and social organization, but grew at the same time, owing to the compulsion under which culture placed them, incapable of understanding in what way culture went beyond such integration. What has become alien to men is the human component of culture, its closest part, which upholds them against the world. They make common cause with the world against themselves, and the most

1. August Stramm (1874–1915) was a laconic expressionist poet before the First World War; Oskar Kokoschka (born 1886), before acquiring prominence as a painter, wrote a series of imagistic dramas in the period 1907–1919.

alienated condition of all, the omnipresence of commodities, their own conversion into appendages of machinery, is for them a mirage of closeness. The great works of art and philosophical constructions have remained uncomprehended not through their too great distance from the heart of human experience, but the opposite; and this incomprehension could itself be accounted for easily enough by too great comprehension: shame at involvement in universal injustice that would become overwhelming as soon as one allowed oneself to understand. Instead, people cling to what mocks them in confirming the mutilation of their essence by the smoothness of its own appearance. On such inevitable delusions lackeys of the existing order have in all phases of urban civilization parasitically dwelt: later Attic comedy, Hellenistic arts and crafts, are already kitsch, even though they have not yet at their disposal the technique of mechanical reproduction and that industrial apparatus whose archetype the ruins of Pompeii readily conjure up. Reading popular novels a hundred years old like those of Cooper, one finds in rudimentary form the whole pattern of Hollywood. The stagnation of the culture industry is probably not the result of monopolization, but was a property of so-called entertainment from the first. Kitsch is composed of that structure of invariables which the philosophical lie ascribes to its solemn designs. On principle, nothing in them must change, since the whole mischief is intended to hammer into men that nothing must change. But as long as civilization followed its course randomly and anonymously, the objective spirit was not aware of this barbaric element as a necessary part of itself. Under the illusion of directly helping freedom, when it was mediating domination, it at least disdained to assist in directly reproducing the latter. It proscribed kitsch, that followed it like a shadow, with a fervour certainly itself expressive of the bad conscience of high culture, half aware that under domination it ceases to be culture, and reminded by kitsch of its own degradation. Today, when the consciousness of rulers is beginning to coincide with the overall tendency of society, the tension between culture and kitsch is breaking down. Culture no longer impotently drags its despised opponent behind it, but is taking it under its direction. In administering the whole of mankind, it administers also the breach between man and culture. Even the coarseness, insensitivity and narrowness objectively imposed on the oppressed, are manipulated with subjective mastery in humour. Nothing more exactly

characterizes the condition of being at once integral and antagonistic than this incorporation of barbarity. Here, however, the
will of the controllers can invoke that of the world. Their mass
society did not first produce the trash for the customers, but the
customers themselves. It is they who hungered for films, radio and
magazines; whatever remained unsatisfied in them through the
order which takes from them without giving in exchange what it
promises, only burned with impatience for their gaoler to remember
them, and at last offer them stones in his left hand for the hunger
from which he withholds bread in his right. Unresistingly, for a
quarter of a century, elderly citizens, who should have known of
something different, have been falling into the arms of the culture
industry which so accurately calculates their famished hearts. They
have no cause to take umbrage at a youth corrupted to the marrow
by Fascism. This subjectless, culturally disinherited generation are
the true heirs of culture.

97

Monad. – The individual owes his crystallization to the forms of
political economy, particularly to those of the urban market. Even
as the opponent of the pressure of socialization he remains the
latter's most particular product and its likeness. What enables him
to resist, that streak of independence in him, springs from monadological individual interest and its precipitate, character. The
individual mirrors in his individuation the preordained social laws
of exploitation, however mediated. This means too, however, that
his decay in the present phase must itself not be deduced individual-
istically, but from the social tendency which asserts itself by means
of individuation and not merely as its enemy. On this point reactionary cultural criticism diverges from the other kind. Reactionary
criticism often enough attains insight into the decay of individuality and the crisis of society, but places the ontological responsibility for this on the individual as such, as something discrete and
internal: for this reason the accusation of shallowness, lack of faith
and substance, is the last word it has to say, and return to the past
its solace. Individualists like Huxley and Jaspers damn the individual for his mechanical emptiness and neurotic weakness, but
the trend of their condemnation is rather to sacrifice the individual

himself than to criticize the social *principium individuationis*. As half-truths their polemics are already the whole untruth. Society is seen by them as an unmediated community of men, from whose attitudes the whole follows, instead of as a system not only encompassing and deforming them, but even reaching down into that humanity which once conditioned them as individuals. By this exclusively human interpretation of the situation as it is, the crude material reality that binds human beings to inhumanity is accepted even while being accused. In its better days, when it reflected historically, the bourgeoisie was well aware of such interconnections, and it is only since its doctrine has degenerated to obtuse apologetics against socialism that it has forgotten them. It is not the least merit of Jakob Burckhardt's history of Greek civilization to have connected the drying-up of Hellenistic individuality not only with the objective decline of the *polis*, but precisely with the cult of the individual: 'But following the deaths of Demosthenes and Phocion, the city is surprisingly depleted of political personalities, and not only of them: Epicurus, born as early as 342 of an Attic cleruch family on Samos, is the last Athenian of any kind to have world-historical importance.' The situation in which the individual was vanishing was at the same time one of unbridled individualism, where 'all was possible': 'Above all, individuals are now worshipped instead of gods.'[1] That the setting-free of the individual by the undermining of the *polis* did not strengthen his resistance, but eliminated him and individuality itself, in the consummation of dictatorial states, provides a model of one of the central contradictions which drove society from the nineteenth century to Fascism. Beethoven's music, which works within the forms transmitted by society and is ascetic towards the expression of private feelings, resounds with the guided echo of social conflict, drawing precisely from this asceticism the whole fullness and power of individuality. That of Richard Strauss, wholly at the service of individual claims and dedicated to the glorification of the self-sufficient individual, thereby reduces the latter to a mere receptive organ of the market, an imitator of arbitrarily chosen ideas and styles. Within repressive society the individual's emancipation not only benefits but damages him. Freedom from society robs him of the strength for freedom. For however real he may be in his relations to others, he is, con-

1. Jakob Burckhardt, *Griechische Kulturgeschichte*, Berlin 1902, Vol. IV, pp. 515–16.

sidered absolutely, a mere abstraction. He has no content that is not socially constituted, no impulse transcending society that is not directed at assisting the social situation to transcend itself. Even the Christian doctrine of death and immortality, in which the notion of absolute individuality is rooted, would be wholly void if it did not embrace humanity. The single man who hoped for immortality absolutely and for himself alone, would in such limitation only inflate to preposterous dimensions the principle of self-preservation which the injunction that 'He that loses his life, shall save it' holds in check. Socially, the absolute status granted to the individual marks the transition from the universal mediation of social relation – a mediation which, as exchange, always also requires curtailment of the particular interests realized through it – to direct domination, where power is seized by the strongest. Through this dissolution of all the mediating elements within the individual himself, by virtue of which he was, in spite of everything, also a part of a social subject, he regresses, impoverished and coarsened, to the state of a mere social object. As something abstractly realized, in Hegel's sense, the individual cancels himself out: the countless people who know nothing but their naked, prowling interest are those who capitulate the moment organization and terror overtake them. If today the trace of humanity seems to persist only in the individual in his decline, it admonishes us to make an end of the fatality which individualizes men, only to break them completely in their isolation. The saving principle is now preserved in its antithesis alone.

98

Bequest. – Dialectical thought is an attempt to break through the coercion of logic by its own means. But since it must use these means, it is at every moment in danger of itself acquiring a coercive character: the ruse of reason would like to hold sway over the dialectic too. The existing cannot be overstepped except by means of a universal derived from the existing order itself. The universal triumphs over the existing through the latter's own concept, and therefore, in its triumph, the power of mere existence constantly threatens to reassert itself by the same violence that broke it. Through the absolute rule of negation, the movement of thought as of history becomes, in accordance with the pattern of immanent antithesis, unambiguously, exclusively, implacably positive. Everything is subsumed under the principal economic phases and their development, which each in turn historically shape the whole of society; thought in its entirety has something of what Parisian artists call le *genre chef d'oeuvre*. That calamity is brought about precisely by the stringency of such development; that this stringency is itself linked to domination, is, at the least, not made explicit in critical theory, which, like traditional theory, awaits salvation from stage-by-stage progression. Stringency and totality, the bourgeois intellectual ideals of necessity and generality, do indeed circumscribe the formula of history, but for just this reason the constitution of society finds its precipitate in those great, immovable, lordly concepts against which dialectical criticism and practice are directed. If Benjamin said that history had hitherto been written from the standpoint of the victor, and needed to be written from that of the vanquished,[1] we might add that knowledge must indeed present the fatally rectilinear succession of victory and defeat, but should also address itself to those things which were not embraced by this dynamic, which fell by the wayside – what might be called the waste products and blind spots that have escaped the dialectic. It is in the nature of the defeated to appear, in their impotence, irrelevant, eccentric, derisory. What transcends the ruling society is not only the potentiality it develops but also all that which did not fit properly into the laws of historical movement. Theory must needs deal with cross-gained, opaque, unassimilated material, which as such admittedly has from the start an anachronistic quality, but is not wholly obsolete since it has outwitted the historical dynamic. This can most readily be seen in art. Children's books like *Alice in Wonderland* or *Struwwelpeter*, of which it would be absurd to ask whether they are progressive or reactionary, contain incomparably more eloquent ciphers even of history than the high drama of Hebbel, concerned though it is with the official themes of tragic guilt, turning points of history, the course of the world and the individual, and in Satie's pert and puerile piano pieces there are flashes of experience undreamed of by the school of Schönberg, with all its rigour and all the pathos of musical development behind it. The very grandeur of logical deductions may inadvertently take on a provincial quality. Benjamin's writings are an attempt in ever

1. Walter Benjamin, *Illuminations*, London 1973, pp. 258–9.

new ways to make philosophically fruitful what has not yet been foreclosed by great intentions. The task he bequeathed was not to abandon such an attempt to the estranging enigmas of thought alone, but to bring the intentionless within the realm of concepts: the obligation to think at the same time dialectically and undialectically.

99

Gold assay. – Among the concepts to which, after the dissolution of its religious and the formalization of its autonomous norms, bourgeois morality has shrunk, that of genuineness ranks highest. If nothing else can be bindingly required of man, then at the least he should be wholly and entirely what he is. In the identity of each individual with himself the postulate of incorruptible truth, together with the glorification of the factual, are transferred from Enlightenment knowledge to ethics. It is just the critically independent late-bourgeois thinkers, sickened by traditional judgements and idealistic phrases, who concur with this view. Ibsen's admittedly violated verdict on the living lie, Kierkegaard's doctrine of existence, have made the ideal of authenticity a centrepiece of metaphysics. In Nietzsche's analysis the word genuine stands unquestioned, exempt from conceptual development. To the converted and unconverted philosophers of Fascism, finally, values like authenticity, heroic endurance of the 'being-in-the-world' of individual existence, frontier-situations, become a means of usurping religious-authoritarian pathos without the least religious content. They lead to the denunciation of anything that is not of sufficiently sterling worth, sound to the core, that is, the Jews: did not Richard Wagner already play off genuine German metal against foreign dross and thus misuse criticism of the culture market as an apology for barbarism? Such abuse, however, is not extrinsic to the concept of genuineness. Now that its worn-out livery is being sold off, seams and patches are coming to light that were invisibly present in the great days of its opposition. The untruth is located in the substratum of genuineness itself, the individual. If it is in the *principium individuationis*, as the antipodes Hegel and Schopenhauer both recognized, that the secret of the world's course is concealed, then the conception of an ultimate and absolute substantiality of the self falls victim to an illusion that protects the established order even while its essence decays. The equation of the genuine and the true is untenable. It is precisely undeviating self-reflection – the practice of which Nietzsche called psychology, that is, insistence on the truth about oneself, that shows again and again, even in the first conscious experiences of childhood, that the impulses reflected upon are not quite 'genuine'. They always contain an element of imitation, play, wanting to be different. The desire, through submergence in one's own individuality, instead of social insight into it, to touch something utterly solid, ultimate being, leads to precisely the false infinity which since Kierkegaard the concept of authenticity has been supposed to exorcise. No-one said so more bluntly than Schopenhauer. This peevish ancestor of existential philosophy and malicious heir of the great speculators knew his way among the hollows and crags of individual absolutism like no other. His insight is coupled to the speculative thesis that the individual is only appearance, not the Thing-in-Itself. 'Every individual', he writes in a footnote in the Fourth Book of *The World as Will and Representation*, 'is on one hand the subject of cognition, that is to say, the complementary condition of the possibility of the whole objective world, and on the other a single manifestation of that same Will, which objectifies itself in each thing. But this duplicity of our being is not founded in a unity existing for itself: otherwise we should be able to have consciousness of ourselves through ourselves and independently of the objects of cognition and willing: but of this we are utterly incapable; as soon as we attempt to do so and, by turning our cognition inwards, strive for once to attain complete self-reflection, we lose ourselves in a bottomless void, find ourselves resembling the hollow glass ball out of whose emptiness a voice speaks that has no cause within the ball, and, in trying to grasp ourselves, we clutch, shuddering, at nothing but an insubstantial ghost.'[1] Thus he called the mythical deception of the pure self by its name, null and void. It is an abstraction. What presents itself as an original entity, a monad, is only the result of a social division of the social process. Precisely as an absolute, the individual is a mere reflection of property relations. In him the fictitious claim is made that what is biologically one must logically precede the social whole, from which it is only isolated by force,

1. Schopenhauer, *Die Welt als Wille und Vorstellung*, Leipzig 1877, p. 327 (*The World as Will and Idea*, London, 1950, p. 358).

and its contingency is held up as a standard of truth. Not only is the self entwined in society; it owes society its existence in the most literal sense. All its content comes from society, or at any rate from its relation to the object. It grows richer the more freely it develops and reflects this relation, while it is limited, impoverished and reduced by the separation and hardening that it lays claim to as an origin. Attempts like Kierkegaard's, in which the individual seeks abundance by retreat within himself, did not by accident end up in the sacrifice of the individual and in the same abstraction that he denounced in the systems of idealism. Genuineness is nothing other than a defiant and obstinate insistence on the monadological form which social oppression imposes on man. Anything that does not wish to wither should rather take on itself the stigma of the inauthentic. For it lives on the mimetic heritage. The human is indissolubly linked with imitation: a human being only becomes human at all by imitating other human beings. In such behaviour, the primal form of love, the priests of authenticity scent traces of the utopia which could shake the structure of domination. That Nietzsche, whose reflection penetrated even the concept of truth, drew back dogmatically before that of genuineness, makes him what in the end he wanted to be, a Lutheran, and his fulminations against play-acting bear the stamp of the anti-Semitism which infuriated him in the arch-actor Wagner. It is not with play-acting that he ought to have reproached Wagner – for all art, and music first of all, is related to drama, and in every one of Nietzsche's periods there resounds the millenial echo of rhetorical voices in the Roman Senate – but with the actor's denial of play-acting. Indeed, not only inauthenticity that poses as veridical ought to be convicted of lying: authenticity itself becomes a lie the moment it becomes authentic, that is, in reflecting on itself, in postulating itself as genuine, in which it already oversteps the identity that it lays claim to in the same breath. The self should not be spoken of as the ontological ground, but at the most theologically, in the name of its likeness to God. He who holds fast the self and does away with theological concepts helps to justify the diabolical positive, naked interest. He borrows from the latter an aura of significance and makes the power of command of self-preserving reason into a lofty superstructure, while the real self has already become in the world what Schopenhauer recognized it to be in introspection, a phantom. Its illusory character can be understood from the historical implications of the concept of genuineness as such. In it dwells the notion of the supremacy of the original over the derived. This notion, however, is always linked with social legitimism. All ruling strata claim to be the oldest settlers, autochthonous. The whole philosophy of inwardness, with its professed contempt for the world, is the last sublimation of the brutal, barbaric lore whereby he who was there first has the greatest rights; and the priority of the self is as untrue as that of all who feel at home where they live. None of this is changed if authenticity falls back on the oppositions of *physei* and *thesei*, the idea that what exists without human interference is better than the artificial. The more tightly the world is enclosed by the net of man-made things, the more stridently those who are responsible for this condition proclaim their natural primitiveness. The discovery of genuineness as a last bulwark of individualistic ethics is a reflection of industrial mass-production. Only when countless standardized commodities project, for the sake of profit, the illusion of being unique, does the idea take shape, as their antithesis yet in keeping with the same criteria, that the non-reproducible is the truly genuine. Previously, the question of authenticity was doubtless as little asked of intellectual products as that of originality, a concept unknown in Bach's era. The fraud of genuineness goes back to bourgeois blindness to the exchange process. Genuine things are those to which commodities and other means of exchange can be reduced, particularly gold. But like gold, genuineness, abstracted as the proportion of fine metal, becomes a fetish. Both are treated as if they were the foundation, which in reality is a social relation, while gold and genuineness precisely express only the fungibility, the comparability of things; it is they that are not in-themselves, but for-others. The ungenuineness of the genuine stems from its need to claim, in a society dominated by exchange, to be what it stands for yet is never able to be. The apostles of genuineness, in the service of the power that now masters circulation, dignify the demise of the latter with the dance of the money veils.

100

Sur l'Eau.[1] – He who asks what is the goal of an emancipated society is given answers such as the fulfilment of human possibilities or the

1. Title of a book of sketches about sailing by Maupassant.

richness of life. Just as the inevitable question is illegitimate, so the repellent assurance of the answer is inevitable, calling to mind the social-democratic ideal of the personality expounded by heavily-bearded Naturalists of the 'nineties, who were out to have a good time. There is tenderness only in the coarsest demand: that no-one shall go hungry any more. Every other seeks to apply to a condition that ought to be determined by human needs, a mode of human conduct adapted to production as an end in itself. Into the wishful image of an uninhibited, vital, creative man has seeped the very fetishism of commodities which in bourgeois society brings with it inhibition, impotence, the sterility of the never-changing. The concept of dynamism, which is the necessary complement of bourgeois 'a-historicity', is raised to an absolute, whereas it ought, as an anthropological reflex of the laws of production, to be itself critically confronted, in an emancipated society, with need. The conception of unfettered activity, of uninterrupted procreation, of chubby insatiability, of freedom as frantic bustle, feeds on the bourgeois concept of nature that has always served solely to proclaim social violence as unchangeable, as a piece of healthy eternity. It was in this, and not in their alleged levelling-down, that the positive blue-prints of socialism, resisted by Marx, were rooted in barbarism. It is not man's lapse into luxurious indolence that is to be feared, but the savage spread of the social under the mask of universal nature, the collective as a blind fury of activity. The naive supposition of an unambiguous development towards increased production is itself a piece of that bourgeois outlook which permits development in only one direction because, integrated into a totality, dominated by quantification, it is hostile to qualitative difference. If we imagine emancipated society as emancipation from precisely such totality, then vanishing-lines come into view that have little in common with increased production and its human reflections. If uninhibited people are by no means the most agreeable or even the freest, a society rid of its fetters might take thought that even the forces of production are not the deepest substratum of man, but represent his historical form adapted to the production of commodities. Perhaps the true society will grow tired of development and, out of freedom, leave possibilities unused, instead of storming under a confused compulsion to the conquest of strange stars. A mankind which no longer knows want will begin to have an inkling of the delusory, futile nature of all the arrangements hitherto made in order to escape want, which used wealth to reproduce want on a larger scale. Enjoyment itself would be affected, just as its present framework is inseparable from operating, planning, having one's way, subjugating. *Rien faire comme une bete*, lying on water and looking peacefully at the sky, 'being, nothing else, without any further definition and fulfilment', might take the place of process, act, satisfaction, and so truly keep the promise of dialectical logic that it would culminate in its origin. None of the abstract concepts comes closer to fulfilled utopia than that of eternal peace. Spectators on the sidelines of progress like Maupassant and Sternheim[1] have helped this intention to find expression, timidly, in the only way that its fragility permits.

1. Carl Sternheim (1878–1942): German playwright who wrote a series of satirical comedies about Wilhelmine society, in a spirit not unlike that of Maupassant.

Minima Moralia

Avalanche, veux-tu m'emporter dans ta chute?

Baudelaire

Hothouse plant. – The talk about early and late maturers, seldom free of the death-wish for the former, is specious. He who matures early lives in anticipation. His experience is a-prioristic, an intuitive sensibility feeling out in images and words what things and people will realize only later. Such anticipation, saturated, as it were, with itself, withdraws from the outer world and infuses its relation to it with the colour of neurotic playfulness If the early maturer is more than a possessor of dexterities, he is obliged to catch himself up, a compulsion which normal people are fond of dressing up as a moral imperative. Painfully he must win for the relation to objects the space that is occupied by his imagination: even suffering he has to learn. Contact with the non-self, which in the alleged late-maturer is scarcely ever disturbed from within, becomes for the early-maturer an urgent need. The narcissistic direction of his impulses, indicated by the preponderance of imagination in his experience, positively delays his maturing. Only later does he live through, in their crude violence, situations, fears, passions, that had been greatly softened in imagination, and they change, in conflict with his narcissism, into a consuming sickness. So he relapses into the childishness that he had once surmounted with too little exertion and which now exacts its price; he becomes immature, while the mature are the others who were at each stage what they were expected to be, puerile too, and who now find unpardonable the force which gains disproportionate ascendancy over the erstwhile early-maturer. He is struck down by passion; lulled too long in the security of his autarky, he reels helplessly where he had once built his airy bridges. The infantile traits in the hand-writing of the precocious are not an empty warning. For they are an irritation to the natural order, and spiteful health feasts on the danger threatening them, just as society mistrusts them as a visible negation of the equation of success with effort. In their inner economy, unconsciously but implacably, the punishment is meted out that has always been thought their due. What was proffered to them with deceptive benevolence is revoked. Even in psychological fate there is an authority to see that everything is repaid. The individual law is a puzzle-picture of the exchange of equivalents.

More haste, less speed. – Running in the street conveys an impression of terror. The victim's fall is already mimed in his attempt to escape it. The position of the head, trying to hold itself up, is that of a drowning man, and the straining face grimaces as if under torture. He has to look ahead, can hardly glance back without stumbling, as if treading the shadow of a foe whose features freeze the limbs. Once people ran from dangers that were too desperate to turn and face, and someone running after a bus unwittingly bears witness to past terror. Traffic regulations no longer need allow for wild animals, but they have not pacified running. It estranges us from bourgeois walking. The truth becomes visible that something is amiss with security, that the unleashed powers of life, be they mere vehicles, have to be escaped. The body's habituation to walking as normal stems from the good old days. It was the bourgeois form of locomotion: physical demythologization, free of the spell of hieratic pacing, roofless wandering, breathless flight. Human dignity insisted on the right to walk, a rhythm not extorted from the body by command or terror. The walk, the stroll, were private ways of passing time, the heritage of the feudal promenade in the nineteenth century. With the liberal era walking too is dying out, even where people do not go by car. The Youth Movement, sensing these tendencies with infallible masochism, challenged the parental Sunday excursions and replaced them by voluntary forced marches, naming them, in medieval fashion, *Fahrt* [journey, drive] when the Ford model was about to become available for such purposes. Perhaps the cult of technical speed as of sport conceals an impulse to master the terror of running by deflecting it from one's own body and at the same time effortlessly surpassing it. The triumph of mounting mileage ritually appeases the fear of the fugitive. But if someone is shouted at to 'run', from the child who has to fetch his mother a forgotten handbag from the first floor, to the prisoner ordered by his escort to flee so that they have a pretext for murdering him, the archaic power makes itself heard that otherwise inaudibly guides our every step.

Boy from the heath.[1] – Things one fears for no real reason, apparently obsessed by an *idée fixe*, have an impertinent tendency to come about. The question one most shuns is raised with perfidiously amiable interest by a subordinate; the person one wishes most anxiously to keep away from one's beloved will unfailingly invite her, be it from a distance of three thousand miles, thanks to well-meaning introductions, and bring about ominous acquaintances. It is debatable how far one promotes these terrors oneself: whether one's over-anxious silence puts the question into the insidious listener's mouth; whether one provokes the fatal contact by asking the mediator, in foolishly destructive confidence, not to mediate. Psychology knows that he who imagines disasters in some way desires them. But why do they come so eagerly to meet him? Something in reality strikes a chord in paranoid fantasy and is warped by it. The sadism latent in everyone unerringly divines the weakness latent in everyone. And the fantasy of persecution is contagious: wherever it occurs spectators are driven irresistibly to imitate it. This succeeds most easily when one gives the fantasy a helping hand by doing what the other fears. 'One fool makes many' – the bottomless solitude of the deluded has a tendency to collectivization and so quotes the delusion into existence. This pathic mechanism harmonizes with the social one prevalent today, whereby those socialized into desperate isolation hunger for community and flock together in cold mobs. So folly becomes an epidemic: insane sects grow with the same rhythm as big organizations. It is the rhythm of total destruction. The fulfilment of persecution-fantasies springs from their affinity to bloody realities. Violence, on which civilization is based, means the persecution of all by all, and the persecution-maniac puts himself at a disadvantage only by blaming on his neighbour what is perpetrated by the whole, in a helpless attempt to make the incommensurable commensurable. He is burnt because he seeks to grasp directly, as with his bare hands, the objective delusion which he resembles, whereas the absurd order consists precisely in its perfected indirectness. He is sacrificed to safeguard the tissue of beguilement. Even the worst, most senseless representations of events, the wildest projections, contain the

1. *Der Heideknabe*: a ballad by Hebbel (1844) in which every misfortune feared by the boy of the title invariably befalls him.

unconscious effort of consciousness to recognize the fatal law by which society perpetuates its existence. Aberration is really only short-circuited adaptation: the patent imbecility of one calls the imbecility of the whole by its right name mistakenly in another, and the paranoiac is a caricature of the right life, in that he chooses on his own initiative to emulate the wrong one. But just as in a short-circuit sparks are scattered, in reality one delusion communicates like lightning with another. The points of communication are the overwhelming confirmations of persecution-fantasies which, mocking the invalid with being right, only plunge him deeper in them. The surface of life then at once closes together again, proving to him that things are not so bad and he is insane. He subjectively anticipates the state where objective madness and individual helplessness merge directly, as when Fascism, a dictatorship by persecution-maniacs, realizes all the persecution-fears of its victims. Whether exaggerated suspicions are paranoiac or true to reality, a faint private echo of the turmoil of history, can therefore only be decided retrospectively. Horror is beyond the reach of psychology.

104

Golden Gate. – Someone who has been offended, slighted, has an illumination as vivid as when agonizing pain lights up one's own body. He becomes aware that in the innermost blindness of love, that must remain oblivious, lives a demand not to be blinded. He was wronged; from this he deduces a claim to right and must at the same time reject it, for what he desires can only be given in freedom. In such distress he who is rebuffed becomes human. Just as love uncompromisingly betrays the general to the particular in which alone justice is done to the former, so now the general, as the autonomy of others, turns fatally against it. The very rebuttal through which the general has exerted its influence appears to the individual as exclusion from the general; he who has lost love knows himself deserted by all, and this is why he scorns consolation. In the senselessness of his deprivation he is made to feel the untruth of all merely individual fulfilment. But he thereby awakens to the paradoxical consciousness of generality: of the inalienable and unindictable human right to be loved by the beloved. With his plea, founded on

no titles or claims, he appeals to an unknown court, which accords
to him as grace what is his own and yet not his own. The secret of
justice in love is the annulment of all rights, to which love mutely
points. 'So forever/cheated and foolish must love be.'[1]

105

Expiry. – Sleepless night: so there is a formula for those tormented
hours, drawn out without prospect of end or dawn, in the vain
effort to forget time's empty passing. But truly terrifying are the
sleepless nights when time seems to contract and run fruitlessly
through our hands. We put out the light in the hope of long hours
of rest that can bring succour. But as our thoughts run wild the
night's healing store is squandered, and before we have banished
all sights from beneath our burning lids, we know that it is too late,
that we shall soon feel the rough shake of morning. In a similar way
the condemned man may see his last moments slip away unarrested,
unused. But what is revealed in such contraction of the hours is the
reverse of time fulfilled. If in the latter the power of experience
breaks the spell of duration and gathers past and future into the
present, in the hasteful sleepless night duration causes unendurable
dread. Man's life becomes a moment, not by suspending duration
but by lapsing into nothingness, waking to its own futility in face
of the bad eternity of time itself. In the clock's over-loud ticking
we hear the mockery of light-years for the span of our existence.
The hours that are past as seconds before the inner sense has
registered them, and sweep it away in their cataract, proclaim that
like all memory our inner experience is doomed to oblivion in
cosmic night. Of this people are today made forcibly aware. In his
state of complete powerlessness the individual perceives the time he
has left to live as a brief reprieve. He does not expect to live out his
life to the end. The prospect of violent death and torture, present to
everyone, is prolonged in the fear that the days are numbered, that
the length of one's own life is subject to statistics; that growing old
has become a kind of unfair advantage gained over the average.
Perhaps the life quota allocated revocably by society is already

1. *So muss übervorteilt, / Albern doch überall sein die Liebe*: lines from
Hölderlin's ode *Tränen*.

spent. Such fear is registered by the body in the flight of the hours. Time flies.

All the little flowers.[1] – The pronouncement, probably by Jean Paul, that memories are the only possessions which no-one can take from us, belongs in the storehouse of impotently sentimental consolations that the subject, resignedly withdrawing into inwardness, would like to believe the very fulfilment that he has given up. In setting up his own archives, the subject seizes his own stock of experience as property, so making it something wholly external to himself. Past inner life is turned into furniture just as, conversely, every Biedermeier piece was memory made wood. The interior where the soul accommodates its collection of memoirs and curios is derelict. Memories cannot be conserved in drawers and pigeon-holes; in them the past is indissolubly woven into the present. No-one has them at his disposal in the free and voluntary way that is praised in Jean Paul's fulsome sentences. Precisely where they become controllable and objectified, where the subject believes himself entirely sure of them, memories fade like delicate wallpapers in bright sunlight. But where, protected by oblivion, they keep their strength, they are endangered like all that is alive. This is why Bergson's and Proust's conception, intended to combat reification, that the present, immediacy, is constituted only through the mediation of memory, has not only a redeeming but an infernal aspect. Just as no earlier experience is real that has not been loosed by involuntary remembrance from the deathly fixity of its isolated existence, so conversely, no memory is guaranteed, existent in itself, indifferent to the future of him who harbours it; nothing past is proof, through its translation into mere imagination, against the curse of the empirical present. The most blissful memory of a person can be revoked in its very substance by later experience. He who has loved and who betrays love does harm not only to the image of the past, but to the past itself. Irresistibly evident, an impatient movement

1. Allusion to line from Schubert's song *Trockne Blumen* (1823) from the cycle *Die Schöne Müllerin,* which starts: *Ihr Blümlein alle, die sie mir gab* (All the little flowers that she gave me). The theme of the song is the fading of the flowers and the sentiment avowed by them.

while waking up, a distraught tone of voice, a faint hypocrisy in pleasure, obtrudes itself in the memory and turns the earlier closeness even then into the distance that it has since become. Despair has the accent of irrevocability not because things cannot improve, but because it draws the past too into its vortex. Therefore it is foolish and sentimental to try to keep the past untainted by the present's turbid flood. No other hope is left to the past than that, exposed defencelessly to disaster, it shall emerge from it as something different. But he who dies in despair has lived his whole life in vain.

107

Ne cherchez plus mon coeur.[1] – The heir to Balzacian obsession, Proust, for whom every social invitation seems an 'open Sesame' to restored life, escorts us into labyrinths where primeval gossip conveys to him the dark secrets of all splendour, until this becomes, under his too close and yearning gaze, dull and cracked. Yet the *placet futile*,[2] the preoccupation with a historically-condemned luxury class whose superfluity any bourgeois could show by calculations, the absurd energy squandered on the squanderers, is more thoroughly rewarded than the unclouded eye for the relevant. The framework of decline within which Proust quotes the portrait of his society, turns out to be that of a major social tendency. What meets its downfall in Charlus, Saint-Loup and Swann is the same thing that is lacking in the whole succeeding generation, who do not even know the name of the last poet. The eccentric psychology of decadence traces the negative anthropology of mass society: Proust gave an allergic account of what was about to befall all love. The exchange relationship that love partially withstood throughout the bourgeois age has completely absorbed it; the last immediacy falls victim to the distance of all the contracting parties from all others. Love is chilled by the value that the ego places on itself. Loving at all seems to it like loving more, and he who loves more puts himself in the wrong. This arouses his mistress's suspicion, and his emotion,

1. Line from Baudelaire's poem *Causerie* in *Les Fleurs du Mal*.
2. Futile petition: Latin title of an early poem by Mallarmé, addressed to a princess.

thrown back on itself, grows sick with possessive cruelty and self-destructive imagining. 'The relationship to the beloved', Proust writes in *Le Temps retrouvé*, 'can remain platonic for reasons quite other than the woman's purity or the sensual character of the love she arouses. Perhaps the lover is unable, in the excess of his love, to await the moment of fulfilment with sufficient dissemblance or indifference. He approaches her incessantly, never stops writing to her, tries to see her; she refuses herself, and he despairs. From this moment on she realizes that if she accords him only her company or her friendship, this favour will seem so great to one who has already given up hope that she can spare herself the trouble of granting him anything more, so that she can wait confidently until he, incapable of not seeing her any longer, is ready to end the war at any price: then she can dictate a peace with the platonic character of their relationship as its first condition. . . . All this the woman divines instinctively, knowing that she can permit herself the luxury of never giving herself to the man whose insatiable desire she feels, if he is too exalted to conceal it from her from the first.' The callow Morel is stronger than his high and mighty lover. 'He always kept the upper hand by merely refusing himself, and in order to refuse himself it was probably enough to know himself loved.'[1] The private motif of Balzac's Duchesse de Langeais has become universal.[2] The quality of every one of the countless automobiles which return to New York on Sunday evenings corresponds exactly to the attractiveness of the girl sitting in it. – The objective dissolution of society is subjectively manifested in the weakening of the erotic urge, no longer able to bind together self-preserving monads, just as if mankind were imitating the physicists' theory of the exploding universe. The frigid aloofness of the loved one, by now an acknowledged institution of mass culture, is answered by the 'insatiable desire' of the lover. When Casanova called a woman unprejudiced, he meant that no religious convention prevented her from giving herself; today the unprejudiced woman is the one who no longer believes in love, who will not be hoodwinked into investing more than she can expect in return. Sexuality, the supposed instigator of all the bustle, has become the delusion that was earlier

1. *A La Recherche du Temps Perdu*, Vol. III, Paris 1954, pp. 818–19, 820 (*Time Regained*, London 1960, pp. 148–9, 150).

2. The Duchesse de Langeais, in Balzac's novel of the same name, combined coquetry with cold refusal.

comprised by abnegation. As the arrangements of life no longer allow time for pleasure conscious of itself, replacing it by the performance of physiological functions, de-inhibited sex is itself de-sexualized. Really, they no longer want ecstasy at all, but merely compensation for an outlay that, best of all, they would like to save as superfluous.

108

Princess Lizard.[1] – Imagination is inflamed by women who lack, precisely, imagination. They have the brightest aureoles who, turned unwaveringly outward, are wholly matter-of-fact. Their attraction stems from their lack of awareness of themselves, indeed of a self at all: Oscar Wilde coined the name unenigmatic Sphinxes for them. They resemble the image designated for them: the more they are pure appearance, undisturbed by any impulse of their own, the greater their likeness to archetypes, Preziosa, Peregrina, Albertine,[2] who convey a sense of the illusoriness of all individuation, and yet must again and again disappoint by what they are. Their lives are construed as illustrations, or a perpetual children's festival, and such perception does no justice to their needy empirical existence. Storm touched on this in the deeper meaning of his children's story 'Pole Poppenspäler'.[3] The Frisian boy falls in love with the little girl of the travelling players from Bavaria. 'When at length I turned round, I saw a little red dress coming towards me; and truly, and truly, it was the little puppet player; in spite of her faded clothes she seemed surrounded by a fairy-tale radiance. I plucked up courage and spoke to her: 'Will you come for a walk, Lizzy?' She looked at me mistrustfully with her black eyes. 'A walk?' she repeated slowly – 'Ah – you're a fine one!' 'Where would you like to go then?' – 'To the drapers shop, that's where!' 'Do you want to

1. In North-German folk-lore, lizards are reputed to be princesses, transformed into them by magicians, for their vanity.
2. Preziosa: heroine of the play of the same name by Pius-Alexander Wolff (1821), set to music by Carl Maria von Weber. Peregrina: subject of the cycle of love-poems by Eduard Mörike (1804–75), originally in his novel *Maler Nolten*. Albertine: mistress of the narrator in Proust's *A La Recherche du Temps Perdu*.
3. Theodor Storm (1817–88): Frisian writer, friend of Mörike; his main works were melancholy novellae. *Pole Poppenspäler* was written in 1874.

buy yourself a new dress?' I asked, awkwardly enough. She laughed out loud. 'Go on with you! – No, just rags and tatters!' 'Rags and tatters, Lizzy?' 'Of course. Just a few rags to make clothes for the puppets; they never cost much!' Poverty compels Lizzy to make shabbiness – 'rags and tatters' – her guide-line, although she would herself like something else. Uncomprehending, she must mistrust as eccentric anything that has no practical justification. Imagination gives offence to poverty. For shabbiness has charm only for the onlooker. And yet imagination needs poverty, to which it does violence: the happiness it pursues is inscribed in the features of suffering. So Sade's Justine, who falls from one torture-trap into the next, is called 'notre intéressante héroine', and likewise Mignon, at the moment of being beaten, the interesting child.[1] Dream princess and whipping-girl are the same, and she suspects nothing of it. There are traces of this in the relation of northern peoples to the southern: the prosperous Puritans vainly try to get from the dark-haired denizens of foreign countries what the course of the world, which they control, denies not only to them but all the more to the vagrants. The sedentary man envies the nomadic existence, the quest for fresh pastures, and the painted waggon is the house on wheels whose course follows the stars. Infantility, fixated in desultory motion, the joylessly restless, momentary urge to survive, stands in for the undistorted, for fulfilment, and yet excludes it, inwardly resembling the self-preservation from which it falsely promises deliverance. This is the circle of bourgeois nostalgia for naivety. The soullessness of those in the margins of civilization, forbidden self-determination by daily need, at once appealing and tormenting, becomes a phantasm of soul to the well-provided-for, whom civilization has taught to be ashamed of the soul. Love falls for the soulless as a cipher of living spirit, because the living are the theatre of its desperate desire to save, which can exercise itself only on the lost: soul dawns on love only in its absence. So the expression called human is precisely that of the eyes closest to those of the animal, the creaturely ones, remote from the reflection of the self. At the last, soul itself is the longing of the soulless for redemption.

1. Mignon: leading female character in Goethe's novel *Wilhelm Meisters Lehrjahre*.

L'Inutile Beauté.[2] – Women of exceptional beauty are doomed to unhappiness. Even those favoured by every circumstance, who have birth, wealth, talent on their side, seem as if hounded or obsessed by the urge to destroy themselves and all the human relationships they contract. An oracle gives them the choice between calamities. Either they shrewdly exchange beauty for success. Then they pay with happiness for its condition; being no longer able to love, they poison the love felt for them and are left empty-handed. Or the privilege of beauty gives them the courage and confidence to repudiate the exchange agreement. They take seriously the happiness that their person promises, and are unstinting with themselves, assured by the admiration of all that they do not need first to prove their worth. In their youth they are free to choose. This makes them anything but choosy: nothing is definitive, everything can be replaced at any time. Quite early on, without much forethought, they marry and thereby commit themselves to pedestrian conditions, forfeit the privilege of infinite possibility, abase themselves to human beings. At the same time, however, they cling to the childish dream of omnipotence with which their lives have beguiled them, and – un-bourgeois in this – continue to throw away what tomorrow may be replaced by something better. Thus they are the type of the destructive character. Just because they were once *hors de concours* they are unsuccessful in competition, for which they now develop a mania. The gesture of irresistibility remains when the reality has passed away; magic perishes the moment it ceases merely to stand for hope and settles in domesticity. But her resistibility makes her also a victim: she becomes subject to the order she once soared above. Her generosity is punished. The fallen woman like the obsessive one are martyrs of happiness. Incorporated beauty has in time become a calculable element of existence, a mere substitute for non-existent life, without having ever been anything more. To herself and others she has broken her promise of happiness. Yet she who keeps it takes on an aura of doom and is herself overtaken by disaster. In this way the enlightened world has entirely absorbed myth. Their jealousy has outlived the gods.

1. *L'Inutile Beauté*: title of Maupassant's last book of short stories, written in 1890, dominated by the tale of the same name.

Constanze.[1] – Everywhere bourgeois society insists on the exertion of will; only love is supposed to be involuntary, pure immediacy of feeling. In its longing for this, which means a dispensation from work, the bourgeois idea of love transcends bourgeois society. But in erecting truth directly amid the general untruth, it perverts the former into the latter. It is not merely that pure feeling, so far as it is still possible within the determinate system of the economy, becomes precisely thereby society's alibi for the domination of interests and bears witness to a humanity that does not exist. The very involuntariness of love, even where it has not found itself a practical accommodation beforehand, contributes to the whole as soon as it is established as a principle. If love in society is to represent a better one, it cannot do so as a peaceful enclave, but only by conscious opposition. This, however, demands precisely the element of voluntariness that the bourgeois, for whom love can never be natural enough, forbid it. Loving means not letting immediacy wither under the omnipresent weight of mediation and economics, and in such fidelity it becomes itself mediated, as a stubborn counter-pressure. He alone loves who has the strength to hold fast to love. Even though social advantage, sublimated, preforms the sexual impulse, using a thousand nuances sanctioned by the order to make now this, now that person seem spontaneously attractive, an attachment once formed opposes this by persisting where the force of social pressure, in advance of all the intrigues that the latter then invariably takes into its service, does not want it. It is the test of feeling whether it goes beyond feeling through permanence, even though it be as obsession. The love, however, which in the guise of unreflecting spontaneity and proud of its alleged integrity, relies exclusively on what it takes to be the voice of the heart, and runs away as soon as it no longer thinks it can hear that voice, is in this supreme independence precisely the tool of society. Passive without knowing it, it registers whatever numbers come out in the roulette of interests. In betraying the loved one it betrays itself. The fidelity exacted by society is a means to unfreedom, but only through fidelity can freedom achieve insubordination to society's command.

1. Constanze: faithful heroine of Mozart's opera *Die Entführung aus dem Serail*, and name of his wife.

Philemon and Baucis. – The domestic tyrant has his wife help him on with his coat. She eagerly performs this service of love, following him with a look that says: what else should I do, let him have his little pleasure, that's how he is, only a man. The patriarchal marriage takes its revenge on the master in the wife's indulgent considerateness, which in its ironic laments over masculine self-pity and inadequacy has become a formula. Beneath the lying ideology which sets up the man as superior, there is a secret one, no less untrue, that sees him as inferior, the victim of manipulation, manoeuvring, fraud. The hen-pecked husband is the shadow of him who has to go out to face the hostile world. With the same narrow-minded percipience that the wife shows for her husband, grown-ups are judged by children. In the incongruity between his authoritarian pretensions and his helplessness, that emerges of necessity in the private sphere, there is something ridiculous. Every married couple appearing together is comic, and this the wife's patient understanding tries to offset. There is hardly a woman who has been for some time in the married state who does not, by whispering about his little weaknesses, disavow her husband. False nearness incites malice, and in the sphere of consumption the stronger party is the one who controls the commodities. Hegel's dialectic of master and servant applies as much as ever to the archaic order of the household, and is reinforced by the wife's dogged clinging to its anachronism. As the repressed matriarch she becomes the master precisely where she has to serve, and the patriarch needs only to appear as such in order to be a caricature. This simultaneous dialectic of epochs has presented itself to individualistic eyes as the 'battle of the sexes'. Both opponents are in the wrong. In demystifying the husband, whose power rests on his money-earning trumped up as human worth, the wife too expresses the falsehood of marriage, in which she seeks her whole truth. No emancipation without that of society.

Et dona ferentes. – Philistine German freedom-mongers have always prided themselves particularly on the poem about the God and the bayadere, with its closing fanfare to the effect that immortals bear aloft wanton children in arms of fire.[1] The approved broad-mindedness is not to be trusted. It fully adopts the bourgeois judgement on venal love; the effect of God-the-Fatherly understanding and forgiveness is attained only by vilifying the charming object of redemption with horrified fascination as a profligate. The act of grace is tied to reservations that make it illusory. In order to deserve redemption – as if a deserved redemption were one at all – the girl herself is allowed to partake of 'the couch's pleasing celebrations' 'not for pleasure or for gain'. Well, for what else? Does not the pure love foisted on her crudely disrupt the magic with which Goethe's dance rhythms entwine her figure, a magic, to be sure, not subsequently effaced even by the talk of deep perdition. But it is quite imperative that she be made into one of those good souls who have forgotten themselves but once. To be admitted to the preserves of humanity, the harlot, for whom humanity vaunts its tolerance, must first stop being one. The gods look in pleasure on penitent sinners. The whole expedition to the place where the last houses are is a kind of metaphysical slumming party, a show put on by patriarchal meanness to puff itself up twice over, first by widening beyond all measure the gap between masculine spirit and feminine nature, and then by decking out the total power that enables it to revoke this self-made difference as supreme goodness. The bourgeois needs the bayadere, not merely for pleasure, which he grudges her, but to feel himself a god. The nearer he gets to the edge of his domain and the more he forgets his dignity, the more blatant becomes the ritual of power. The night has its joy, but the whore is burned notwithstanding. The rest is the Idea.

113

Spoilsport. – The affinity noted by homespun psychology between asceticism and intoxication, the love-hate relationship of saints and prostitutes, has an objectively valid basis in the fact that asceticism allows to fulfilment more of its rights than do cultural instalment payments. Hostility to pleasure can certainly not be separated from connivance at the discipline of a society whose nature is to demand

1. The reference is to Goethe's poem *Der Gott und die Bayadere*. A bayadere is a Hindu dancing-girl.

more than it gives. But there is also a mistrust of pleasure stemming from the intuition that pleasure in this world is none. A construction of Schopenhauer's expresses something of this intuition. The transition from affirmation to denial of the will to live is effected by developing the thought that every restriction on the Will by an obstacle 'interposed between it and its eventual goal, suffers; whereas its attainment of this goal is satisfaction, contentment, happiness'. But while such 'suffering', according to Schopenhauer's intransigent insight, tends to increase to such an extent that death can easily enough become desirable, the state of 'satisfaction' is itself unsatisfying, because 'as soon as need and danger grant man respite, boredom is so near that amusements become an imperative need. What keeps all living things occupied and in motion is the striving for existence. With existence, however, once secured, they do not know what to do: thus the second force that sets them in motion is the striving to be rid of the burden of existence, to make it imperceptible, to "kill time", i.e. to escape boredom'.[1] But this concept of boredom, raised to such unsuspected dignity, is – and this is the last thing that Schopenhauer's anti-historical mind would admit – bourgeois through and through. It is the complement of alienated labour, being the experience of antithetically 'free time', whether because this latter is intended only to restore the energy expended, or because the appropriation of alien labour weighs on it like a mortgage. Free time remains the reflex-action to a production rhythm imposed heteronomously on the subject, compulsively maintained even in the weary pauses. Consciousness of the unfreedom of existence in its entirety, suppressed by the demands of earning a living, that is, by unfreedom itself, only emerges in the intermezzo of freedom. The *nostalgie du dimanche* is not a longing for the working week, but for the state of being emancipated from it; Sunday fails to satisfy, not because it is a day off work, but because its own promise is felt directly as unfulfilled; like the English one, every Sunday is too little Sunday. The man for whom time stretches out painfully is one waiting in vain, disappointed at not finding tomorrow already continuing yesterday. The boredom of those who have no need to work, however, is not fundamentally different. Society as a totality inflicts on those in power what they do to the others, and what is forbidden to these they will hardly

1. Schopenhauer, *Die Welt als Wille und Vorstellung*, p. 369 (*The World as Will and Idea*, Vol. 1, p. 404).

permit themselves. The bourgeois have made of satiety, which might be akin to bliss, a term of abuse. Because others go hungry, ideology requires that the absence of hunger be thought vulgar. So the bourgeois indict the bourgeois. Their own exemption from work proscribes the praise of idleness: the latter is called boring. The hectic bustle to which Schopenhauer alludes springs less from the unbearableness of a privileged condition than from its ostentation, which, according to the historical situation, is designed either to increase social distance or, by purportedly important displays, apparently to reduce it, to emphasize the usefulness of the masters. If people at the top are really bored, it is not because they suffer from too much happiness, but because they are marked by the general misery; by the commodity character that consigns amusements to idiocy, by the brutality of the command which echoes terribly in the rulers' gaiety, finally by their fear of their own superfluity. None who profit by the profit system may exist within it without shame, and this deforms even the undeformed joys, although the excesses envied by the philosophers may at times have been by no means as boring as they assure us. That in realized freedom boredom would disappear, many experiences snatched from civilization give us reason to believe. The dictum *omne animal post coitum triste est* was concocted by bourgeois contempt for man; nowhere more than here does humanity differ from creaturely gloom. It is not ecstasy but socially approved love that is followed by disgust: it is, to use Ibsen's word, sticky. Deep erotic emotion turns weariness into the plea of tenderness, and momentary sexual incapacity is understood as accidental, quite external to passion. Not without reason Baudelaire thought together both the bondage and the spiritualized illumination of erotic obsession, and called kiss, scent and conversation equally immortal. The transience of pleasure, the mainstay of asceticism, attests that except in the *minutes heureuses,* when the lover's forgotten life shines back in the loved one's limbs, there is, as yet, no pleasure at all. Even the Christian denunciations of sex in Tolstoy's *Kreutzer Sonata* cannot, in the midst of all the monkish sermonizing, entirely eradicate the memory of those moments. What he maintains against sensual love is not only the theological motif of self-abnegation, with its splendid *volte-face* requiring that no man shall make another his object – really a protest, therefore against patriarchal control – but at the same time a concern for the misshapen bourgeois form of sex, murkily enmeshed with every kind of material interest, for marriage as an ignoble compromise, however much Rousseauesque rancour against enjoyment intensified in reflection may also have found its way into his diatribes. The attack on the period of engagement is levelled against the family photograph, with its resemblance to the word 'bridegroom'. 'On top of this there was the repulsive habit of bringing chocolates, the bloating with every kind of sweetmeat, and all the disgusting preparations for the wedding: all around there was talk of nothing but the accommodation, the bedroom, the beds, house-clothes and nightclothes, linen and toilet articles.' In similar vein he ridicules the honeymoon, comparing it to the disappointment after a visit to a much-vaunted, 'highly uninteresting', fairground booth. It is not so much the exhausted senses that are to blame for *dégoût*, as the institutional, permitted, assimilated character of pleasure, its false immanence in an order that cuts it to shape and imparts to it in the very moment of ordaining it a deathly melancholy. Such repugnance can so increase that finally ecstasy prefers to withdraw completely into renunciation, rather than sin by realization against its own principle.

114

Heliotrope. – When a guest comes to stay with his parents, a child's heart beats with more fervent expectation than it ever did before Christmas. It is not presents that are the cause, but transformed existence. The perfume that the lady visitor puts down on the chest of drawers while he is allowed to watch her unpacking, has a scent that resembles memory even though he breathes it for the first time. The cases with the labels from the Suvretta Hotel and Madonna di Campiglio, are chests in which the jewels of Aladdin and Ali Baba, wrapped in precious tissues – the guest's kimonos – are borne hither from the caravanserais of Switzerland and the South Tyrol in sleeping-car sedan chairs for his glutted contemplation. And just as fairies talk to children in fairy-tales, the visitor talks seriously without condescension, to the child of the house. The child asks sensible questions about countries and people and she, in the absence of daily familiarity and seeing nothing but the fascination in his eyes, answers with portentous utterances about a brother-in-law's softening of the brain and a nephew's marital affrays. So, the child feels himself admitted all at once to the mighty and mysterious league of the grown-ups, the magic circle of the people of sense. With the order of the day – perhaps tomorrow he will be allowed to miss school – the boundaries between the generations too are suspended, and he who at eleven o'clock has still not been sent to bed has an inkling of true promiscuity. The single visit makes Thursday a feast-day and in the hubbub one seems to be sitting at table with all mankind. For the guest comes from afar. Her appearing promises the child a world beyond the family, reminding him that it is not the ultimate. The yearning to plunge into unformed joy, into the pool of salamanders and storks that the child has learned painfully to subdue and block with the frightful image of the black man, the demon who wants to take him away – here he finds it again, without fear. Among those nearest him, as their friend, appears the figure of all that is different. The soothsaying gypsy, let in by the front door, is absolved in the lady visitor and transfigured into a rescuing angel. From the joy of greatest proximity she removes the curse by wedding it to utmost distance. For this the child's whole being is waiting, and so too, later, must he be able to wait who does not forget what is best in childhood. Love counts the hours until the one when the guest steps over the threshhold and imperceptibly restores life's washed-out colours: 'Here I am again /returned from the endless world.'[1]

115

Coming clean. – To find out whether a person means us well there is one almost infallible criterion: how he passes on unkind or hostile remarks about us. Usually such reports are superfluous, nothing but pretexts to help ill-will on its way without taking responsibility, indeed in the name of good. Just as all acquaintances feel an inclination to say something disparaging about everyone from time to time, probably in part because they baulk at the greyness of acquaintanceship, so at the same time each is sensitive to the views of all others, and secretly wishes to be loved even where he does not himself love: no less indiscriminate and general than the alienation between people is the longing to breach it. In this climate the

1. *Da bin ich wieder, | hergekommen aus weiter Welt*: lines from Mörike's *Peregrina* cycle.

passer-on flourishes, never short of damaging material and ever secure in the knowledge that those who wish to be liked by everyone are always avidly on the lookout for evidence of the contrary. One ought to transmit denigratory remarks only when they relate directly and transparently to shared decisions, to the assessment of people on whom one has to rely, for example in working with them. The more disinterested the report, the murkier the interest, the warped desire, to cause pain. It is relatively harmless if the teller simply wants to set the two parties against each other while showing off his own qualities. More frequently he comes forward as the appointed mouthpiece of public opinion, and by his very dispassionate objectivity lets the victim feel the whole power of anonymity to which he must bow. The lie is manifest in the unnecessary concern for the honour of the injured party ignorant of his injury, for everything being above board, for inner cleanliness; as soon as these values are asserted by the Gregers Werles[1] of our contorted world the contortion is increased. By dint of moral zeal, the well-meaning become destroyers.

116

Just hear, how bad he was.[2] – Those who have found themselves unexpectedly in danger of their lives, in violent catastrophes, often report that they were surprisingly free of fear. The general terror does not impinge specifically on them, but affects them as mere residents of a town, members of a large association. They are reconciled to a fate which is fortuitous and, as it were, inanimate, as if it did not really concern them. Psychologically, absence of fear is explained by lack of preparedness for fear in face of the crushing blow. The freedom of eye-witnesses has about it something impaired, akin to apathy. The psychic organism, like the body, is attuned to experience of an order of magnitude bearing some relation to itself. If the object of experience grows out of proportion to the individual, he no longer really experiences it at all, but registers it directly, in concepts divorced from intuitive knowledge, as something external, incommensurable, for which he has the same indifference as the catastrophe has for him. In the moral

1. Gregers Werle: central character in Ibsen's play *The Wild Duck*.
2. *Und höre nur, wie bös er war*: lines from *Struwwelpeter*.

179

sphere there is an analogous situation. Someone who acts in a manner that by accepted norms is grievously wrong, like taking revenge on an enemy or refusing pity, will hardly feel spontaneous guilt, but rather summon the feeling up by a painful exertion. This is not without relevance to the doctrine of reason of state, the severance of morality from politics. It conceives the extreme contrast between public affairs and private existence in the same way. A major crime appears to the individual very largely as a mere infringement of conventions, not only because the norms it offends are themselves conventional, ossified, unbinding on the living subject, but because their objectification as such, even when they have underlying substance, holds them at a distance from the moral innervations, the sphere of conscience. The thought of particular indelicacies, however, micro-organisms of wrongdoing, unnoticed perhaps by anyone else – that at a social gathering one sat down too early at table, or at a tea reception put cards with the guests' names at their places, though this is done only at dinners – such trifles can fill the delinquent with unconquerable remorse and a passionately bad conscience, and on occasion with such burning shame that he shrinks from confessing them even to himself. There is nothing particularly noble in this, for he knows that society, having no objections to inhumanity, has all the more to impropriety, and that a man who turns his mistress out of doors, so proving himself a fine fellow, can be sure of social approbation, while he who respectfully kisses the hand of a well-connected girl who is somewhat too young, exposes himself to ridicule. These luxuriously narcissistic worries have, however, a second aspect: that of a refuge for experience rebounding from the objectified order. The subject can measure up to these minute traits of the mistaken or the correct and pass muster as capable of right or wrong actions; but his indifference to moral guilt is tinged with the awareness that the incapacity for personal decision grows with the dimensions of its object. If one afterwards finds out that when one parted from one's girl-friend on bad terms without telephoning her again, one did indeed cast her out, there is in the idea of this something faintly comic; it sounds like the dumb girl of Portici.[1] 'Murder', we read in a detective novel by Ellery Queen, 'is so . . . newspapery. It doesn't happen to you. You read about it in a paper, or in a detective story,

1. *La Muette de Portici*: the first French grand opera, by Daniel François Auber (1828).

and it makes you wriggle with disgust, or sympathy. But it doesn't mean anything.' Authors like Thomas Mann have therefore described newsworthy catastrophes, from the railway accident to the murder by the jilted girl, grotesquely, exorcising the laughter that is otherwise irresistibly provoked by the solemn pomp of a funeral by making it the affair of the poetic subject. In contrast, the minimal offences are so relevant because in them we can be good or evil without smiling over it, even if our seriousness is a little delusive. Through them we get the feel of morality in our very skin – when we blush – and assimilate it to the subject, who looks on the gigantic moral law within himself as helplessly as at the starry sky, of which the former is a poor imitation. That such occurrences may be intrinsically amoral, while spontaneously good impulses, acts of human compassion without the pathos of maxims do, after all, also happen, does not devalue a predilection for propriety. For while the good impulse, caring nothing for alienation, straightway expresses the general, it easily enough shows the subject as alienated from himself, a mere agent of the precepts with which he imagines himself at one: as a fine human being. Conversely, he whose moral impulse responds to the wholly external, to fetishized convention, is able, in suffering under the insurmountable divergence between inner and outer, a split that he holds fast in its petrification, to grasp the general without thereby sacrificing himself and the truth of his experience. His accentuation of the gap aims at reconciliation. Moreover the monomaniac's behaviour is not entirely without justification in its object. In the sphere of social manners on which he whimsically fixes his attention, all the inaccessible problems of false life reappear, and his obstinacy has to contend with the whole, but with the difference that here the conflict that was otherwise beyond his reach can be worked out paradigmatically, with rigour and in freedom. The man, on the other hand, who conforms in his reactions to social reality, has a private life that is formless in exact proportion as his form is stamped on him by the assessment of power relationships. He has a tendency, whenever he escapes the supervision of the external world, whenever he feels at home in the expanded circumference of his own self, to be ruthless and brutal. On those near him he avenges all the discipline and all the renunciation of directly vented aggression that is imposed on him by those far away. To the outside world, towards his objective enemies, he behaves courteously and amicably, but on friendly ground he is all coldness and hostility. Where civilization as self-preservation does not force on him civilization as humanity, he gives free rein to his fury against the latter, and refutes his own ideology of home, family and community. It is this that is combated by micrological moral myopia. It detects in the formless familiarity and slackness a mere pretext for violence, a show of being nice in order to be nasty, to our heart's desire. It subjects the intimate sphere to critical scrutiny because intimacies estrange, violate the imponderably delicate aura of the other which is his condition as a subject. Only by the recognition of distance in our neighbour is strangeness alleviated: accepted into consciousness. The presumption of un-diminished nearness present from the first, however, the flat denial of strangeness, does the other supreme wrong, virtually negates him as a particular human being and therefore the humanity in him, 'counts him in', incorporates him in the inventory of property. Wherever immediateness posits and entrenches itself, the bad mediateness of society is insidiously asserted. The cause of im-mediacy is now espoused only by the most circumspect reflection. This is tested on the smallest scale.

117

Il servo padrone.[1] – The mindless tasks imposed by authoritarian culture on the subject classes can be performed only at the cost of permanent regression. Their formlessness is, precisely, the product of social form. The barbarians engendered by culture have, how-ever, always been used by it to keep alive its own barbaric nature. Domination delegates the physical violence on which it rests to the dominated. In being allowed the satisfaction of exercising their distorted instincts in collectively approved and proper ways, they learn to do those things which the noble need for the continued indulgence of their nobility. The self-education of the ruling clique, with all its concomitant discipline, stifling of spontaneous impulses, cynical scepticism and blind lust to command, would not be possible if the oppressors did not themselves submit, through hirelings among the oppressed, to a part of the oppression they inflict on others. This is doubtless why the psychological differences between

1. Allusion to the title of the comic opera by Giovanni Pergolesi, *La Serva Padrone* (The Maid as Mistress, 1733).

the classes are so much less than the objective economic gap. The harmony of the irreconcilable helps to perpetuate the bad totality. The baseness of the superior puts him on a level with his upstart subordinate. From the domestic servants and governesses tormenting upper-class children to show them what life is like, by way of the teachers from Westerwald extirpating in them, along with the use of foreign words, all joy in language, and then the officials and employees leaving them to stand in queues, the non-commissioned officers treading on them, there is a straight line to Gestapo torturers and the bureaucrats of the gas-chambers. The delegation of power to the lower orders finds a prompt and sympathetic response in the upper orders themselves. Someone appalled by the good-breeding of his parents will seek refuge in the kitchen, basking in the cook's vitality that secretly reflects the principle of the parental good breeding. The refined are drawn to the unrefined, whose coarseness deceptively promises what their own culture denies. They do not know that the indelicacy that appears to them as anarchic nature, is nothing but a reflex-action produced by the compulsion they struggle to resist. Mediating between the class solidarity of the higher orders and their blandishments to delegates of the lower classes, is a justified feeling of guilt towards the poor. But the rebel who has been put in his place, who has been made to feel to the core of his being 'how things are done here', has ended up one of them himself. Bettelheim's observation on the identification of the victims of the Nazi camps with their executioners implies a verdict on the higher nurseries of social horticulture, the English public school, the German military academy. Topsy-turviness perpetuates itself: domination is propagated by the dominated.

118

Downwards, ever downwards.[1] – Private relations between people seem modelled on the industrial bottleneck. In even the smallest community the level is determined by the most subaltern of its members. Anyone who, in conversation, talks over the head of even one person, is tactless. For the sake of humanity talk is restricted to the most obvious, dullest and tritest matters, if just one inhuman

1. *Hinunter und immer weiter*: title of a *Lied* set by Schubert.

face is present. Now that the world has made men speechless, not to be on speaking terms is to be in the right. The wordless need only stick immovably to their interests and their natures to get their way. It is enough that the other, vainly seeking contact, falls into a pleading or soliciting tone, for him to be at a disadvantage. Since the bottleneck knows of no court of appeal higher than that of fact, while thought and speech necessarily point to one, intelligence becomes naivety, and blockheads seize on this as irrefutable fact. The common consent to the positive is a gravitational force that pulls all downwards. It shows itself superior to the opposing impulse by declining to engage it. The more complex personality, unwilling to be pulled down, has to observe the strictest consideration for the inconsiderate. The latter need no longer be plagued by the disquiet of consciousness. Intellectual debility, affirmed as a universal principle, appears as vital force. A formalistic, administrative way of settling problems, a compartmentalized separation of everything that is, by its meaning, inseparable, hidebound insistence on arbitrary opinion in the absence of any proof, in short the practice of reifying every feature of an aborted, unformed self, withdrawing it from the process of experience and asserting it as the ultimate That's-the-way-I-am, suffices to overrun impregnable positions. Such people can be as sure of the assent of others, similarly deformed, as of their own advantage. The cynical trumpeting of their own defect betrays an awareness that at the present stage the objective spirit liquidates the subjective. They are down to earth like their zoological forbears, before they got up on their hind-legs.

119

Model of virtue. – Everyone has heard of the connection between repression and morality as instinctual renunciation. But moral ideas not only suppress the rest, they are directly derived from the existence of the suppressors. Since Homer Greek linguistic usage has intertwined the concepts of goodness and wealth. *Kalokagathia*, held up by the humanists to modern society as a model of aesthetico-moral harmony, always laid heavy stress on possessions, and Aristotle's *Politics* openly admits the fusion of inner worth with status in its definition of nobility as 'inherited wealth, combined with excellence'. The conception of the *polis* in the classical age, embracing both inward and outward existence, the individual's position in the city state and his self as a unity, made it possible to attribute moral rank to riches without arousing the crude suspicions even at that time befitting the doctrine. If visible influence in the existing state is the measure of a man, then it is only consistent to accredit the material wealth which tangibly underwrites his influence to his character, since moral substance itself is seen, no differently than in Hegel's philosophy of later years, as constituted by his participation in objective social reality. It was the advent of Christianity that first negated this identification, with its proposition that a camel could pass more easily through a needle's eye than a rich man enter heaven. But the special theological premium on poverty indicates how deeply the general consciousness was stamped by the morality of possessions. Fixed property was a means of differentiation from nomadic disorder, against which all norms were directed; to be good and to have goods coincided from the beginning. The good man is he who rules himself as he does his own property: his autonomous being is modelled on material power. The rich should therefore not be accused of immorality – the reproach has ever been part of the armature of political repression – but rather made aware that, to the others, they represent morality. In it goods are reflected. Wealth as goodness is an element in the world's mortar: the tenacious illusion of their identity prevents the confrontation of moral ideas with the order in which the rich are right, while at the same time it has been impossible to conceive concrete definitions of morality other than those derived from wealth. The further the individual and society diverge in later periods through the competition of interests, and the more the individual is thrown back on himself, the more doggedly he clings to the notion of the moral nature of wealth. Wealth shall vouch for the possibility of reuniting what is sundered, the inward and the outward. Such is the secret of intramundane asceticism, the businessman's boundless exertion – falsely hypostasized by Max Weber – *ad maiorem dei gloriam*. Material success joins individual and society not merely in the comfortable and by now questionable sense that the rich man can escape solitude, but far more radically: if blind, isolated self-interest is pursued far enough it turns, as economic power, into social predominance and manifests itself as an incarnation of the all-uniting principle. He who is rich or attains riches, feels that he has accomplished 'on his own initiative', as a self, what the objective spirit, the truly irrational predestination of a society held together by brutal economic inequality, intends. So the rich man can claim as goodness what really only betokens its absence. He himself and others perceive him as the realization of the general principle. Because this is one of injustice, the unjust man regularly becomes just, and not merely in illusion, but supported by the supreme might of the law by which society reproduces itself. The wealth of individuals is inseparable from the progress of society in 'prehistory'. The rich control the means of production. Technical advances in which society as a whole participates are therefore put down primarily to 'their' – today industry's – progress, and the Fords necessarily seem benefactors to the extent that they actually are so within the framework of the existing relations of production. Their pre-established privilege makes it appear as if they are relinquishing something belonging to them – that is, the increase of use-values, while they are really, in the blessings they administer, only letting a part of the profit flow back where it came from. Hence the delusive character of the moral hierarchy. Certainly, poverty has always been glorified as asceticism, the social condition for gaining the very riches in which morality becomes manifest; nevertheless, as is known, 'what a man is worth' means his bank balance, and in German commercial jargon to say 'the man is good' means that he can pay. However, what the reason of state of an omnipotent economy confesses so cynically, extends unavowed to the behaviour of individuals. The private generosity that the rich can supposedly afford, the aura of happiness surrounding them, some of which is reflected on those they allow to approach them, all this helps to veil them. They remain the nice, the right people, the better sort, the good. Wealth insulates from overt injustice. While the policeman beats up strikers with a rubber truncheon, the factory-owner's son can drink an occasional whisky with a progressive writer. By all the desiderata of private morality, even the most advanced, the rich man could – if only he could – indeed be better than the poor. This possibility, admittedly neglected in reality, plays a part in the ideology of those without it: even the confidence-trickster, who may in any case be preferable to the legitimate corporation bosses, enjoys the fame, after his arrest, of having had such a lovely house, and the highly-paid executive acquires human warmth by serving opulent dinners.

The barbaric success-religion of today is consequently not simply contrary to morality: it is the homecoming of the West to the venerable morals of our ancestors. Even the norms which condemn the present world are themselves the fruits of its iniquities. All morality has been modelled on immorality and to this day has reinstated it at every level. The slave morality is indeed bad: it is still the master morality.

120

Rosenkavalier. – The elegant attract by the expectation that they will be free in private from greed for advantages already theirs, and from the blinkered myopia that results from constricting circumstances. One imagines them capable of adventurous thinking, serene indifference to their own interests, sophisticated reactions, and believes that their sensitivity must recoil, at least in thought, from the brutality on which their privilege depends, whereas the victims have scarcely even the possibility of perceiving what makes them such. If, however, the severance of production from the private sphere turns out to be itself a piece of necessary social illusion, this expectation of spiritual unrestraint must be disappointed. Not even the subtlest snobism has *dégoût* for its objective precondition, but rather insulates the snob from its realization. It is an open question how far the eighteenth-century French aristocracy did indeed have the playfully suicidal share in the Enlightenment and the preparation for the Revolution that revulsion from the terrorists of virtue is so fond of imagining. The bourgeoisie, at any rate, has remained pure even in its late phase from any such penchants. None but the *déclassés* dance out of line on the volcano. Subjectively too, society life is so thoroughly stamped by the economic principle, whose kind of rationality spreads to the whole, that emancipation from egoistic interests, even merely as an intellectual luxury, is denied to it. Just as they are incapable of themselves enjoying their immeasurably increased wealth, they are unable to think against themselves. To no avail the quest for frivolity. The perpetuation of the real difference between upper and lower strata is assisted by the progressive disappearance of differences in the mode of consciousness between the two. The poor are prevented from thinking by the discipline of others, the rich by their own. The rulers' consciousness is inflicting on all intellect what earlier was done to religion. Culture is being turned by the *haute bourgeoisie* into an element of ostentation. A person's intelligence or education is ranked among the qualities that make him suitable for inviting or marrying, like good horsemanship, love of nature, charm, or a faultlessly fitting dinner-jacket. About knowledge they are incurious. Usually these blithe spirits are as totally absorbed by everyday practicalities as the petty bourgeoisie. They furnish houses, prepare parties, show virtuosity in booking hotel and airline reservations. For the rest, they sustain themselves on the offal of European irrationalism. They bluntly justify their own hostility to mind, sensing subversion – not even wrongly – in thought itself, in its independence of anything given, existent. Just as in Nietzsche's day educated philistines believed in progress, the unfaltering elevation of the masses and the greatest possible happiness for the greatest possible number, so today they believe, without quite knowing it themselves, in the opposite, the revocation of 1789, the incorrigibility of human nature, the anthropological impossibility of happiness – in other words, that the workers are too well-off. The profound insights of the day before yesterday have been reduced to the ultimate in banality. Of Nietzsche and Bergson, the last socially accepted philosophies, nothing is left but the murkiest anti-intellectualism in the name of the nature its apologists despoil. 'What most vexes me about the Third Reich', a general director's Jewish wife, later murdered in Poland, said in 1933, 'is that we can no longer use the word "earthy", because it has been commandeered by the Nazis', and even after the defeat of the Fascists, a fine-featured Austrian lady of the manor, meeting at a cocktail party a workers' leader mistakenly thought radical, could do nothing in her enthusiasm for his personality but repeat bestially: 'and moreover he's so utterly unintellectual, so utterly unintellectual'. I remember my fright when an aristocratic girl of vague origins, scarcely able to speak German without an affectedly foreign accent, confessed to me her sympathy for Hitler, with whose image hers seemed incompatible. At the time I thought a winsome feeble-mindedness must be concealing from her who she was. But she was shrewder than I, for what she represented no longer existed, and her class-consciousness, in deleting her individual destiny, helped her being-in-itself, her social character, to emerge. People at the top are closing ranks so tightly that all possibility of subjective deviation has gone, and difference can be sought only in the more distinguished cut of an evening dress.

121

Requiem for Odette. – The Anglomania of the upper classes in continental Europe arises from the ritualization on the island of feudal practices intended to be sufficient unto themselves. Culture is not maintained there as a separate sphere of the objective mind, as dabbling in art or philosophy, but as a form of empirical existence. The high life aspires to be the beautiful life. It affords those engaging in it ideological pleasure-gains. Because the formalization of life becomes a task requiring the adherence to rules, the artificial preservation of a style, the maintenance of a delicate balance between correctness and independence, existence itself appears endowed with meaning, so appeasing the bad conscience of the socially superfluous. The constant injunction to do and say what exactly befits one's status and situation demands a kind of moral effort. By making it difficult to be the person one is, one gains the feeling of living up to a patriarchal *noblesse oblige*. At the same time the displacement of culture from its objective manifestations to immediate life dispels the risk of one's immediacy being shaken by intellect. The latter is spurned as a disruption of aplomb, a want of taste, but this is done, not with the embarrassing coarseness of an East Prussian Junker, but by a seemingly intellectual criterion, that of aestheticizing everyday life. The flattering illusion is produced that one has been spared any cleavage into superstructure and infrastructure, culture and corporeal reality. But for all its aristocratic trappings, ritual falls into the late-bourgeois habit of hypostasizing a performance in itself meaningless as meaning, of degrading mind to the duplication of what is there in any case. The norm followed is fictitious; its social preconditions, like its model, court ceremony, have ceased to exist, and it is acknowledged not because it is felt as binding, but in order to legitimize an order advantageously illegitimate. So Proust, with the infallibility of one himself susceptible, observed that Anglomania and the cult of formally stylized living are found less among aristocrats than among those aspiring to rise: from the snob to the parvenu it is only a step. Hence the relation between snobbery and *art nouveau*, the attempt of a class defined by exchange to project itself into an image of vegetable beauty pure of exchange. That this self-fêting in no way enriches life is manifest in the boredom of the cocktail parties, the weekend invitations to the country, the golf, symbolic of the whole sphere, the organization of the social round – privileges giving real enjoyment to none, and serving only to conceal from the privileged how much in the joyless whole they too are without the possibility of pleasure. In its most recent phase the beautiful life has been reduced to what Veblen took it to be throughout the ages, ostentation, mere being select, and the park no longer offers any other satisfaction than the wall against which those on the outside flatten their noses. The misdemeanours of the upper classes – now in any case being irresistibly democratized – reveal in all its crassness what has long been true of society: that life has become the ideology of its own absence.

122

Monograms. – *Odi profanum vulgus et arceo* [I hate the vulgar rabble and shun it],[1] said the son of the freed slave.

Very evil people cannot really be imagined dying.

To say 'we' and mean 'I' is one of the most recondite insults.

Between 'there came to me in a dream' [*es träumte mir*] and 'I dreamt' lie the ages of the world. But which is the more true? No more than it is spirits who send the dream, is it the ego that dreams.

Before the eighty-fifth birthday of a man well provided for in every respect, I asked myself in a dream what I could give him to cause him real pleasure, and at once answered my own question: a guide to the realm of the dead.

That Leporello has to complain of meagre diet and shortage of money casts doubt on the existence of Don Juan.

In early childhood I saw the first snow-shovellers in thin shabby clothes. Asking about them, I was told they were men without work who were given this job so that they could earn their bread. Then they get what they deserve, having to shovel snow, I cried out in rage, bursting uncontrollably into tears.

1. Horace, whose father was a freed slave.

Love is the power to see similarity in the dissimilar.

A Paris circus advertisement before the Second War: *Plus sport que le théâtre, plus vivant que le cinéma.* [More sporting than the theatre, more living than the cinema].

Perhaps a film that strictly and in all respects satisfied the code of the Hays Office might turn out a great work of art, but not in a world in which there is a Hays Office.

Verlaine: the venial mortal sin.

Brideshead Revisited by Evelyn Waugh: socialized snobbery.

Zille gives penury a smack on the bottom.[1]

Scheler: *Le boudoir dans la philosophie.*[2]

A poem by Liliencron describes military music.[3] It starts: 'Round the corner brasses bray, like tubas on the Judgement Day', and finishes: 'Came a bright-winged butterfly/clash-clash-bang round the corner?' Poeticized historical-philosophy of power, with the Judgement Day at the beginning, the butterfly at the end.

In Trakl's 'Along' there is the line: 'Tell how long it is we have been dead'; in Däubler's 'Golden Sonnets': 'How true that we are all long dead.'[4] The unity of Expressionism consists in expressing that people wholly estranged from one another, life having receded within them, have thereby become, precisely, dead.

Among the forms tried out by Borchardt there was no lack of remodelled folk-songs.[5] Shunning the phrase 'In popular style' he calls them instead: 'In the style of the people'. But that sounds like: 'In the name of the law'. In the renovator-poet lurks the Prussian policeman.

1. Heinrich Zille (1858–1929): jocular cartoonist of Berlin plebeian life after 1900.
2. Max Scheler (1874–1928): phenomenological philosopher and theorist of a sociology of knowledge. Inversion of De Sade's *La Philosophie dans le Boudoir*.
3. Detlev von Liliencron (1844–1909): naturalist poet and short-story writer.
4. Georg Trakl (1887–1914): Austrian lyric poet of great pessimism. Theodor Däubler (1876–1934): German writer whose expressionist poems, mystical in inspiration, were written between 1915 and 1919.
5. Rudolf Borchardt (1877–1945): conservative and anti-rationalist poet and essayist, early influenced by Swinburne.

Not least among the tasks now confronting thought is that of placing all the reactionary arguments against Western culture in the service of progressive enlightenment.

True thoughts are those alone which do not understand themselves.

Seeing the little old woman dragging faggots to his pyre, Hus cried out: *Sancta simplicitas*. But what of the reason for his sacrifice, the Last Supper in both its forms? Every thought seems naive beside a higher one, and nothing is simple-minded, since all grows simple on the desolate vanishing-line of oblivion.

Love you will find only where you may show yourself weak without provoking strength.

123

The bad comrade.[1] – In a real sense, I ought to be able to deduce Fascism from the memories of my childhood. As a conqueror dispatches envoys to the remotest provinces, Fascism had sent its advance guard there long before it marched in: my schoolfellows. If the bourgeois class has from time immemorial nurtured the dream of a brutal national community, of oppression of all by all; children already equipped with Christian-names like Horst and Jürgen and surnames like Bergenroth, Bojunga and Eckhardt enacted the dream before the adults were historically ripe for its realization. I felt with such excessive clarity the force of the horror towards which they were straining, that all subsequent happiness seemed revocable, borrowed. The outbreak of the Third Reich did, it is true, surprise my political judgement, but not my unconscious fear. So closely had all the motifs of permanent catastrophe brushed me, so deeply were the warning signs of the German awakening burned into me, that I recognized them all in the features of Hitler's dictatorship: and it often seemed to my foolish terror as if the total State had been invented expressly against me, to inflict on me after all those things from which, in my childhood, its primeval form, I had been temporarily dispensed. The five patriots who set upon a single schoolfellow, thrashed him and, when he complained to the

1. *Der böse Kamerad*: allusion to the song *Der gute Kamerad* (The Good Comrade) popularized by the nazis.

teacher, defamed him a traitor to the class – are they not the same as those who tortured prisoners to refute claims by foreigners that prisoners were tortured? They whose hallooing knew no end when the top boy blundered – did they not stand grinning and sheepish round the Jewish detainee, poking fun at his maladroit attempt to hang himself? They who could not put together a correct sentence but found all of mine too long – did they not abolish German literature and replace it by their 'writ' [*Schrifttum*]? Some covered their chests with mysterious insignia and wanted, far from the sea, to become naval officers when the navy had long ceased to exist: they proclaimed themselves detachment and unit leaders, legitimists of the illegitimate. The crabbed intelligent ones who had as little success in class as the gifted amateur constructor without connections had under liberalism; who therefore, to please their parents, busied themselves with fret-saw work or even, for their own pleasure, spun out intricate designs in coloured inks at their drawing boards on long afternoons, helped the Third Reich to its cruel efficiency, and are being cheated once again. Those, however, who were always truculently at loggerheads with the teachers, interrupting the lessons, nevertheless sat down, from the day, indeed the very hour of their matriculation, with the same teachers, at the same table and the same beer, in male confederacy, vassals by vocation, rebels who, crashing their fists on the table, already signalled their worship for their masters. They needed only to miss promotion to the next class to overtake those who had left their class, and take revenge on them. Now that they, officials and recruits, have stepped visibly out of my dream and dispossessed me of my past life and my language, I no longer need to dream of them. In Fascism the nightmare of childhood has come true.

1935

124

Puzzle-picture. – Why, despite a historical development that has reached the point of oligarchy, the workers are less and less aware that they are such, can be surmised from a number of observations. While objectively the relation of owners and producers to the productive apparatus grows ever more rigid, subjective class membership becomes all the more fluctuating. This tendency is fostered by economic development itself. The organic composition of capital demands, as has often been noted, control through technical experts rather than through factory owners. The latter were the counterpart, as it were, of living labour, the former correspond to the share of machinery in capital. The quantification of technical processes, however, their dissection into minute operations largely independent of education and experience, makes the expertise of these new-style managers to a large degree illusory, a pretence concealing the privilege of being appointed. That technical development has reached a state which makes every function really open to all – this immanently socialist element in progress has been travestied under late industrialism. Membership of the élite seems attainable to everyone. One only waits to be co-opted. Suitability consists in affinity, from the libidinal garnishing of all goings-on, by way of the healthy technocratic outlook, to hearty *realpolitik*. Such men are expert only at control. That anyone could do as much has not brought their demise but the possibility that anyone can be appointed. Preference goes to those who fit in most exactly. The elect, of course, remain a negligible minority, but the structural possibility suffices to preserve the illusion of equal opportunities under a system which has eliminated the free competition that lived on that illusion. That technical forces might permit a condition free of privileges is accredited by all, even those in the shadow, to the social relations which prevent it. In general, subjective class-membership today shows a mobility that allows the rigidity of the economic order itself to be forgotten: rigid things can always be moved about. Even the individual's powerlessness to calculate his economic fate in advance makes its own contribution to this comforting mobility. Downfall is decided not by incompetence but by an opaque hierarchical structure in which no-one, scarcely even those at the very top, can feel secure: an egalitarian threat. When, in the most successful film of a year, the heroic squadron leader returns to be harrassed by petty-bourgeois caricatures as a drug-store jerk, he not only gives the spectators an occasion for unconscious gloating but in addition strengthens them in their consciousness that all men are really brothers. Extreme injustice becomes a deceptive facsimile of justice, disqualification of equality. Sociologists, however, ponder the grimly comic riddle: where is the proletariat?

Olet.[1] – In Europe the pre-bourgeois past survives in the shame felt at being paid for personal services or favours. The new continent knows nothing of this. In the old world too nothing was done for nothing, but this was felt as a wound. Doubtless, a distinction that itself derives from nothing better than a monopoly of land, is ideology. But it had penetrated characters deeply enough to stiffen their necks against the market. The German ruling class disdained to earn money other than by privilege or control of production until deep into the twentieth century. What was thought disreputable about artists and scholars was what they themselves most rebelled against, remuneration, and Hölderlin, the private tutor, as much as Liszt, the pianist, underwent precisely in employment those experiences which led them into their opposition to the dominant consciousness. Up to our days a man's membership of the upper or lower classes has been crudely determined by whether or not he accepted money. At times false pride became conscious criticism. Every child of the European upper classes blushed at a monetary gift made by relations, and even if the greater force of bourgeois utility overcame and overcompensated such reactions, the doubt nevertheless remained whether man was made merely to exchange. The remnants of the old were, in the European consciousness, ferments of the new. In America, on the other hand, no child of even well-off parents has inhibitions about earning a few cents by newspaper rounds, and this nonchalance has found its way into the demeanour of adults. This is why, to the uninformed European, Americans in their entirety can so easily appear as people without dignity, predisposed to paid services, just as, conversely, they are inclined to take him for a vagabond and aper of princes. The self-evidence of the maxim that work is no disgrace, the guileless absence of all snobbery concerning the ignominy, in the feudal sense, of market relationships, the democracy of the earnings-principle, contribute to the persistence of what is utterly anti-democratic, economic injustice, human degradation. It occurs to nobody that there might be services that are not expressible in terms of exchange value. This is the real pre-condition for the triumph of that subjective reason which is incapable of thinking a truth intrinsically binding, and perceives it solely as existing for

1. Inversion of Juvenal's dictum *pecunia non olet*: money does not smell.

others, as exchangeable. If across the Atlantic the ideology was pride, here it is delivering the goods. This applies also to the products of the objective spirit. The direct advantage to each party in the exchange act, in other words subjectively the most limited attitude, prohibits subjective expression. Profitability, the *a priori* condition of consequentially marketable production, nips the spontaneous need for subjectivity, for the thing itself, in the bud. Even cultural products introduced and distributed with the maximum display of expense repeat, though it be by virtue of impenetrable machinery, the public-house musician's sidelong glance at the plate on the piano while he hammers their favourite melody into his patrons' ears. The culture industry's budget runs to billions, but the formal law of its performances is that of the tip. The excessively glossy, hygienic quality of industrialized culture is the sole rudiment of primal shame, an exorcising image, comparable to the tail-coats of the highest hotel managers, who, in their eagerness not to look like head-waiters, outdo aristocrats in elegance, so giving themselves away as head-waiters.

126

I.Q. – The modes of behaviour appropriate to the most advanced state of technical development are not confined to the sectors in which they are actually required. So thinking submits to the social checks on its performance not merely where they are professionally imposed, but adapts to them its whole complexion. Because thought has by now been perverted into the solving of assigned problems, even what is not assigned is processed like a problem. Thought, having lost autonomy, no longer trusts itself to comprehend reality, in freedom, for its own sake. This it leaves, respectfully deluded, to the highest-paid, thereby making itself measurable. It behaves, even in its own eyes, as if it had constantly to demonstrate its fitness. Even where there is no nut to crack, thinking becomes training for no matter what exercise. It sees its objects as mere hurdles, a permanent test of its own form. Considerations that wish to take responsibility for their subject-matter and therefore for themselves, arouse suspicion of being vain, windy, asocial self-gratification. Just as for neo-positivists knowledge is split into accumulated sense-experience and logical formalism, the mental activity of the type for whom unitary knowledge is made to measure, is polarized into the inventory of what he knows and the spot-check on his thinking-power: every thought becomes for him a quiz either of his knowledgeability or his aptitude. Somewhere the right answers must be already recorded. Instrumentalism, the latest version of pragmatism, has long been concerned not merely with the application of thought but the *a priori* condition of its form. When oppositional intellectuals endeavour, within the confines of these influences, to imagine a new content for society, they are paralysed by the form of their own consciousness, which is modelled in advance to suit the needs of this society. While thought has forgotten how to think itself, it has at the same time become its own watchdog. Thinking no longer means anything more than checking at each moment whether one can indeed think. Hence the impression of suffocation conveyed even by all apparently independent intellectual productions, theoretical no less than artistic. The socialization of mind keeps it boxed in, isolated in a glass case, as long as society is itself imprisoned. As thought earlier internalized the duties exacted from without, today it has assimilated to itself its integration into the surrounding apparatus, and is thus condemned even before the economic and political verdicts on it come fully into force.

127

Wishful thinking. – Intelligence is a moral category. The separation of feeling and understanding, that makes it possible to absolve and beatify the blockhead, hypostasizes the dismemberment of man into functions. Praise of the simpleton has an undertone of anxiety lest the severed parts reunite and put an end to the derangement. 'If you have understanding and a heart', a verse of Hölderlin's runs, 'show only one. Both they will damn, if both you show together.'[1] The defamation of limited understanding in comparison to infinite – but because infinite, to the finite subject forever unfathomable – reason, which resounds throughout philosophy, chimes in, despite its critical claims, with the catch-tune: 'Be honest

1. *Hast du Verstand und ein Herz, so zeige nur eines von beiden. | Beides verdammen sie dir, zeigst du beides zugleich*: the two-line poem which Hölderlin entitled 'Good Advice'.

evermore and true.'¹ When Hegel demonstrates the stupidity of understanding,² he not only accords isolated reflection, positivism of every designation, its full measure of untruth, but he also connives at the prohibition on thought, cuts back the negative labour of the concept which his method itself claims to perform, and endorses on the highest peak of speculation the Protestant pastor urging his flock to remain one instead of relying on their own feeble light. It is rather for philosophy to seek, in the opposition of feeling and understanding, their – precisely moral – unity. Intelligence, in asserting its power of judgement, opposes anything given in advance, by at the same time expressing it. The very judgement that excludes instinctual impulses compensates them by a moment of counter-pressure against the force exerted by society. The power of judgement is measured by the cohesion of the self. But therefore also by that dynamic of instincts which is entrusted by the psychic division of labour to feeling. Instinct, the will to withstand, is implicit in the meaning of logic. It is because, in logic, the judging subject forgets itself, shows itself incorruptible, that it wins its victories. Just as, on the other hand, people within the narrowest horizons grow stupid at the point where their interest begins, and then vent their rancour on what they do not want to understand because they could understand it only too well, so the planetary stupidity which prevents the present world from perceiving the absurdity of its own order is a further product of the unsublimated, unsuperseded interest of the rulers. Short-run yet irresistible, this hardens into the anonymous schema of the course of history. To it corresponds the stupidity and obstinacy of the individual; inability consciously to link the power of prejudice and business. Such stupidity regularly consorts with moral deficiency, lack of autonomy and responsibility, whereas so much is true in Socratic rationalism that one can scarcely imagine a seriously intelligent man, whose thoughts are directed at objects and do not circle formalistically within themselves, as wicked. For the motivation of evil, blind absorption by contingent self-interest, tends to dissolve in the medium of thought. Scheler's dictum that all knowledge is founded in love was a lie, because he demanded immediate love of the contemplated. But it would become truth if love urged the

1. *Üb' immer Treu und Redlichkeit*: from the *Lied* set by Mozart.
2. Understanding: *Verstand* – the limited analytic intellect opposed by Hegel to the infinite grasp of *Vernunft* or Reason.

dissolution of all sham immediacy and thus, of course, became incompatible with the object of knowledge. The severance of thought is not remedied by the synthesis of mutually estranged psychic departments, nor by therapeutically imbuing reason with irrational ferments, but by self-conscious reflection on the element of wish that antithetically constitutes thinking as thinking. Only when that element is dissolved purely, without heteronomous residues, in the objectivity of thought, will it become an impulse towards Utopia.

128

Regressions. – My earliest memory of Brahms, and certainly not only mine, is 'Cradle Song'. Complete misunderstanding of the text: I did not know that the word used there for carnations – *Näglein* – referred to flowers, but took it to mean the little nails, drawing pins, with which the curtain round the cot, my own, was thickly studded, so that the child, shielded from every chink of light, could sleep in an unending peace without fear. How much the flowers fell short of the tenderness of those curtains. Nothing, for us, can fill the place of undiminished brightness except the unconscious dark; nothing that of what once we might have been, except the dream that we had never been born.

'Sleep in gentle ease / little eyes shut please, / hear the raindrops in the dark, / hear the neighbour's doggy bark. / Doggy bit the beggar-man, / tore his coat, away he ran, / to the gate the beggar flees, / sleep in gentle ease.' The first strophe of Taubert's lullaby is frightening. And yet its two last lines bless sleep with a promise of peace. But this is not entirely due to bourgeois callousness, the comforting knowledge that the intruder has been warded off. The sleepy child has already half forgotten the expulsion of the stranger, who in Schott's song-book looks like a Jew, and in the line 'to the gate the beggar flees' he glimpses peace without the wretchedness of others. So long as there is still a single beggar, Benjamin writes in a fragment, there is still myth; only with the last beggar's disappearance would myth be appeased. But would not violence then be forgotten as in the child's drowsiness? Would not, in the end, the disappearance of the beggar make good everything that was ever done to him and can never be made good? Is there not concealed in all persecution by human beings, who, with the little dog, set the whole of nature on the weak, the hope to see effaced the last trace of persecution, which is itself the portion of nature? Would not the beggar, driven out of the gate of civilization, find refuge in his homeland, freed from exile on earth? 'Have now peaceful mind, beggar home shall find.'

As long as I have been able to think, I have derived happiness from the song: 'Between the mountain and the deep, deep vale': about the two rabbits who, regaling themselves on the grass, were shot down by the hunter, and, on realizing they were still alive, made off in haste. But only later did I understand the moral of this: sense can only endure in despair and extremity; it needs absurdity, in order not to fall victim to objective madness. One ought to follow the example of the two rabbits; when the shot comes, fall down giddily, half-dead with fright, collect one's wits and then, if one still has breath, show a clean pair of heels. The capacity for fear and for happiness are the same, the unrestricted openness to experience amounting to self-abandonment in which the vanquished rediscovers himself. What would happiness be that was not measured by the immeasurable grief at what is? For the world is deeply ailing. He who cautiously adapts to it by this very act shares in its madness, while the eccentric alone would stand his ground and bid it rave no more. He alone could pause to think on the illusoriness of disaster, the 'unreality of despair', and realize not merely that he is still alive but that there is still life. The ruse of the dazed rabbits redeems, with them, even the hunter, whose guilt they purloin.

129

Service to the customer. – The culture industry piously claims to be guided by its customers and to supply them with what they ask for. But while assiduously dismissing any thought of its own autonomy and proclaiming its victims its judges, it outdoes, in its veiled autocracy, all the excesses of autonomous art. The culture industry not so much adapts to the reactions of its customers as it counterfeits them. It drills them in their attitudes by behaving as if it were itself a customer. One might suspect that the whole ideal of adjustment which it also professes to obey, is ideology; that people aspire more to adapt to others and to the whole, the more they are intent, by exaggerated equality, the public oath of social impotence, on having a stake in power and so subverting equality. 'Music does the listening for the listener', and the film perpetrates on trust-scale the odious trick of grown-ups who, palming something off on children, belabour the recipients with the language it would suit them to hear from them, and present the usually dubious gift with the expressions of lip-smacking delight that they wish to elicit. The culture industry is geared to mimetic regression, to the manipulation of repressed impulses to copy. Its method is to anticipate the spectator's imitation of itself, so making it appear as if the agreement already exists which it intends to create. It can do so all the better because in a stabilized system it can indeed count on such agreement, having rather to reiterate it ritualistically than actually to produce it. Its product is not a stimulus at all, but a model for reactions to non-existent stimuli. Hence in the picture-house the enthusiastic music-titles, the idiotic nursery-talk, the winking folksiness; even the close-up of the start seems to shout: how super! With these techniques the cultural apparatus assails the spectator with the frontal force of the express-train coming towards him at the climax of cinematic tension. But the tone adopted by every film is that of the witch handing food to the child she wants to enchant or devour, while mumbling horribly: 'Lovely, lovely soup. How you're going to enjoy it!' In art this kitchen-fire witchcraft was invented by Wagner, whose linguistic intimacies and musical spices are forever tasting themselves, and he also, with a genius's compulsion to confess, laid bare the whole process in the scene of the 'Ring' where Mime offers Siegfried the poisoned potion. But who is to strike off the monster's head, now that it has itself lain long, with its fair locks, under the linden tree?

130

Grey and grey. – Even its bad conscience cannot help the culture industry. So objective has its spirit become that it slaps its own subjects in the face, so that they, its agents all, are in the know and attempt, by means of mental reservations, to distance themselves from the mischief they cause. The admission that films disseminate ideologies is itself disseminated ideology. It is accommodated administratively in the rigid distinction between synthetic day-dreams on one hand, vehicles of refuge from everyday life, 'escape'; and on the other well-meaning products that spur us on to correct social behaviour, 'convey a message'. Their prompt subsumption under escape and message expresses the untruth of both types. The scorn for escapism, the standardized indignation at superficiality, is nothing but the pitiful echo of the old-established ethos that fulminates against gambling because in the dominant practice it cannot play the game. It is not because they turn their back on washed-out existence that escape-films are so repugnant, but because they do not do so energetically enough, because they are themselves just as washed-out, because the satisfactions they fake coincide with the ignominy of reality, of denial. The dreams have no dream. Just as the technicolour heroes do not allow us to forget for a second that they are normal people, type-cast public faces and investments, so under the thin tinsel of schematically produced fantasy emerges in unmistakable outline the skeleton of cinema-ontology, the whole obligatory hierarchy of values, the canon of the undesirable or the exemplary. There is nothing more practical than escape, nothing more fervently espoused to big business: we are abducted into the distance only to have the laws of empiricist living hammered from afar, unhampered by empirical possibilities of evasion, into our consciousness. The escape is full of message. And message, the opposite, looks what it is: the wish to flee from flight. It reifies the resistance to reification. One need only hear experts praising a celluloid masterpiece for having, beside other merits, moral seriousness, in the same tone as a glamorous actress is certified as having personality too. The executive conference could easily decide to include in the escape-film, along with more expensive extras, an ideal: the Goethean call that man should be noble, helpful and kind. Severed from the immanent logic of the work, its subject matter, this ideal becomes itself a piece of matter, to be provided from stock, therefore at once palpable and null, amounting to no more than reform of remediable abuses, glorified social work. The favourite theme of such films is the rehabilitation of drunkards, whose miserable intoxication they envy. When society, now petrifying according to anonymous laws, is presented as if good-will were enough to remove its faults, it is defended even where it is honestly attacked. A kind of Popular Front of all right-thinking men is invoked. The practical spirit of the message, the tangible demonstration of how things can be improved, joins forces with the system in the fiction that a subject encompassing the whole of society, such as does not at present exist, can put everything right if only everyone will sit down together and make up their minds about the root of the trouble. It is very agreeable to be able thus to prove one's capacities. Message becomes escape: he who sets about cleaning up the house he lives in energetically enough, forgets the foundation it is built on. Escape in earnest, an image of revulsion from the whole, down to its formal constituents, could become a message without expressing one, indeed just because of its unbending asceticism towards practical proposals.

131

Wolf as grandmother. – The strongest argument in the arsenal of apologists for the cinema is the crudest, its mass-consumption. They declare it, this drastic medium of the culture industry, popular art. Their independence of the norms of the autonomous work is supposed to relieve films of aesthetic responsibility, such standards proving in their case reactionary, just as all intentions to ennoble films artistically do indeed look awry, falsely elevated, out of keeping with the form – imports for the connoisseur. The more pretensions a film has to art, the more bogus it becomes. The protagonists of the cinema can point to this and, moreover, as critics of an inwardness now become kitsch, can picture themselves, with their coarse outward kitsch, as the *avant-garde.* If one is once drawn onto this ground, such arguments, fortified with technical experience and professional fluency, become almost irresistible. The film is not a mass art, but merely manipulated to deceive the masses? But through the market the wishes of the public are ceaselessly asserted; collective production by itself guarantees the film's collective nature; only someone out of touch with reality could suspect its producers of being sly string-pullers; most lack talent, to be sure, but where the necessary gifts do come together, then, despite all the limitations of the system, success is possible. The mass taste with which the film complies is not that of the masses themselves, but foisted on them? But to talk of a different mass taste than that which the masses actually display is absurd, and everything that has ever been called folk art has always reflected domination. Only in the competent adaptation of production to given needs, not in orientation to an utopian audience, can the unformulated general will, by this logic, be given form. The film is full of lying stereotypes? But the stereotype is of the essence of folk art; fairy-tales are as familiar with the rescuing prince and the devil as the film with the hero and the villain, and even the barbaric cruelty that divides the world into good and evil the film has in common with the greatest fairy-tales, which have the stepmother dance to death in red-hot iron shoes.

All this could be answered only by reflecting on the basic concepts presupposed by the apologists. Bad films cannot be put down to incompetence; the most gifted are broken by the business set-up, and that the untalented flock to it is due to the affinity between lying and the swindler. The mindlessness is objective; improved personnel could not found a folk art. Its concept arose out of agrarian relationships or an economy of simple commodity production. Such relations and the characters expressing them are those of masters and servants, gainers and losers, but in an immediate, not wholly objectified form. Of course they are no less seamed with class distinctions than late industrial society, but their members are not yet encompassed by the total structure, which first reduces the individual subjects to mere moments, in order then to unite them, impotent and discrete, in the collective. That there is no longer a folk does not mean, however, as the Romantics propagated, that the masses are worse. Rather, it is precisely in the new, radically alienated form of society that the untruth of the old is first being revealed. The very traits which the culture industry claims as the heritage of folk art, become, through the industry itself, suspect. The film has a retroactive effect: its optimistic horror brings to light in the fairy-tale what always served injustice, and shows dimly in the reprimanded miscreants the faces of those whom integral society condemns, and to condemn whom has from the first been the dream of socialization. For this reason the demise of individualist art is no justification for one that deports itself as if its subject and its archaic reactions were natural, whereas its real subject is the syndicate, unconscious certainly, of a few big firms. Even if the masses have, as customers, an influence on the cinema, it remains as abstract as the box-office returns which have replaced discriminating applause: the mere choice between Yes and No to what is offered, an integral part of the disproportion between concentrated power and dispersed impotence. The fact, finally, that in the making of a film numerous experts, and also simple technicians, have a say, no more guarantees its humanity than decisions by qualified scientific advisory boards ensure that of bombs and poison gas.

The rarified talk about the film as an art doubtless befits hacks wishing to recommend themselves; but the conscious appeal to naivety, to the servants' obtuseness that has long since permeated the thoughts of the masters, is equally worthless. The film, which today attaches itself inescapably to men as if it were a part of them, is at the same time remotest of all from their human destiny, which might be realized from one day to the next; and apologetics for it are sustained by resistence to thinking this antinomy. That the people who make films are in no way schemers is no counter-argument. The objective spirit of manipulation asserts itself in experiential rules, appraisals of the situation, technical criteria, economically inevitable calculations, the whole specific weight of the industrial apparatus, without any special censorship being needed, and even if the masses were asked they would reflect back the ubiquity of the system. The producers no more function as subjects than do their workers and consumers, but merely as components in a self-regulating machinery. The Hegelian-sounding precept, however, that mass-art should reflect the real taste of the masses and not that of carping intellectuals, is usurpation. The film's opposition, as an all-encompassing ideology, to the objective interests of mankind, its interlacement with the status quo of profit-motivation, bad conscience and deceit can be conclusively demonstrated. No appeal to an actually existent state of consciousness could ever have the right to veto insight which transcended this state of consciousness by discerning its contradiction to itself and to objective conditions. It is possible that the German Fascist professor was right and that real folk-songs already lived on cultural values that had sunk down from the upper stratum. Not for nothing is all folk art fissured and, like the film, not 'organic'. But between the old injustice, in whose voice a lament is audible even where it glorifies itself, and alienation proclaiming itself togetherness, insidiously creating an appearance of human closeness with loud-speakers and advertising psychology, is a difference equal to that between the mother telling her child, to allay its terror of demons, the fairy-tale in which the good are rewarded and the bad punished, and the cinema product which forces the justice of each and every world order, in every country, stridently and threateningly into the audience's eyes and ears, in order to teach them anew, and more thoroughly, the old fear. The fairy-tale dreams, appealing so eagerly to the child in the man, are nothing other than regression organized by total enlightenment, and where they pat the onlooker most confidentially on the shoulder, they most thoroughly betray him. Immediacy, the popular community concocted by films, amounts to mediation without residue, reducing men and everything human so perfectly to things, that their contrast to things, indeed the spell of reification itself, becomes imperceptible. The film has succeeded in transforming subjects so indistinguishably into social functions, that those wholly encompassed, no longer aware of any conflict, enjoy their own dehumanization as something human, as the joy of warmth. The total interconnectedness of the culture industry, omitting nothing, is one with total social delusion. Which is why it makes such light work of counter-arguments.

132

Expensive reproduction. – Society is integral even before it undergoes totalitarian rule. Its organization also embraces those at war with it by co-ordinating their consciousness to its own. Even those intellectuals who have all the political arguments against bourgeois ideology at their fingertips, undergo a process of standardization which – despite crassly contrasting content, through readiness on their part to accommodate themselves – approximates them to the prevalent mentality to the extent that the substance of their viewpoint becomes increasingly incidental, dependent merely on their preferences or the assessment of their own chances. What they subjectively fancy radical, belongs objectively so entirely to the compartment in the pattern reserved for their like, that radicalism is debased to abstract prestige, legitimation for those who know what an intellectual nowadays has to be for and what against. The good things they opt for have long since been just as accepted, in numbers just as restricted, in their hierarchy of values just as fixed, as those of student fraternities. While they inveigh against official kitsch, their views, like dutiful children, are allowed to partake only of pre-selected nutrition, clichés against clichés. The habitations of such young bohemians resemble their intellectual household. On the walls the deceptively faithful colour reproductions of famous Van Goghs like the 'Sunflowers' or the 'Café at Arles', on the bookshelf the boiled-down socialism and psycho-analysis and a little sexology for libertines with inhibitions. Added to this the Random House edition of Proust – Scott Moncrieff's translation deserved a better fate, cut-price exclusivity even in its appearance, the compactly economical 'omnibus' shape, a mockery of the author whose every sentence put out of action some received opinion, while now as a prize-winning homosexual he fills a similar need for youth as do the books about forest animals and the North Pole expedition in the German home. Also the gramophone with the *Lincoln*-cantata of some stalwart spirit deeply concerned with railway stations, together with the duly marvelled-at Oklahoma folklore and a few noisy jazz records that make you feel at once collective, audacious and comfortable. Every opinion earns the approbation of friends, every argument is known by them beforehand. That all cultural products, even non-conformist ones, have been incorporated into the distribution-mechanisms of large-scale capital, that in the most developed country a product that does not bear the imprimatur of mass-production can scarcely reach a reader, viewer, listener at all, denies deviationary longings their subject matter in advance. Even Kafka is becoming a fixture in the sub-let studio. The intellectuals themselves are already so heavily committed to what is endorsed in their isolated sphere, that they no longer desire anything that does not carry the highbrow tag. Ambition aims solely at expertise in the accepted stock-in-trade, hitting on the correct slogan. The outsiderishness of the initiates is an illusion, they are merely biding their time. To see them as renegades is to assess them too high; they mask mediocre faces with horn-rimmed spectacles betokening 'brilliance', though with plain-glass lenses, solely in order to better themselves in their own eyes and in the general rat-race. They are already just like the rest. The subjective precondition of opposition, unco-ordinated judgement, is dying out, while its gesticulations continue to be performed as a group ritual. Stalin only needs to clear his throat and they throw Kafka and Van Gogh on the rubbish-heap.

Contribution to intellectual history. – At the back of my edition of *Zarathustra*, dated 1910, are publisher's notices. All are slanted at the tribe of Nietzsche-readers as conceived by Alfred Kröner in Leipzig, who must have been an expert on the subject. *'Ideal Goals of Life*, by Adalbert Svoboda. Svoboda has lit in his work a far-shining beacon of enlightenment, spreading bright illumination over all the problems of the questing human mind and bringing the true ideals of reason, art and culture clearly before our eyes. Grand in scale and splendidly produced, it is excitingly written from beginning to end, gripping, stimulating and instructive, and has a reinvigorating effect on all truly free minds, like a nerve-steeling bath or refreshing mountain air.' Signed: 'Humanity', and almost as recommendable as David Friedrich Strauss. *'On Zarathustra*, by Max Zerbst. There are two Nietzsches. One is the world-famous "philosopher-in-fashion", the dazzling poet and prodigious master of style, who is now on all lips and from whose works a few misunderstood slogans have become the dubious common-property of the "educated". The other Nietzsche is the unfathomable, inexhaustible thinker and psychologist, the great prober of man and valuer of life unequalled in power of spirit and might of mind, to whom the farthest future belongs. To bring this other Nietzsche closer to the percipient and serious among modern men is the intention of the two discourses contained in this little book.' Even so, I should prefer just the one. For the other is called: *'Philosopher and Noble Human-Being*. A Contribution to the Characterization of Friedrich Nietzsche by Meta von Salis-Marschlins. The book arrests our attention by its honest recording of all the emotions that Nietzsche's personality has aroused in a self-aware womanly soul.' Don't forget the whip, Zarathustra taught. Instead, we are offered: *'The Philosophy of Joy*, by Max Zerbst. Dr Max Zerbst takes Nietzsche as his starting-point, but strives to transcend a certain one-sidedness in Nietzsche. . . . Cool abstractions are not the author's affair, it is more a hymn, a philosophical hymn to joy that he intones.' Like a student spree. None of that one-sidedness. Rather a bee-line to the atheist's paradise: *'The Four Gospels*, in German, with an Introduction and Notes by Dr Heinrich Schmidt. In contrast to the corrupt form, worked over many times, in which the Gospel has been handed down to us in literature, this new edition goes back to the sources and may well be of high value not only for truly religious people, but also for those "Antichrists" who feel an urge to social action.' It is a difficult choice, but one can assume with some confidence that both élites are about as bearable as the synoptists: '*The Gospel of the New Man* (A Synthesis: Nietzsche and Christ), by Carl Martin. A wonderfully edifying book. Everything, in the science and art of the present, that has taken up the fight against the spectres of the past, all this has put out roots and blossom in this ripe and yet so youthful heart and mind. And the remarkable thing is that this "new", utterly new man draws the revivifying draught, for himself and for us, from an ancient spring of rejuvenescence: those other tidings of redemption whose purest notes are heard in the Sermon on the Mount. . . . In the form, too, the simplicity and majesty of those words!' Signed: Ethical Culture. The miracle passed from among us all but forty years ago, plus twenty more, of course, the genius in Nietzsche having rightly decided to break off prematurely its communication with the world. But all to no avail – inspirited, unbelieving priests and exponents of that organized ethical culture that was later to cause emigrant ladies in New York, who once enjoyed a comfortable existence, to finish up as waitresses, have done themselves proud on the estate of the man who once anxiously wondered whether anyone was listening when he sang to himself 'a secret barcarole'. Even at that time the hope of leaving behind messages in bottles on the flood of barbarism bursting on Europe was an amiable illusion: the desperate letters stuck in the mud of the spring of rejuvenescence and were worked up by a band of Noble Human-Beings and other riff-raff into highly artistic but inexpensive wall-adornments. Only since then has progress in communications really got into its stride. Who, in the end, is to take it amiss if even the freest of free spirits no longer write for an imaginary posterity, more trusting, if possible, than even their contemporaries, but only for the dead God?

134

Juvenal's error.[1] – Difficult to write satire. Not only because our situation, which needs it more than any ever did, makes a mockery

1. Allusion to Juvenal's remark *difficile est satyras non scribere*: it is difficult not to write satire.

of mockery. The medium of irony has itself come into contradiction with truth. Irony convicts its object by presenting it as what it purports to be; and without passing judgement, as if leaving a blank for the observing subject, measures it against its being-in-itself. It shows up the negative by confronting the positive with its own claim to positivity. It cancels itself out the moment it adds a word of interpretation. In this it presupposes the idea of the self-evident, originally of social resonance. Only when a compelling consensus of subjects is assumed, is subjective reflection, the performance of the conceptual act, superfluous. He who has laughter on his side has no need of proof. Historically, therefore, satire has for thousands of years, up to Voltaire's age, preferred to side with the stronger party which could be relied on, with authority. Usually it acted on behalf of older strata threatened by more recent stages of enlightenment, which sought to support their traditionalism with enlightened means: its inexhaustible theme was the decay of morals. For this reason what was once a deft rapier appears to later generations as a decidedly cumbersome cudgel. This double-tongued spiritualization of appearances is always intended to show the satirist as amusing, on the crest of progress; the yardstick applied, however, is that of whatever is endangered by progress, while the latter is nevertheless so far presupposed as the prevalent ideology that the phenomenon pronounced degenerate is condemned without being done the justice of rational debate. Aristophanean comedy, in which obscenity is supposed to expose loose living, counted, as a modernistic *laudatio temporis acti*, on the mob it slandered. With the triumph of the bourgeois class in the Christian era the function of irony then slackened. It early defected to the oppressed, especially those who in reality were no longer so. Certainly, as prisoner of its own form, it never entirely divested itself of its authoritarian inheritance, its unrebellious malice. Only with the bourgeois decline was it sublimated into an appeal to ideas of humanity which no longer tolerated any reconciliation with the established order and its consciousness. But even these ideas included their own self-evidence: no doubt concerning objective, immediate obviousness was entertained; no witticism of Karl Kraus wavers over the decision who is decent and who a scoundrel, what is intelligence and what stupidity, what is language and what journalism. To this presence of mind his formulations owe their force. Just as, in their instantaneous grasp of the matter in hand, no question holds them up, so they admit no question. The more emphatically, however, Kraus's prose posits its humanity as invariant, the more backward-looking it becomes. It condemns corruption and decadence, the *literati* and the Futurists, without having any other advantage over the zealots of an intellectual state of nature than a perception of its worthlessness. That in the end his intransigence towards Hitler showed itself pliable towards Schuschnigg, attests not to want of courage but to the antinomy of satire. It needs something to hold on to, and the self-styled malcontent had to bow to its positivity. Even the denunciation of the hack journalist contains, besides its truth, its critical element, something of the common sense which cannot bear the inflated windbag. The hatred for those who would seem more than they are, nailed them down to their real nature as an undisputed fact. The infallible eye for anything trumped-up, for unsubstantiated but commercially-angled intellectual pretensions, unmasks those who failed to measure up to their own higher standard. This higher standard is power and success, and manifests itself, in their bungled attempt to reach it, as itself a lie. But equally these impostors have always incarnated utopia: even false jewellery gleams with a helpless childhood dream, and this too is damned, called before the forum of success, because it failed. All satire is blind to the forces liberated by decay. Which is why total decay has absorbed the forces of satire. The scorn of the leaders of the Third Reich for emigrants and liberal statesmen, a scorn whose power was now no more than that of mere biceps, was the last. The impossibility of satire today should not be blamed, as sentimentality is apt to do, on the relativism of values, the absence of binding norms. Rather, agreement itself, the formal *a priori* of irony, has given way to universal agreement of content. As such it presents the only fitting target for irony and at the same time pulls the ground from under its feet. Irony's medium, the difference between ideology and reality, has disappeared. The former resigns itself to confirmation of reality by its mere duplication. Irony used to say: such it claims to be, but such it is; today, however, the world, even in its most radical lie, falls back on the argument that things are like this, a simple finding which coincides, for it, with the good. There is not a crevice in the cliff of the established order into which the ironist might hook a fingernail. Crashing down, he is pursued by the mocking laughter of the insidious object that disempowered him. The gesture of the unthinking That's-how-it-is is the exact means by which the world dispatches each of its victims, and the transcendental agreement inherent in irony becomes ridiculous in face of the real unanimity of those it ought to attack. Pitted against the deadly seriousness of total society, which has absorbed the opposing voice, the impotent objection earlier quashed by irony, there is now only the deadly seriousness of comprehended truth.

135

Sacrificial lamb. – Dictating is not only more comfortable, more conducive to concentration, it has an additional substantive benefit. Dictation makes it possible for the writer, in the earliest phases of production, to manoeuvre himself into the position of critic. What he sets down is tentative, provisional, mere material for revision, yet appears to him, once transcribed, as something estranged and in some measure objective. He need have no fear of committing something inadequate to paper, for he is not the one who has to write it: he outwits responsibility in its interests. The risk of formulation takes the innocuous form first of the casually delivered memorandum and then of work on something already existing, so that he no longer properly perceives his own audacity. In face of the difficulty, now grown to desperate proportions, of every theoretical utterance, such tricks become a blessing. They are technical aids to the dialectical procedure which makes statements in order to withdraw them and yet to hold them fast. But thanks are due to the person taking down the dictation, if at the right moment he pulls up the writer by contradiction, irony, nervosity, impatience and disrespect. He incurs wrath, so diverting it from the store of bad conscience with which otherwise the writer would mistrust his own work and therefore dig in his heels all the more defiantly over his supposedly sacred text. The emotion that turns ungratefully on his troublesome helper, benignly purifies his relation to his subject.

136

Exhibitionist. – Artists do not sublimate. That they neither satisfy nor repress their desires, but transform them into socially desirable

212

achievements, their works, is a psycho-analytical illusion; incidentally, legitimate works of art are today without exception socially undesired. Rather, artists display violent instincts, free-floating and yet colliding with reality, marked by neurosis. Even the philistine's dream of the actor or violinist as the synthesis of a bundle of nerves and a tugger of heart-strings, has more truth than the no less philistine economic theory of instincts according to which the favourite children of renunciation get rid of the stuff in symphonies and novels. Their lot is rather a hysterically excessive lack of inhibition over every conceivable fear; narcissism taken to its paranoiac limit. To anything sublimated they oppose idiosyncrasies. They are implacable towards aesthetes, indifferent to a carefully-tended environment, and in tastefully-conducted lives they recognize diminished reactions against pressures to diminution as surely as do the psychologists, by whom they are themselves misunderstood. From Mozart's letters to his little Augsburg cousin to the jibes of the embittered private tutor, they have been attracted by the coarse, the inane, the indecent. They do not fit into Freudian theory because it lacks an adequate concept of expression, despite all its insight into the workings of symbolism in dream and neuroses. That an instinctual impulse expressed uncensored cannot be called repressed even though it no longer wishes to reach the goal it cannot find, is no doubt obvious. On the other hand, the analytic distinction between motor – 'real' – and hallucinatory satisfaction is an extension of that between satisfaction and undisguised expression. But expression is not hallucination. It is appearance, measured by the reality principle that it wishes to circumvent. Never, however, does subjective material attempt through appearance, as it does through the symptom, to substitute itself delusively for reality. Expression negates reality by holding up to it what is unlike it, but it never denies reality; it looks straight in the eye the conflict that results blindly in the symptom. What expression has in common with repression is that its movement is blocked by reality. That movement, and the whole complex of experience of which it is a part, is denied direct communication with its object. As expression it achieves unfalsified manifestation of itself and so of the resistance to it, in sensuous imitation. It is so strong that it suffers modification to a mere image, the price of survival, without mutilation on its outward path. In place of the goal, and of subjective, censorial 'elaboration', it sets an objective, polemical self-revelation. This distinguishes it from sublimation: each successful expression of the subject, one might say, is a small victory over the play of forces in its own psychology. The pathos of art is bound up with the fact that precisely by withdrawing into imagination it renders the superior power of reality its due, and yet does not resign itself to adaptation, does not prolong external violence in internal deformation. Those who accomplish this, have without exception to pay dearly for it as individuals, left helplessly behind by their expression, which has outstripped their psychology. Thereby, however, they no less than their products instil doubts as to the ranking of art-works as cultural achievements by definition. No work of art, within the organization of society, can escape its involvement in culture, but there is none, if it is more than mere handicraft, which does not make culture a dismissive gesture: that of having become a work of art. Art is as inimical to 'art' as are artists. In renouncing the goal of instinct they remain faithful to it, and unmask the socially desirable activity naively glorified by Freud as sublimation – which probably does not exist.

137

Small sorrows, great songs.[1] – Contemporary mass-culture is historically necessary not merely as a result of the encompassment of life in its totality by monster enterprises, but as a consequence of what seems most utterly opposed to the standardization of consciousness predominant today, aesthetic subjectivism. True, the more artists have journeyed into the interior, the more they have learned to forgo the infantile fun of imitating external reality. But at the same time, by dint of reflecting on the psyche, they have found out more and more how to control themselves. The progress in technique that brought them ever greater freedom and independence of anything heterogeneous, has resulted in a kind of reification, technification of the inward as such. The more masterfully the artist expresses himself, the less he has to 'be' what he expresses, and the more what he expresses, indeed the content of subjectivity itself, becomes a mere function of the production process. Nietzsche

1. Inversion of the lines by Heine: *Aus meinem grossen Schmerzen / mach' ich die kleinen Lieder* (From my great sorrows, I make small songs), in his *Lyrisches Intermezzo*, XXXVI.

had an inkling of this when he taxed Wagner, that tamer of expression, with hypocrisy, without perceiving that this was not a
matter of psychology but of a historical tendency. The transformation of expressive content from an undirected impulse into
material for manipulation makes it palpable, exhibitable, saleable.
The lyrical subjectivism of Heine, for example, does not stand in
simple contradiction to his commercial traits; the saleable is itself
subjectivity administrated by subjectivity. The virtuoso use of the
'scale' characteristic of nineteenth-century performers is transformed by an internal impulsion, without any need for betrayal,
into journalism, spectacle, calculation. The law of motion of art,
which amounts to the control and therefore the objectification of
the subject by itself, means its downfall: the hostility to art of film,
which passes in administrative review all materials and emotions in
order to sell them most effectively to the public, the second stage of
externality, has its source in art, in the growing domination over
inner nature. The much-lauded play-acting of modern artists, their
exhibitionism, is the gesture whereby they put themselves as goods
on the market.

138

Who is who. – The artist's or scholar's flattering conviction of his
own naivety and purity is prolonged in his propensity to explain
difficulties by the devious interests, the practical, calculating mentality of those who contract his services. But just as every construction that acquits oneself and convicts the world, all insistence
on one's own qualifications, tends precisely to acquit the world in
oneself, so the same holds good for the antithesis of pure intentions
and cunning. Premeditating, guided by a thousand political and
tactical considerations, cautious and suspicious – just such is the
attitude adopted today by the intellectual outsider who knows
what to expect. The insiders, however, whose realm has long since
coalesced across party frontiers into 'living-space', no longer need
the calculation ascribed to them. They are so dependably committed
to the rules of reason's game, their interests have so unquestionably
sedimented in their thinking, that they have again become ingenuous. In seeking out their dark designs, one's judgement is indeed
metaphysically true, in that they are akin to the sombre course of

the world, but psychologically false: one succumbs to the objective increase of persecution-mania. They who, through their function, commit base and treacherous acts, who sell themselves and their friends to power, need no cunning or *arrière-pensée*, no plans elaborated by the ego, rather they need only give way to their own reactions, unthinkingly satisfy the demands of the moment, to perform effortlessly what others could achieve only by unfathomable scheming. They inspire trust just by proclaiming it. They see their own advantage, live from hand to mouth and commend themselves as both unegoistic and subscribers to a state of things which can be relied on to let them go short of nothing. Because all pursue without conflict solely their own particular interests, these appear in turn as universal and, in this way, disinterested. Their gestures are candid, spontaneous, disarming. They are nice and their opponents unpleasant. Since they no longer have the independence to perform an act in opposition to their interests, they rely on the goodwill of others, and themselves radiate it. Abstract interest, being wholly mediated, creates a second immediacy, while the man not yet wholly encompassed compromises himself as unnatural. If he is not to come to grief he must ceremoniously outdo the world in worldliness and is easily convicted of his maladroit excess. Suspicion, power-greed, lack of comradeship, deceit, vanity and inconsistency are a compelling reproach to him. Social witchcraft inescapably turns him who does not play the game into a self-seeker, and he who, lacking a self, lives by the principle of reality, is called selfless.

139

Addressee unknown. – Cultivated philistines are in the habit of requiring that a work of art 'give' them something. They no longer take umbrage at works that are radical, but fall back on the shamelessly modest assertion that they do not understand. This eliminates even opposition, their last negative relationship to truth, and the offending object is smilingly catalogued among its kind, consumer commodities that can be chosen or refused without even having to take responsibility for doing so. One is just too stupid, too old-fashioned, one simply can't keep up, and the more one belittles oneself the more one can be sure of swelling the mighty unison of the *vox inhumana populi,* the judging power of the petrified *Zeitgeist.* Incomprehensibility, that benefits no-one, from being an inflammatory crime becomes pitiable folly. Together with the barb one deflects the temptation. That one must be given something, apparently the postulate of substantiality and fullness, cuts both off and impoverishes giving. In this, however, human relationships are like aesthetic. The reproach that someone gives one nothing is pitiful. If the relation has grown sterile, it should be broken off. But he who holds it fast and yet complains, is always devoid of the organ of receiving: fantasy. Both must give something, happiness, as precisely what is not exchangeable, not open to complaint, but such giving is inseparable from taking. All is over if what one finds for the other no longer reaches him. There is no love that is not an echo. In myths the warrant of grace was the acceptance of sacrifice; it is this acceptance that love, the re-enactment of sacrifice, beseeches if it is not to feel under a curse. The decay of giving is today matched by a hardness towards receiving. But this comes to the same thing as the denial of real happiness, that alone permits men to cling to their kind of happiness. The rampart would only be breached if they were to accept from others what, with a wry face, they refuse themselves. But this they find difficult because of the effort demanded by taking. Besotted with technique, they transfer their hatred for the superfluous exertion of their existence, to the expense of energy that pleasure, as a moment of their being, needs even in all its sublimations. Though facilitated in countless ways, their practice remains absurd toil; yet to squander strength on their lives' secret, happiness, is something they cannot endure. Here the watchword is 'relax and take it easy', a formula borrowed from the language of the nursing-home, not of exuberance. Happiness is obsolete: uneconomic. For its idea, sexual union, is the opposite of slackness, a blessed straining, just as that of all subjected labour is cursed.

140

Consecutio temporum.[1] – When my first composition teacher, trying to knock the atonal nonsense out of me, found his tales of erotic scandals about the new composers proving ineffective, he switched

1. 'Sequence of tenses.'

his attack to what he suspected as my weak spot, by showing himself up-to-date. The ultra-modern, his argument ran, was no longer modern, the stimulations I sought were already numb, the expressive figures that excited me belonged to an outdated sentimentality, and the new youth had, as he liked to put it, more red blood-corpuscles. His own pieces, in which oriental themes were regularly extended by the chromatic scale, betrayed the same ultra-subtle deliberations as the manoeuvres of a conservatory director with a bad conscience. But I was soon to discover that the fashion he opposed to my modernity did actually resemble, in the primeval habitat of the great *salons,* what he had hatched up in the provinces. Neo-classicism, that form of reaction which not only fails to acknowledge itself as such but even passes off its reactionary moment as ahead of its time, was the advance-guard of a massive tendency which under Fascism and mass-culture quickly learned to be rid of tender concern for the endlessly tiresome sensibilities of artists, and to combine the spirit of Courths-Mahler[1] with that of technical progress. The modern has really become unmodern. Modernity is a qualitative, not a chronological, category. Just as it cannot be reduced to abstract form, with equal necessity it must turn its back on conventional surface coherence, the appearance of harmony, the order corroborated merely by replication. The stalwarts of the Fascist fighting leagues, thundering fulsomely against Futurism, saw more clearly in their rage than did the Moscow censors who placed Cubism on the Index because, in its private impropriety, it failed to measure up to the spirit of the collective age, or the brazen theatre critics who find a play by Strindberg or Wedekind *passé* but a piece of underground reportage up-to-date. All the same, their blasé philistinism utters an appalling truth: that the procession of total society which would like to force its organization on all expression, is in fact leaving behind the power which opposes what Lindbergh's wife called the wave of the future, that is, the critical construction of being. This is not merely outlawed by a corrupt public opinion, but the prevailing absurdity affects its very substance. The might of what is, constraining the mind to follow its example, is so overwhelming that even the unassimilated expression of protest assumes in face of it a home-spun, aimless, inexperienced quality reminiscent of the provincialism that once so

1. Hedwig Courths-Maler (1867–1950): best-seller novelist of popular sentimental romances.

prophetically suspected modernity of backwardness. Matching the psychological regression of individuals who exist without a self, is a regression of the objective spirit, in which obtuseness, primitivism and the bargain-sale set up what historically has long since decayed as the newest historical power, and consign to the day before yesterday everything that does not zealously join the march of regression. This *quid pro quo* of progress and reaction makes orientation in contemporary art almost as difficult as in politics, and furthermore paralyses production itself, where anyone who clings to extreme intentions is made to feel like a backwoodsman, while the conformist no longer lingers bashfully in arbours, literary or horticultural,[1] but hurtles forward, rocket-powered, into the pluperfect.

141

La nuance | encor'.[2] – The demand that thinking and information dispense with nuances cannot be summarily dismissed as bowing to the prevalent obtuseness. Were linguistic nuance no longer perceptible, it would be itself implicated, not merely reception. Language is by its own objective substance social expression, even where it has abruptly severed itself from society as individual. Changes that it undergoes in communication involve the writer's uncommunicative material. Words and phrases spoilt by use do not reach the secluded workshop intact. And the historical damage cannot be repaired there. History does not merely touch on language, but takes place in it. What continues to be used in spite of usage smacks of simple-minded provincialism or cosy restoration. So thoroughly have all nuances been perverted and sold off as 'flavour' that even advanced literary subtleties recall debased words like 'gloaming', 'pensive', 'verdant', 'fragrant'. The measures against banality are becoming banal, arty-crafty, with an undertone of moping consolation from that womanly world whose soulfulness complete with lutes and traditional costume, was politically co-ordinated in Germany. In the cultivated superior trash with which

1. Allusion to *Die Gartenlaube*, an illustrated family magazine of patriotic-conservative tendency in the late nineteenth century.
2. *Car nous voulons la nuance encor', | Pas la couleur, rien que la nuance!* – lines from Verlaine's poem *Art Poétique*, a symbolist manifesto.

the intellectuals who survive there happily compete for the vacant posts of culture, what yesterday had a linguistically conscious air hostile to convention, reads today as olde-worlde prettifying. German culture seems faced with the alternative between a loathsome second *Biedermeier* or paper administrative philistinism. Yet this simplification, suggested not only by market interests but by cogent political motives and finally by the historical state of the language itself, does not so much overcome nuances as it tyrannically furthers their decay. It offers sacrifices to omnipotent society. But the latter, by virtue of its very omnipotence, is as incommensurable and alien to the subject of knowledge and expression as it ever was in the milder days when it spurned the language of common speech. The fact that human beings are absorbed by the totality without being humanly equal to it, makes institutionalized linguistic forms as vacuous as naively individualistic tone-values, and equally fruitless is the attempt to turn the tables on the former by admitting them to the literary medium: people incapable of reading a diagram posing as engineers. The collective language attractive to the writer who suspects his isolation of romanticism, is no less romantic: he usurps the voice of those for whom he cannot speak directly, as one of them, because his language, through reification, is as divorced from them as all are from each other; because the present form of the collective is in itself speechless. No collective entrusted today with expressing the subject, thereby becomes a subject. He who does not chime in with the official hymnic tone of festivals to liberation supervised by totalitarians, but seriously espouses the *aridité* recommended ambiguously enough by Roger Caillois, merely submits to an objective discipline as privation, without receiving anything concrete and general in exchange. The contradiction between the abstractness of the language that wants to do away with bourgeois subjectivism, and its emphatically concrete objects, does not reside in the incapacity of writers but in a historical antinomy. The subject wants to cede himself to the collective without being cancelled by it. Therefore his very forfeiture of the private becomes private, chimerical. His language, imitating single-handed the taut construction of society, fondly believes it has wakened cement to speech. As punishment, this unauthorized communal language commits incessant *faux pas*, matter-of-factness at the expense of matter and fact, not so very different from a bourgeois waxing eloquent. The conclusion to be drawn from the decay of nuance is not to cling obstinately to forms that have decayed, nor yet to extirpate them altogether, but rather to try to out-nuance them, to push them to the point where from subjective shading they switch to being a pure, specific definition of the object. The writer must combine the tightest control in ensuring that the word refers, without sidelong glances, to the matter alone, with the shedding of all phrases, the patient effort to detect what linguistically, in itself, carries meaning and what does not But those in fear of falling in spite of everything behind the *Zeitgeist*, of being cast on the refuse-heap of discarded subjectivity, should be reminded that *arriviste* timeliness and progressive content are no longer the same. In an order which liquidates the modern as backward, this backwardness, once condemned, can be invested with the truth over which the historical process obliviously rolls. Because no other truth can be expressed than that which is able to fill the subject, anachronism becomes the refuge of modernity.

142

By this does German song abide.[1] – Free verse was rejected by artists like George as a miscarried form, a hybrid between metre and prose. They are refuted by Goethe and by Hölderlin's late hymns. Their technical eye takes free verse at face value. They stop their ears to history by which free verse is stamped. Only in the period of their decay are free rhythms no more than prose periods printed one below the other, in elevated tone. Where free verse proves a form in its own right, it has emerged from the metrical strophe, transcending subjectivity. It turns the pathos of metre against its own claims, a strict negation of ultimate strictness, just as musical prose, emancipated from the symmetry of the eight-beat rhythm, owes its existence to the implacable principles of construction which matured in the articulation of tonal regularity. In free rhythms the ruins of the artistically rhymeless classical strophe grow eloquent. Jutting their alien contours into the newer languages, they are suited by their strangeness to express what is not exhausted by communication. But they yield, unrescuable, to the flood of the languages in which they once stood erect. Only brokenly, marooned in the

1. *Dem folgt deutscher Gesang*: last line of Hölderlin's poem *Patmos*.

realm of communication and distinguishable from it by no capricious convolutions, do they signify distance and stylization, as if incognito, and without privilege, until in poetry like Trakl's the waves of dream close over the helpless verses. Not without reason was the epoch of free rhythms that of the French Revolution, the solemn entrance of human dignity and equality. But does not the conscious practice of such verses resemble the law followed by language as a whole in its unconscious history? Is not all carefully-fashioned prose really a system of free rhythms, an attempt to make the magic charm of the absolute coincide with the negation of its appearance, an effort of the mind to save the metaphysical power of expression by means of its own secularization? Were this so, a ray of light would fall on the sisyphean burden that every prose-writer has shouldered, now that demythologization has led to the destruction of language itself. Linguistic quixotry has become obligatory, since the putting-together of each sentence contributes to the decision whether language as such, ambiguous since primeval times, will succumb to commercialism and the consecrated lie that is a part of it, or whether it will make itself a sacred text by diffidence towards the sacral element on which it lives. Prose isolates itself so ascetically from poetry for the sake of invoking song.

143

In nuce. – The task of art today is to bring chaos into order.

Artistic productivity is the capacity for being voluntarily involuntary.

Art is magic delivered from the lie of being truth.

Since works of art are sprung, for better or worse, from fetishes – are artists to be blamed if their attitude to their products is slightly fetishistic?

The art-form which has from earliest times laid the highest claims to spirituality, as representation of Ideas, drama, depends equally, by its innermost presuppositions, on an audience.

Just as, according to Benjamin, painting and sculpture translate the mute language of things into a higher but similar one, so it might be supposed that music rescues name as pure sound – but at the cost of severing it from things.

Perhaps the strict and pure concept of art is applicable only to music, while great poetry ,or great painting – precisely the greatest – necessarily brings with it an element of subject-matter transcending aesthetic confines, undissolved in the autonomy of form. The more profound and consequential an aesthetic theory, the more inappropriate it becomes to such works as the major novels of the nineteenth century. Hegel seized this advantage in his polemic against Kant.

The belief put about by aesthetic theorists that a work of art is to be understood as an object of immediate contemplation, purely on its own terms, is unsound. It is limited not merely by the cultural presuppositions of each work, its 'language', which only the initiate can follow. Even where there are no such difficulties, the work of art demands more than that one should merely abandon oneself to it. Anyone wishing to find the *Fledermaus* beautiful must know that it is the *Fledermaus*: his mother must have told him that it is not about the winged animal but a fancy-dress costume; he must remember having been told: tomorrow you can go to see the *Fledermaus*. To be within tradition used to mean: to experience the work of art as something sanctioned, valid: to participate through it in all the reactions of those who had seen it previously. Once this falls away, the work is exposed in its nakedness and fallibility. The plot, from a ritual, becomes idiocy, the music, from a canon of significant figures, flat and stale. It is really no longer so beautiful. From this mass-culture draws its right of adaptation. The weakness of all traditional culture outside its tradition provides the pretext for improving, and so barbarically mutilating it.

The comfort that flows from great works of art lies less in what they express than in the fact that they have manged to struggle out of existence. Hope is soonest found among the comfortless.

Kafka: the solipsist without ipseity.

Kafka, though an avid reader of Kierkegaard, is connected with existentialist philosophy only to the extent that one speaks of down-and-outs as 'annihilated existences'.

Surrealism breaks the *promesse du bonheur*. It sacrifices, to the appearance of happiness transmitted by any integral form, concern for its truth.

Magic Flute. – The ideology of cultural conservatism which sees enlightenment and art as simple antitheses is false, among other reasons, in overlooking the moment of enlightenment in the genesis of beauty. Enlightenment does not merely dissolve all the qualities that beauty adheres to, but posits the quality of beauty in the first place. The disinterested pleasure that according to Kant is aroused by works of art, can only be understood by virtue of historical antitheses still at work in each aesthetic object. The thing disinterestedly contemplated pleases because it once claimed the utmost interest and thus precluded contemplation. The latter is a triumph of enlightened self-discipline. Gold and precious stones, in the perception of which beauty and luxury still coexist undistinguished, were honoured as magical. The radiance they reflect was thought their own essence. Under their power falls whatever is touched by their light. This was early used in the mastering of nature. Jewels were seen as instruments for subjugating the course of the world by its own cunningly usurped power. The magic adhered to the illusion of omnipotence. This illusion was dispelled by mind's self-enlightenment, but the magic has survived as the power of radiant things over men, in whom they once instilled a dread that continues to hold their eyes spellbound, even after they have seen through its claim to domination. Contemplation, as a residue of fetishist worship, is at the same time a stage in overcoming it. As radiant things give up their magic claims, renounce the power with which the subject invested them and hoped with their help himself to wield, they become transformed into images of gentleness, promises of a happiness cured of domination over nature. This is the primeval history of luxury, that has migrated into the meaning of all art. In the magic of what reveals itself in absolute powerlessness, of beauty, at once perfection and nothingness, the illusion of omnipotence is mirrored negatively as hope. It has escaped every trial of strength. Total purposelessness gives the lie to the totality of purposefulness in the world of domination, and only by virtue of this negation, which consummates the established order by drawing the conclusion from its own principle of reason, has existing society up to now become aware of another that is possible. The bliss of contemplation consists in disenchanted charm. Radiance is the appeasement of myth.

145

Art-object. – Accumulated domestic monstrosities can shock the unwary by their relation to works of art. Even the hemispherical paper-weight with a fir-tree landscape submerged under glass and below it a greeting from Bad Wildungen has some resemblance to Stifter's green Fichtau,[1] even the polychrome garden dwarf to a little wight from Balzac or Dickens. This is the fault neither simply of the subjects nor of the abstract similarity of all aesthetic appearance. Rather the existence of trash expresses inanely and undisguisedly the fact that men have succeeded in reproducing from within themselves a piece of what otherwise imprisons them in toil, and in symbolically breaking the compulsion of adaptation by themselves creating what they feared; and an echo of the same triumph resounds in the mightiest works, though they seek to forgo it, imagining themselves pure self unrelated to any model. In both cases freedom from nature is celebrated, yet remains mythically entrapped. What men trembled before, they have placed at their own disposal. Great paintings and picture-postcards have in common that they have put primeval images at our fingertips. The illustration of *L'automne* in the schoolbook is a *déjà-vu*, the Eroica, like great philosophy, represents the idea as a total process, yet as if it were directly, sensuously present. In the end indignation over kitsch is anger at its shameless revelling in the joy of imitation, now placed under taboo, while the power of works of art still continues to be secretly nourished by imitation. What escapes the jurisdiction of existence and its purposes is not only a protesting better world but also a more stupid one incapable of self-assertion. This stupidity grows, the more autonomous art idolizes its isolated, allegedly innocent self-assertion instead of its real one, guilty and imperious. The subjective act, by presenting itself as the successful rescue of objective meaning, becomes untrue. Of this it is convicted

1. Fichtau is the idyllic valley that appears in Adalbert Stifter's tales *Die Narrenburg* and *Prokopus*.

by kitsch; the latter's lie does not even feign truth. It incurs hostility because it blurts out the secret of art and the affinity of culture to savagery. Every work of art has its irresoluble contradiction in the 'purposefulness without purpose' by which Kant defined the aesthetic; in the fact that it is an apotheosis of making, of the nature-ruling capacity that, as a second creation, postulates itself as absolute, purpose-free, existing in itself, whereas after all the act of making, indeed the very glorification of the artefact, is itself inseparable from the rational purposefulness from which art seeks to break away. The contradiction between what is and what is made, is the vital element of art and circumscribes its law of development, but it is also art's shame: by following, however indirectly, the existing pattern of material production and 'making' its objects, art as akin to production cannot escape the question 'what for?' which it aims to negate. The closer the mode of production of artefacts comes to material mass-production, the more naively it provokes that fatal question. Works of art, however, try to silence it. 'Perfection', as Nietzsche put it, 'must not have become',[1] that is, it should not appear made. Yet the more consequentially it distances itself, through perfection, from making, the more fragile its own made existence necessarily becomes: the endless pains to eradicate the traces of making, injure works of art and condemn them to be fragmentary. Art, following the decay of magic, has taken upon itself the transmission of images to posterity. But in this task it employs the same principle that destroyed images: the stem of its Greek name is the same as that of technique. Its paradoxical entanglement in the process of civilization brings it into conflict with its own idea. The archetypes of our time, synthetically concocted by film and hit-song for the bleak contemplation of the late industrial era, do not merely liquidate art but, by their blatant feeblemindedness, blast into daylight the delusion that was always immured in the oldest works of art and which still gives the maturest their power. Luridly the horror of the ending lights up the deception of the origin. – It is the fortune and limitation of French art never to have entirely eradicated the pride in making little pictures, just as it differs most obviously from German art in not acknowledging the concept of kitsch. In countless significant manifestations it casts a conciliatory glance at what pleases because it was skilfully

1. Nietzsche, *Werke*, Munich 1954, Vol. I, p. 545 (*Human All-Too-Human*, Edinburgh–London 1910, p. 153).

made: sublime artistry keep a hold on sensuous life by a moment of harmless pleasure in the *bien fait*. While the absolute claim of perfection without becoming, the dialectic of truth and appearance, is thus renounced, the untruth of those dubbed by Haydn the Grand Moguls is also avoided; they, determined to have no truck with the winsome vignette or figurine, succumb to fetishism by driving out all fetishes. Taste is the ability to keep in balance the contradiction in art between the made and the apparent not-having-become; true works of art, however, never at one with taste, are those which push this contradiction to the extreme, and realize themselves in their resultant downfall.

146

Toy shop. – Hebbel, in a surprising entry in his diary, asks what takes away 'life's magic in later years'. 'It is because in all the brightly-coloured contorted marionettes, we see the revolving cylinder that sets them in motion, and because for this very reason the captivating variety of life is reduced to wooden monotony. A child seeing the tightrope-walkers singing, the pipers playing, the girls fetching water, the coachmen driving, thinks all this is happening for the joy of doing so; he can't imagine that these people also have to eat and drink, go to bed and get up again. We however, know what is at stake.' Namely, earning a living, which commandeers all those activities as mere means, reduces them to interchangeable, abstract labour-time. The quality of things ceases to be their essence and becomes the accidental appearance of their value. The 'equivalent form'[1] mars all perceptions: what is no longer irradiated by the light of its own self-determination as 'joy in doing', pales to the eye. Our organs grasp nothing sensuous in isolation, but notice whether a colour, a sound, a movement is there for its own sake or for something else; wearied by a false variety, they steep all in grey, disappointed by the deceptive claim of qualities still to be there at all, while they conform to the purposes of appropriation, indeed largely owe their existence to it alone. Disenchantment with the contemplated world is the sensorium's reaction to its objective role as a 'commodity world'. Only when purified of appropriation would things be colourful and useful at

1. See Marx, *Capital*, Vol. I, Moscow 1961, p. 55ff.

once: under universal compulsion the two cannot be reconciled. Children, however, are not so much, as Hebbel thought, subject to illusions of 'captivating variety', as still aware, in their spontaneous perception, of the contradiction between phenomenon and fungibility that the resigned adult no longer sees, and they shun it. Play is their defence. The unerring child is struck by the 'peculiarity of the equivalent form': 'use-value becomes the form of manifestation, the phenomenal form of its opposite, value.'[1]

In his purposeless activity the child, by a subterfuge, sides with use-value against exchange value. Just because he deprives the things with which he plays of their mediated usefulness, he seeks to rescue in them what is benign towards men and not what subserves the exchange relation that equally deforms men and things. The little trucks travel nowhere and the tiny barrels on them are empty; yet they remain true to their destiny by not performing, not participating in the process of abstraction that levels down that destiny, but instead abide as allegories of what they are specifically for. Scattered, it is true, but not ensnared, they wait to see whether society will finally remove the social stigma on them; whether the vital process between men and things, praxis, will cease to be practical. The unreality of games gives notice that reality is not yet real. Unconsciously they rehearse the right life. The relation of children to animals depends entirely on the fact that Utopia goes disguised in the creatures whom Marx even begrudged the surplus value they contribute as workers. In existing without any purpose recognizable to men, animals hold out, as if for expression, their own names, utterly impossible to exchange. This make them so beloved of children, their contemplation so blissful. I am a rhinoceros, signifies the shape of the rhinoceros. Fairy-tales and operettas know such images, and the ridiculous question of the woman: how do we know that Orion is really called Orion, rises to the stars.

147

Novissimum organum.[2] – It has long been demonstrated that wage-labour formed the masses of the modern epoch, indeed created the worker himself. As a general principle the individual is not merely

1. Marx, *Capital*, Vol. I, p. 56.
2. Superlatization of the title of Bacon's treatise *Novum Organum*.

the biological basis, but the reflection of the social process; his consciousness of himself as something in-itself is the illusion needed to raise his level of performance, whereas in fact the individuated function in the modern economy as mere agents of the law of value. The inner constitution of the individual, not merely his social role, could be deduced from this. Decisive here, in the present phase, is the category of the organic composition of capital. By this the theory of accumulation meant the 'growth in the mass of the means of production, as compared with the mass of the labour-power that vivifies them'.[1] If the integration of society, particularly in totalitarian states, designates subjects more and more exclusively as partial moments in the network of material production, then the 'alteration of the technical composition of capital' is prolonged within those encompassed, and indeed constituted, by the technological demands of the production process. The organic composition of man is growing. That which determines subjects as means of production and not as living purposes, increases with the proportion of machines to variable capital. The pat phrase about the 'mechanization' of man is deceptive because it thinks of him as something static which, through an 'influence' from outside, an adaptation to conditions of production external to him, suffers certain deformations. But there is no substratum beneath such 'deformations', no ontic interior on which social mechanisms merely act externally: the deformation is not a sickness in men but in the society which begets its children with the 'hereditary taint' that biologism projects on to nature. Only when the process that begins with the metamorphosis of labour-power into a commodity has permeated men through and through and objectified each of their impulses as formally commensurable variations of the exchange relationship, is it possible for life to reproduce itself under the prevailing relations of production. Its consummate organization demands the coordination of people that are dead. The will to live finds itself dependent on the denial of the will to live: self-preservation annuls all life in subjectivity. Compared to this, all the achievements of adaptation, all the acts of conformity described by social psychology and cultural anthropology, are mere epiphenomena. The organic composition of man refers by no means only to his specialized technical faculties, but – and this the usual cultural criticism will not at any price admit – equally to their opposite, the

1. Marx, *Capital*, Vol. I, p. 622.

moments of naturalness which once themselves sprung from the social dialectic and are now succumbing to it. Even what differs from technology in man is now being incorporated into it as a kind of lubrication. Psychological differentiation, originally the outcome both of the division of labour that dissects man according to sectors of the production process and of freedom, is finally itself entering the service of production. 'The specialized "virtuoso" ', one dialectician wrote thirty years ago, 'the vendor of his objectified and reified faculties . . . lapses into a contemplative attitude towards the workings of his own objectified and reified faculties. This phenomenon can be seen at its most grotesque in journalism. Here it is subjectivity itself, knowledge, temperament and powers of expression that are reduced to an abstract mechanism, functioning autonomously and divorced both from the personality of their "owner" and from the material and concrete nature of the subject-matter in hand. The journalist's "lack of convictions", the prostitution of his experiences and beliefs is comprehensible only as the apogee of capitalist reification.'[1] What was here noted among the 'degenerate manifestations' of the bourgeoisie, which it still itself denounced, has since emerged as the social norm, as the character of irreproachable existence under late industrialism. It has long ceased to be a matter of the mere sale of the living. Under *a priori* saleability the living has made itself, as something living, a thing, equipment. The ego consciously takes the whole man into its service as a piece of apparatus. In this re-organization the ego as business-manager delegates so much of itself to the ego as business-mechanism, that it becomes quite abstract, a mere reference-point: self-preservation forfeits its self. Character traits, from genuine kindness to the hysterical fit of rage, become capable of manipulation, until they coincide exactly with the demands of a given situation. With their mobilization they change. All that is left are the light, rigid, empty husks of emotions, matter transportable at will, devoid of anything personal. They are no longer the subject; rather, the subject responds to them as to his internal object. In their unbounded docility towards the ego they are at the same time estranged from it: being wholly passive they nourish it no longer. This is the social pathogenesis of schizophrenia. The severance of character traits both from their instinctual basis and from the self, which commands them where it formerly merely held them together, causes

1. Georg Lukács, *History and Class-Consciousness*, London 1971, p. 100.

man to pay for his increasing inner organization with increasing disintegration. The consummation of the division of labour within the individual, his radical objectification, leads to his morbid scission. Hence the 'psychotic character', the anthropological pre-condition of all totalitarian mass-movements. Precisely this transition from firm characteristics to push-button behaviour-patterns – though apparently enlivening – is an expression of the rising organic composition of man. Quick reactions, unballasted by a mediating constitution, do not restore spontaneity, but establish the person as a measuring instrument deployed and calibrated by a central authority. The more immediate its response, the more deeply in reality mediation has advanced: in the prompt, unresistant reflexes the subject is entirely extinguished. So too, biological reflexes, the models of the present social ones, are – when measured against subjectivity – objectified, alien: not without reason are they often called 'mechanical'. The closer organisms are to death, the more they regress to such twitching. Accordingly the destructive tendencies of the masses that explode in both varieties of totalitarian state are not so much death-wishes as manifestations of what they have already become. They murder so that whatever to them seems living, shall resemble themselves.

148

Knackery. – Metaphysical categories are not merely an ideology concealing the social system; at the same time they express its nature, the truth about it, and in their changes are precipitated those in its most central experiences. Thus death comes within the scope of history, and the latter in turn can only be understood through it. Its dignity used to resemble that of the individual. His autonomy, economic in origin, culminated in the conception of his absoluteness once the theological hope of immortality, that had empirically relativized it, began to pale. To this corresponded the emphatic image of death in which the individual, the basis of all bourgeois behaviour and thinking, was entirely wiped out. Death was the absolute price of absolute value. Now it shares the ruin of the socially defunct individual. Where it is draped in the old dignity, it exudes the lie that was always latent in it: that of naming the impenetrable, predicating the subjectless, incorporating the unassimilable. In contemporary consciousness, however, the truth and untruth of its dignity are done with, not because of otherwordly hopes, but in face of the hopeless debility of the here-and-now. 'The modern world', the radical catholic Charles Péguy noted as early as 1907, 'has succeeded in debasing what is perhaps the most difficult thing in the world to debase, because this thing has in it, as if in its very texture, a particular kind of dignity, a singular incapacity to be debased: it debases death.'[1] If the individual whom death annihilates is himself nothing, bereft of self-command and of his own being, then the annihilating power becomes also nothing, as if in a facetious application of Heidegger's formula of the nothing that nihilates. The radical replaceability of the individual makes his death practically – and in utter contempt – revocable, as it was once conceived to be with paradoxical pathos by Christianity. But as a 'negligible quantity' death is entirely assimilated. For every person, with all his functions, society has a stand-in ready, to whom the former is in any case no more than an intrusive occupier of his workplace, a candidate for death. So the experience of death is turned into that of the exchange of functionaries, and anything in the natural relationship to death that is not wholly absorbed into the social one is turned over to hygiene. In being seen as no more than the exit of a living creature from the social combine, death has been finally domesticated: dying merely confirms the absolute irrelevance of the natural organism in face of the social absolute. If the culture industry anywhere bears witness to the changes in the organic composition of society, it is in the scarcely veiled admission of this state of affairs. Under its lens death begins to be comic. Certainly, the laughter that greets it in a certain genre of production is ambiguous. It still announces fear of the amorphous thing under the net that society has woven over the whole of nature. But the webbing is so thick and dense that remembrance of nature's uncovered state seems childish, sentimental. After the breakdown of the detective story in the books of Edgar Wallace, which seemed by their less rational construction, their unsolved riddles and their crude exaggeration to ridicule their readers, and yet in so doing magnificently anticipated the collective imago of total terror, the type of the murder comedy has come into being. While continuing to claim to make fun of a bogus awe, it demolishes the images of death. It presents the corpse as what it has become, a stage prop. It still looks

1. *Men and Saints*, New York 1944, p. 98.

human and is yet a thing, as in the film 'A Slight Case of Murder', where corpses are continuously transported to and fro, allegories of what they already are. Comedy savours to the full the false abolition of death that Kafka had long before described in panic in the story of Gracchus the hunter: for the same reason, no doubt, music too is starting to become comic. What the National Socialists perpetrated against millions of people, the parading and patterning of the living like dead matter, then the mass-production and cost-cutting of death, threw its prefiguring shadow on those who felt moved to chortle over corpses. What is decisive is the absorption of biological destruction by conscious social will. Only a humanity to whom death has become as indifferent as its members, that has itself died, can inflict it administratively on innumerable people. Rilke's prayer for 'one's own death' is a piteous attempt to conceal the fact that nowadays people merely snuff out.

149

Don't exaggerate. – Criticism of tendencies in modern society is automatically countered, before it is fully uttered, by the argument that things have always been like this. Excitement – so promptly resisted – merely shows want of insight into the invariability of history, an unreasonableness proudly diagnosed by all as hysteria. The accuser is further informed that the motive of his attack is self-aggrandizement, a desire for special privileges, whereas the grounds for his indignation are common knowledge, trivial, so that no-one can be expected to waste his interest on them. The obviousness of disaster becomes an asset to its apologists – what everyone knows no-one need say – and under cover of silence is allowed to proceed unopposed. Assent is given to what has been drummed into people's heads by philosophy of every hue: that whatever has the persistent momentum of existence on its side is thereby proved right. One need only be discontented to be at once suspect as a world reformer. Connivance makes use of the trick of attributing to its opponent a reactionary and untenable theory of decline – for is not horror indeed perennial? – in order by the alleged error in his thinking to discredit his concrete insight into the negative, and to blacken him who remonstrates against darkness as an obfuscator. But even if things have always been so, although

neither Timur nor Genghis Khan nor the English colonial administration in India systematically burst the lungs of millions of people
with gas, the eternity of horror nevertheless manifests itself in the
fact that each of its new forms outdoes the old. What is constant is
not an invariable quantity of suffering, but its progress towards
hell: that is the meaning of the thesis of the intensification of antagonisms. Any other would be innocuous and would give way to
conciliatory phrases, abandoning the qualitative leap. He who
registers the death-camps as a technical mishap in civilization's
triumphal procession, the martyrdom of the Jews as world-his-
torically irrelevant, not only falls short of the dialectical vision but
reverses the meaning of his own politics: to hold ultimate calamity
in check. Not only in the development of forces of production but
also in the increasing pressure of domination does quantity change
into quality. If the Jews as a group are eradicated while society
continues to reproduce the life of the workers, then the argument
that the former were bourgeois and their fate unimportant for the
great dynamic of history, becomes economic sophistry, even in so
far as mass-murder is indeed explicable by the falling rate of profit.
Horror consists in its always remaining the same – the persistence
of 'pre-history' – but is realized as constantly different, unforeseen,
exceeding all expectation, the faithful shadow of developing productive forces. The same duality defines violence as Marx demonstrated in material production: 'There are characteristics which all
stages of production have in common, and which are established as
general ones by the mind; but the so-called *general pre-conditions* of
all production are nothing more than . . . abstract moments with
which no real historical stage of production can be grasped.'[1] In
other words, to abstract out historically unchanged elements is not
to observe neutral scientific objectivity, but to spread, even when
correct, a smoke-screen behind which whatever is tangible and
therefore assailable is lost to sight. Precisely this the apologists will
not admit. On one hand they rave about the *dernière nouveauté* and
on the other they deny the infernal machine that is history. Ausch-
witz cannot be brought into analogy with the destruction of the
Greek city-states as a mere gradual increase in horror, before which
one can preserve tranquillity of mind. Certainly, the unprecedented
torture and humiliation of those abducted in cattle-trucks does shed
a deathly-livid light on the most distant past, in whose mindless,

1. Marx, *Grundrisse*, Harmondsworth 1973, p. 88.

planless violence the scientifically confected was already teleologically latent. The identity lies in the non-identity, in what, not having yet come to pass, denounces what has. The statement that things are always the same is false in its immediateness, and true only when introduced into the dynamics of totality. He who relinquishes awareness of the growth of horror not merely succumbs to cold-hearted contemplation, but fails to perceive, together with the specific difference between the newest and that preceding it, the true identity of the whole, of terror without end.

150

Late extra. – In central passages of Poe and Baudelaire the concept of newness emerges. In the former, in the description of the maelstrom and the shudder it inspires – equated with 'the novel' – of which none of the traditional reports is said to give an adequate idea; in the latter, in the last line of the cycle *La Mort*, which chooses the plunge into the abyss, no matter whether hell or heaven, '*au fond de l'inconnu pour trouver du nouveau*' [in the depths of the unknown to find the new]. In both cases it is an unknown threat that the subject embraces and which, in a dizzy reversal, promises joy. The new, a blank place in consciousness, awaited as if with shut eyes, seems the formula by means of which a stimulus is extracted from dread and despair. It makes evil flower. But its bare contour is a cryptogram for the most unequivocal reaction. It circumscribes the precise reply given by the subject to a world that has turned abstract, the industrial age. The cult of the new, and thus the idea of modernity, is a rebellion against the fact that there is no longer anything new. The never-changing quality of machine-produced goods, the lattice of socialization that enmeshes and assimilates equally objects and the view of them, converts everything encountered into what always was, a fortuitous specimen of a species, the *doppel-gänger* of a model. The layer of unpremeditatedness, freedom from intentions, on which alone intentions flourish, seems consumed. Of it the idea of newness dreams. Itself unattainable, newness installs itself in the place of overthrown divinity amidst the first consciousness of the decay of experience. But its concept remains chained to that sickness, as its abstraction attests, impotently reaching for a receding concreteness. For a 'pre-history of modernity'[1] it would be instructive to analyse the change in the meaning of the word sensation, the exoteric synonym for the Baudelairian *nouveau*. The word became familiar to the educated European through epistemology. In Locke it means simple, direct perception, the opposite of reflection. It then became the great Unknown, and finally the arouser of masses, the destructive intoxicant, shock as a consumer commodity. To be still able to perceive anything at all, regardless of its quality, replaces happiness, since omnipotent quantification has taken away the possibility of perception itself. In place of the fulfilled relation of experience to its subject-matter, we find something merely subjective, physically isolated, feeling that is exhausted in the reading on the pressure-gauge. Thus the historical emancipation from being-in-itself is converted into the form of perception, a process that nineteenth-century sense-psychology accommodated by reducing the underlying level of experience to a mere 'basic stimulus', of whose particular constitution the specific sense-energies were independent. Baudelaire's poetry, however, is full of those lightning flashes seen by a closed eye that has received a blow. As phantasmagoric as these lights is the idea of newness itself. What flashes thus, while serene contemplation now attains merely the socially pre-formed plaster-casts of things, is itself repetition. The new, sought for its own sake, a kind of laboratory product, petrified into a conceptual scheme, becomes in its sudden apparition a compulsive return of the old, not unlike that in traumatic neuroses. To the dazzled vision the veil of temporal succession is rent to reveal the archetypes of perpetual sameness: this is why the discovery of the new is satanic, an eternal recurrence of damnation. Poe's allegory of the 'novel' is that of the breathlessly spinning yet in a sense stationary movement of the helpless boat in the eye of the maelstrom. The sensations in which the masochist abandons himself to the new are as many regressions. So much is true in psycho-analysis that the ontology of Baudelairian modernity, like all those that followed it, answers the description of infantile partial-instincts. Its pluralism is the many-

1. Notion of Walter Benjamin: the whole passage here on Baudelaire and the concept of the 'new' is constructed in implicit contrast to Benjamin's interpretation of them in *Charles Baudelaire – A Lyric Poet in the Era of High Capitalism* (London 1973). For an English translation of Adorno's famous critique of Benjamin's views, see 'Letters to Walter Benjamin', *New Left Review* 81, September–October 1973.

coloured *fata morgana* in which the monism of bourgeois reason sees its self-destruction glitter deceptively as hope. This false promise makes up the idea of modernity, and everything modern, because of its never-changing core, has scarcely aged than it takes on a look of the archaic. The *Tristan* which rises in the middle of the nineteenth century as an obelisk of modernity is at the same time a soaring monument to the compulsion to repeat. The new is ambivalent in its enthronement. While it embraces everything that strives beyond the oneness of an ever more rigid established order, it is at the same time absorption by newness which, under the weight of that oneness, decisively furthers the decomposition of the subject into convulsive moments of illusory living, and so also furthers total society, which modishly ousts the new. Baudelaire's poem about the martyr of sex, the murder victim, allegorically celebrates the sanctity of pleasure in the fearsomely liberating still-life of crime, but his intoxication before the naked headless body already resembles that which drove the prospective victims of Hitler's régime to buy, in paralysed greed, the newspapers in which stood the measures announcing their own doom. Fascism was the absolute sensation: in a statement at the time of the first pogroms, Goebbels boasted that at least the National Socialists were not boring. In the Third Reich the abstract horror of news and rumour was enjoyed as the only stimulus sufficient to incite a momentary glow in the weakened sensorium of the masses. Without the almost irresistible force of the craving for headlines, in which the strangled heart convulsively sought a primeval world, the unspeakable could not have been endured by the spectators or even by the perpetrators. In the course of the war, even news of calamity was finally given full publicity in Germany, and the slow military collapse was not hushed up. Concepts like sadism and masochism no longer suffice. In the mass-society of technical dissemination they are mediated by sensationalism, by comet-like, remote, ultimate newness. It overwhelms a public writhing under shock and oblivious of who has suffered the outrage, itself or others. Compared to its stimulus-value, the content of the shock becomes really irrelevant, as it was ideally in its invocation by poets; it is even possible that the horror savoured by Poe and Baudelaire, when realized by dictators, loses its quality as sensation, burns out. The violent rescuing of all qualities in the new was devoid of quality. Everything can, as the new, divested of itself, become pleasure, just as desensitized morphine addicts finally grab indiscriminately at any drug, including atropine. Sensation has submerged, together with differentiation between qualities, all judgement: it is really this that makes it an agent of catastrophic degeneration. In the terror of regressive dictatorship, modernity, the dialectical image of progress, has culminated in explosion. Newness in collective form, of which there was already a hint in Baudelaire's journalistic streak as in Wagner's drum-beating, is in fact a stimulating and paralysing narcotic extract boiled out of external life: not for nothing were Poe, Baudelaire, Wagner addictive types. Newness only becomes mere evil in its totalitarian format, where all the tension between individual and society, that once gave rise to the category of the new, is dissipated. Today the appeal to newness, of no matter what kind, provided only that it is archaic enough, has become universal, the omnipresent medium of false mimesis. The decomposition of the subject is consummated in his self-abandonment to an ever-changing sameness. This drains all firmness from characters. What Baudelaire commanded through the power of images, comes unbid to will-less fascination. Faithlessness and lack of identity, pathic subservience to situations, are induced by the stimulus of newness, which, as a mere stimulus, no longer stimulates. Perhaps in this lassitude mankind's renunciation of the wish for children is declared, because it is open to everyone to prophesy the worst: the new is the secret figure of all those unborn. Malthus is one of the forefathers of the nineteenth century, and Baudelaire had reason to extol infertile beauty. Mankind, despairing of its reproduction, unconsciously projects its wish for survival into the chimera of the thing never known, but this resembles death. Such a chimera points to the downfall of an all-embracing constitution which virtually no longer needs its members.

151

Theses against occultism. – I. The tendency to occultism is a symptom of regression in consciousness. This has lost the power to think the unconditional and to endure the conditional. Instead of defining both, in their unity and difference, by conceptual labour, it mixes them indiscriminately. The unconditional becomes fact, the conditional an immediate essence. Monotheism is decomposing into a second mythology. 'I believe in astrology because I do not believe in God', one participant in an American socio-psychological investigation answered. Judicious reason, that had elevated itself to the notion of one God, seems ensnared in his fall. Spirit is dissociated into spirits and thereby forfeits the power to recognize that they do not exist. The veiled tendency of society towards disaster lulls its victims in a false revelation, with a hallucinated phenomenon. In vain they hope in its fragmented blatancy to look their total doom in the eye and withstand it. Panic breaks once again, after millennia of enlightenment, over a humanity whose control of nature as control of men far exceeds in horror anything men ever had to fear from nature.

II. The second mythology is more untrue than the first. The latter was the precipitate of the state of knowledge of successive epochs, each of which showed its consciousness to be some degrees more free of blind subservience to nature than had the previous. The former, deranged and bemused, throws away the hard-won knowledge of itself, in the midst of a society which, by the all-encompassing exchange-relationship, eliminates precisely the elemental power the occultists claim to command. The helmsman looking to the Dioscuri, the attribution of animation to tree and spring, in all their deluded bafflement before the unexplained, were historically appropriate to the subject's experience of the objects of his actions. As a rationally exploited reaction to rationalized society, however, in the booths and consulting rooms of seers of all gradations, reborn animism denies the alienation of which it is itself proof and product, and concocts surrogates for non-existent experience. The occultist draws the ultimate conclusion from the fetish-character of commodities: menacingly objectified labour assails him on all sides from demonically grimacing objects. What has been forgotten in a world congealed into products, the fact that it has been produced by men, is split off and misremembered as a being-in-itself added to that of the objects and equivalent to them. Because objects have frozen in the cold light of reason, lost their illusory animation, the social quality that now animates them is given an independent existence both natural and supernatural, a thing among things.

III. By its regression to magic under late capitalism, thought is assimilated to late capitalist forms. The asocial twilight phenomena

239

in the margins of the system, the pathetic attempts to squint through the chinks in its walls, while revealing nothing of what is outside, illuminate all the more clearly the forces of decay within. The bent little fortune-tellers terrorizing their clients with crystal balls are toy models of the great ones who hold the fate of mankind in their hands. Just as hostile and conspiratorial as the obscurantists of psychic research is society itself. The hypnotic power exerted by things occult resembles totalitarian terror: in present-day processes the two are merged. The smiling of auguries is amplified to society's sardonic laughter at itself, gloating over the direct material exploitation of souls. The horoscope corresponds to the official directives to the nations, and number-mysticism is preparation for administrative statistics and cartel prices. Integration itself proves in the end to be an ideology for disintegration into power groups which exterminate each other. He who integrates is lost.

IV. Occultism is a reflex-action to the subjectification of all meaning, the complement of reification. If, to the living, objective reality seems deaf as never before, they try to elicit meaning from it by saying abracadabra. Meaning is attributed indiscriminately to the next worst thing: the rationality of the real, no longer quite convincing, is replaced by hopping tables and rays from heaps of earth. The offal of the phenomenal world becomes, to sick consciousness, the *mundus intelligibilis*. It might almost be speculative truth, just as Kafka's Odradek might almost be an angel, and yet it is, in a positivity that excludes the medium of thought, only barbaric aberration alienated from itself, subjectivity mistaking itself for its object. The more consummate the inanity of what is fobbed off as 'spirit' – and in anything less spiritless the enlightened subject would at once recognize itself, – the more the meaning detected there, which in fact is not there at all, becomes an unconscious, compulsive projection of a subject decomposing historically if not clinically. It would like to make the world resemble its own decay: therefore it has dealings with requisites and evil wishes. 'The third one reads out of my hand,/ She wants to read my doom!' In occultism the mind groans under its own spell like someone in a nightmare, whose torment grows with the feeling that he is dreaming yet cannot wake up.

V. The power of occultism, as of Fascism, to which it is connected by thought-patterns of the ilk of anti-semitism, is not only pathic. Rather it lies in the fact that in the lesser panaceas, as in superimposed pictures, consciousness famished for truth imagines it is grasping a dimly present knowledge diligently denied to it by official progress in all its forms. It is the knowledge that society, by virtually excluding the possibility of spontaneous change, is gravitating towards total catastrophe. The real absurdity is reproduced in the astrological hocus-pocus, which adduces the impenetrable connections of alienated elements – nothing more alien than the stars – as knowledge about the subject. The menace deciphered in the constellations resembles the historical threat that propagates itself precisely through unconsciousness, absence of subjects. That all are prospective victims of a whole made up solely of themselves, they can only make bearable by transferring that whole to something similar but external. In the woeful idiocy they practice, their empty horror, they are able to vent their impracticable woe, their crass fear of death, and yet continue to repress it, as they must if they wish to go on living. The break in the line of life that indicates a lurking cancer is a fraud only in the place where it purports to be found, the individual's hand; where they refrain from diagnosis, in the collective, it would be correct. Occultists rightly feel drawn towards childishly monstrous scientific fantasies. The confusion they sow between their emanations and the isotopes of uranium is ultimate clarity. The mystical rays are modest anticipations of technical ones. Superstition is knowledge, because it sees together the ciphers of destruction scattered on the social surface; it is folly, because in all its death-wish it still clings to illusions: expecting from the transfigured shape of society misplaced in the skies an answer that only a study of real society can give.

VI. Occultism is the metaphysic of dunces. The mediocrity of the mediums is no more accidental than the apocryphal triviality of the revelations. Since the early days of spiritualism the Beyond has communicated nothing more significant than the dead grandmother's greetings and the prophecy of an imminent journey. The excuse that the world of spirits can convey no more to poor human reason than the latter can take in, is equally absurd, an auxiliary hypothesis of the paranoiac system; the *lumen naturale* has, after all, taken us somewhat further than the journey to grandmother, and if the spirits do not wish to acknowledge this, they are ill-mannered hobgoblins with whom it is better to break off all dealings. The platitudinously natural content of the supernatural message betrays its untruth. In pursuing yonder what they have lost, they encounter only the nothing they have. In order not to lose touch with the everyday dreariness in which, as irremediable realists, they are at home, they adapt the meaning they revel in to the meaninglessness they flee. The worthless magic is nothing other than the worthless existence it lights up. This is what makes the prosaic so cosy. Facts which differ from what is the case only by not being facts are trumped up as a fourth dimension. Their non-being alone is their *qualitas occulta*. They supply simpletons with a world outlook. With their blunt, drastic answers to every question, the astrologists and spiritualists do not so much solve problems as remove them by crude premisses from all possibility of solution. Their sublime realm, conceived as analogous to space, no more needs to be thought than chairs and flower-vases. It thus reinforces conformism. Nothing better pleases what is there than that being there should, as such, be meaning.

VII. The great religions have either, like Judaism after the ban on graven images, veiled the redemption of the dead in silence, or preached the resurrection of the flesh. They take the inseparability of the spiritual and physical seriously. For them there was no intention, nothing 'spiritual', that was not somehow founded in bodily perception and sought bodily fulfilment. To the occultists, who consider the idea of resurrection beneath them, and actually do not want to be saved, this is too coarse. Their metaphysics, which even Huxley can no longer distinguish from metaphysics, rest on the axiom: 'The soul can soar to the heights, heigh-ho, / the body stays put on the sofa below.' The heartier the spirituality, the more mechanistic: not even Descartes drew the line so cleanly. Division of labour and reification are taken to the extreme: body and soul severed in a kind of perennial vivisection. The soul is to shake the dust off its feet and in brighter regions forthwith resume its fervent activity at the exact point where it was interrupted. In this declaration of independence, however, the soul becomes a cheap imitation of that from which it had achieved a false emancipation. In place of the interaction that even the most rigid philosophy admitted, the astral body is installed, ignominious concession of hypostasized spirit to its opponent. Only in the metaphor of the body can the concept of pure spirit be grasped at all, and is at the same time cancelled. In their reification the spirits are already negated.

VIII. They inveigh against materialism. But they want to weigh the astral body. The objects of their interest are supposed at once to transcend the possibility of experience, and be experienced. Their procedure is to be strictly scientific; the greater the humbug, the more meticulously the experiment is prepared. The self-importance of scientific checks is taken *ad absurdum* where there is nothing to check. The same rationalistic and empiricist apparatus that threw the spirits out is being used to reimpose them on those who no longer trust their own reason. As if any elemental spirit would not turn tail before the traps that domination of nature sets for such fleeting beings. But even this the occultists turn to advantage. Because the spirits do not like controls, in the midst of all the safety precautions a tiny door must be left open, through which they can make their unimpeded entrance. For the occultists are practical folk. Not driven by vain curiosity, they are looking for tips. From the stars to forward transactions is but a nimble step. Usually the information amounts to no more than that some poor acquaintance has had his dearest hopes dashed.

IX. The cardinal sin of occultism is the contamination of mind and existence, the latter becoming itself an attribute of mind. Mind arose out of existence, as an organ for keeping alive. In reflecting existence, however, it becomes at the same time something else. The existent negates itself as thought upon itself. Such negation is mind's element. To attribute to it positive existence, even of a higher order, would be to deliver it up to what it opposes. Late bourgeois ideology has again made it what it was for pre-animism, a being-in-itself modelled on the social division of labour, on the split between manual and intellectual labour, on the planned domination over the former. In the concept of mind-in-itself, consciousness has ontologically justified and perpetuated privilege by making it independent of the social principle by which it is constituted. Such ideology explodes in occultism: it is Idealism come full circle. Just by virtue of the rigid antithesis of being and mind, the latter becomes a department of being. If Idealism demanded solely on behalf of the whole, the Idea, that being be mind and that the latter exist, occultism draws the absurd conclusion that existence is determinate being: 'Existence, after it has become, is always being with a non-being, so that this non-being is taken up in simple unity with the being. Non-being taken up in being, the fact that the concrete whole is in the form of being, of immediacy, constitutes determinateness as such.'[1] The occultists take literally the non-being in 'simple unity with being', and their kind of concreteness is a surreptitious short-cut from the whole to the determinate which can defend itself by claiming that the whole, having once been determined, is no longer the whole. They call to metaphysics: *Hic Rhodus hic salta*: if the philosophic investment of spirit with existence is determinable, then finally, they sense, any scattered piece of existence must be justifiable as a particular spirit. The doctrine of the existence of the Spirit, the ultimate exaltation of bourgeois consciousness, consequently bore teleologically within it the belief in spirits, its ultimate degradation. The shift to existence, always 'positive' and justifying the world, implies at the same time the thesis of the positivity of mind, pinning it down, transposing the absolute into appearance. Whether the whole objective world, as 'product', is to be spirit, or a particular thing a particular spirit, ceases to matter, and the world-spirit becomes the supreme Spirit, the guardian angel of the established, despiritualized order. On this the occultists live: their mysticism is the *enfant terrible* of the mystical moment in Hegel. They take speculation to the point of fraudulent bankruptcy. In passing off determinate being as mind, or spirit, they put objectified mind to the test of existence, which must prove negative. No spirit exists.

152

Warning: not to be misused. – The dialectic stems from the sophists; it was a mode of discussion whereby dogmatic assertions were shaken and, as the public prosecutors and comic writers put it, the lesser word made the stronger. It subsequently developed, as against *philosophia perennis*, into a perennial method of criticism, a refuge for all the thoughts of the oppressed, even those unthought by them. But as a means of proving oneself right it was also from the first an instrument of domination, a formal technique of apologetics unconcerned with content, serviceable to those who could pay: the principle of constantly and successfully turning the tables. Its truth or untruth, therefore, is not inherent in the method itself, but in its intention in the historical process. The splitting of the

1. Hegel, *Wissenschaft der Logik*, *Werke* 5, p. 116 (*Hegel's Science of Logic*, London 1969, p. 110).

Hegelian school into a left and a right wing was founded in the ambiguity of the theory no less than in the political situation preceding the 1848 revolution. Dialectical thought includes not only the Marxian doctrine that the proletariat as the absolute object of history is capable of becoming its first social subject, and realizing the conscious self-determination of mankind, but also the joke that Gustave Doré[1] attributes to a parliamentary representative of the *ancien régime*: that without Louis XVI there would never have been a revolution, so that he is to be thanked for the rights of man. Negative philosophy, dissolving everything, dissolves even the dissolvent. But the new form in which it claims to suspend and preserve both, dissolved and dissolvent, can never emerge in a pure state from an antagonistic society. As long as domination reproduces itself, the old quality reappears unrefined in the dissolving of the dissolvent: in a radical sense no leap is made at all. That would happen only with the liberating event. Because the dialectical determination of the new quality always finds itself referred back to the violence of the objective tendency that propagates domination, it is placed under the almost inescapable compulsion, whenever it has conceptually achieved the negation of the negation, to substitute, even in thought, the bad old order for the non-existent alternative. The depth to which it penetrates objectivity is bought with complicity in the lie that objectivity is truth. By strictly limiting itself to extrapolating the image of a privilege-free state, from that which owes to the historical process the privilege of existing, it bows to restoration. This is registered by private existence. Hegel taxed the latter with nullity. Mere subjectivity, he argued, insisting on the purity of its own principle, becomes entangled in antinomies. It is brought down by its own mischief, by hypocrisy and evil, in so far as it is not objectified in society and state. Morality, autonomy founded on pure self-certainty, together with conscience, is mere illusion. If 'there is no moral reality',[2] it is consistent that in the *Philosophy of Right* marriage is ranked above conscience, and that the latter, even on its own level, which Hegel, with Romanticism, determines as that of irony, is accused of 'subjective vanity' in its bifocal understanding. This dialectical motif, operating on all levels of the system, is at once true and untrue. True because it unmasks

1. Gustave Doré (1832–83): French painter and illustrator.
2. *Phänomenologie des Geistes, Werke* 3, p. 452 (*The Phenomenology of Mind*, p. 626).

the particular as a necessary illusion, the false consciousness of isolated things as being themselves alone and not moments of the whole; and this false consciousness it breaks down with the power of the whole. Untrue because the motif of objectification, 'alienation', becoming a pretext for bourgeois self-assertion of the subject, is degraded to a mere rationalization, as long as objectivity, contrasted by thought to bad subjectivity, is unfree and does not measure up to the subject's criticism. The word alienation [*Entäusserung*], expressing the expectation of release from private wilfulness through obedience of the private will, acknowledges by the very tenacity with which it views the alien external world as institutionally opposed to the subject – in spite of all its protestations of reconciliation – the continuing irreconcilability of subject and object, which constitutes the theme of dialectical criticism. The act of self-alienation amounts to the renunciation that Goethe called salvation, and thus to a justification of the status quo, now as then. From his insight into, for example, the mutilation of women by patriarchal society, and into the impossibility of eliminating anthropological deformation without its pre-condition, precisely the intransigently realistic dialectician could derive the master-of-the-house standpoint, and lend his voice to the continuance of the patriarchal relationship. In this he lacks neither valid reasons, such as the impossibility of different relations under the present conditions, nor even humanity towards the oppressed, who have to suffer the consequences of false emancipation; but all this truth would become ideology in the hands of male interest. The dialectician knows the unhappiness and vulnerability of the ageing spinster, the murderousness of divorce. But in anti-romantically giving objectified marriage precedence over ephemeral passion which is not preserved in a shared life, he makes himself the mouthpiece of those who practise marriage at the expense of affection, love what they are married to, that is, the abstract property-relationship. The logical conclusion of such wisdom[1] would be that people do not matter, provided they accommodate themselves to the given constellation and do what is asked of them. To protect itself from such temptations an enlightened dialectic needs to guard incessantly against this apologetic, restorative element which is, after all, inherent in sophistication. The threatening relapse of

1. *Dieser Weisheit letzter Schluss*: ironic reprise of the words of Faust's final monologue in Goethe's play.

reflection into unreflectedness gives itself away by the facility with which the dialectical procedure shuttles its arguments, as if it were itself that immediate knowledge of the whole which the very principle of the dialectic precludes. The standpoint of totality is adopted in order, with a schoolmasterly That-is-not-what-I-meant, to deprive one's opponent of any definite negative judgement, and at the same time violently to break off the movement of concepts, to arrest the dialectic by pointing to the insuperable inertia of facts. The harm is done by the *thema probandum*: the thinker uses the dialectic instead of giving himself up to it. In this way thought, masterfully dialectical, reverts to the pre-dialectical stage: the serene demonstration of the fact that there are two sides to everything.

153

Finale. – The only philosophy which can be responsibly practised in face of despair is the attempt to contemplate all things as they would present themselves from the standpoint of redemption. Knowledge has no light but that shed on the world by redemption: all else is reconstruction, mere technique. Perspectives must be fashioned that displace and estrange the world, reveal it to be, with its rifts and crevices, as indigent and distorted as it will appear one day in the messianic light. To gain such perspectives without velleity or violence, entirely from felt contact with its objects – this alone is the task of thought. It is the simplest of all things, because the situation calls imperatively for such knowledge, indeed because consummate negativity, once squarely faced, delineates the mirror-image of its opposite. But it is also the utterly impossible thing, because it presupposes a standpoint removed, even though by a hair's breadth, from the scope of existence, whereas we well know that any possible knowledge must not only be first wrested from what is, if it shall hold good, but is also marked, for this very reason, by the same distortion and indigence which it seeks to escape. The more passionately thought denies its conditionality for the sake of the unconditional, the more unconsciously, and so calamitously, it is delivered up to the world. Even its own impossibility it must at last comprehend for the sake of the possible. But beside the demand thus placed on thought, the question of the reality or unreality of redemption itself hardly matters.

Index